Critical Thinking

Critical Thinking is an exploration of and exposition on the elusive concept of critical thinking that is central to the operation of advanced stages of education and professional development. It draws on a wide-ranging review of literature and discussion. With a substantial section of resources for direct use with learners, the book provides theory and practical support for the teaching process so that learners can become effective critical thinkers.

Topics discussed include:

- a review of the concept of critical thinking, approaches to it, and the activities that it involves;
- issues such as cultural influences, objectivity and subjectivity in critical thinking;
- the significance of the relationship between epistemological development and critical thinking;
- a new concept of depth and quality in critical thinking;
- a new concept of academic assertiveness with wide implications for all aspects of learning;
- the pedagogy of critical thinking, which is addressed through discussion and many exercises;
- the pedagogy of academic assertiveness as a support to critical thinking.

Critical Thinking: an exploration of theory and practice will be of interest to those who support the process of teaching, the teachers themselves, the learners, and those who work in professional education and professional development. Teachers of all disciplines at higher and further education levels in education will find this approach to defining and improving students' critical thinking skills invaluable.

Jennifer Moon works at the Centre for Excellence in Media Practice, Bournemouth University and as a freelance consultant. She is a National Teaching Fellowship Award winner. Her other books include *Learning Journals*, *Handbook of Reflective and Experiential Learning*, *Module and Programme Development Handbook*, *Reflection and Learning in Professional Development* and *Short Courses and Workshops*.

Critical Thinking

An exploration of theory and practice

Jennifer Moon

Routledge
Taylor & Francis Group

LONDON AND NEW YORK

First published 2008
by Routledge
2 Park Square, Milton Park, Abingdon, Oxon OX14 4RN

Simultaneously published in the USA and Canada
by Routledge
270 Madison Ave, New York, NY 10016

Routledge is an imprint of the Taylor & Francis Group, an informa business

© 2008 Jennifer Moon

Typeset in Times New Roman
by Keystroke, 28 High Street, Tettenhall, Wolverhampton
Printed and bound in Great Britain
by TJ International Ltd, Padstow, Cornwall

British Library Cataloguing in Publication Data
A catalogue record for this book is available from the British Library

Library of Congress Cataloging in Publication Data
Library of Congress Cataloging-in-Publication Data
Moon, Jennifer A.
Critical thinking : an exploration of theory and practice / Jennifer Moon.
    p. cm.
Includes bibliographical references and index.
ISBN 0–415–41179–3 (pbk.) – ISBN 0–415–41178–5 (hardback)
1. Critical thinking–Study and teaching. I. Title.
LB2395.35.M66 2007
370.15'2–dc22
2007005441

ISBN10: 0–415–41178–5 (hbk)
ISBN10: 0–415–41179–3 (pbk)
ISBN10: 0–203–94488–7 (ebk)

ISBN13: 978–0–415–41178–3 (hbk)
ISBN13: 978–0–415–41179–0 (pbk)
ISBN13: 978–0–203–94488–2 (ebk)

Contents

Preface

This book is an exploration as well as an exposition. It started from a fascination with the idea of thinking and a sense that, although thinking must surely be at the heart of education, it is not often explicitly taken into consideration in pedagogy. Critical thinking does, however, feature in the rhetoric of education, particularly higher education. Having a word for an idea, however, does not always mean that everyone holds the same conception of it. Early reading around the topic revealed a wide range of different views of what this thing – critical thinking – might be. So the search and the research began to shape themselves around the notion of exploration as well as exposition. More of the background to the book is described in the first chapter.

As with other writings of this author, the intention has been to cover the topic in a broad manner – from the explorations and the theory to the development of a working definition ('defining statement') and then the use of the defining statement as a broad principle around which pedagogical principles and practice could be developed. There are plenty of practical activities described at the end of the book – and many materials to be photocopied and used directly with students.

The book has developed from processes of reading, writing a learning journal on critical thinking, listening and also from running workshops. Several important ideas emerged in listening to what people said in workshops. As time has gone on and the book developed, the workshops also became valuable testing areas for the pedagogical materials that were developed.

The book should be of interest to those who support the process of teaching, the teachers themselves, the learners, and those who work in the professions, professional education and professional development. The notion of critical thinking appears in a number of areas of education. The focus of this book is higher education and professional development, but ideas will also be of interest to those working in post-16 education and in particular, those teaching Critical Thinking at 'A' Level and Theory of Knowledge on the International Baccalaureate courses. In covering the basic subject matter of education, it will be of interest to those who need to think about the theoretical background of critical thinking and for anyone who needs to enact the process of critical thinking as part of an advanced programme of study or as an everyday or professional activity. For some it may simply provide activities to use with learners. It should be of interest too to staff and educational developers and those who support students in study skills development.

A book that is exploration as well as exposition takes a long time to write and so it has been with this one. Something that takes a long time, takes a lot of life as well, and so it has been with this one. I thank those who have borne with my efforts, probably sometimes to the point of tedium. Also I would like to thank those who have attended workshops, unwittingly perhaps, extending my thinking and then trying out the new materials. I apologize to those few who commented that they wanted a workshop about a 'finished thing' and not 'work in progress'. Fortunately or unfortunately, I will never feel happy to claim that I run workshops on 'finished products'. Terms such as 'reflective learning' and 'critical thinking' are always being constructed and reconstructed and are rightly interpreted differently in different contexts.

I want to thank, in particular, colleagues at the Centre for Excellence in Media Practice at Bournemouth University, who, a year ago, in my new post in the Centre, included the writing of this book in my work remit and thus liberated me from a sense of guilt at writing when others thought I should be doing something else.

Jennifer Moon

May 2007

Part 1

Introduction

1 Introduction

The topic, the content, the writer, . . .

Introduction

This book is, as the preface says, an exploration and exposition. Writing it was not just a matter of bringing together existing ideas, but a matter of the use of the format of a book and the activity of writing in order to research this thing – this notion of critical thinking – that seems to be a prominent activity in education and professional development, but about which there is so much uncertainty. This chapter provides the background to this critical thinking project. It contains a range of headings that are generally introductory, but that do not logically flow from beginning to end. It begins by considering some examples of the use of the term 'critical thinking' from tutors and learners. It moves on to ask some questions and review the significance of critical thinking in higher education. The next section describes how the writer began to recognize the issues that she felt needed to be explored, for if this book is research, it is important to place the researcher's orientation into the consideration. There is then a section that summarizes the content of the whole book.

Critical thinking situations

It is tempting to dive into the exploration of critical thinking without any illustration of the kind of situation that might inspire critical thinking in the first place. To dive straight in would be to ignore one of the major points that this book is designed to make – that there are unclear understandings as to just what critical thinking is. We start, therefore, with some scenarios in which critical thinking might be enacted, and one example of critical thinking in action.

> Seth is a student on a drama course. He is asked to attend a performance of a new play and write a critique of it, first for a public newspaper, then as a drama specialist.

> Tim has tried working in oil paint for the first time. He asks Julia to comment on his work. Julia says that she does not want to express her reaction in words, but in a graphic form. She makes a picture. They discuss Tim's work, using Julia's graphic statement as a stimulus.

Sally and Sean are talking of going on holiday and taking their elderly parents. This means that they must take various factors into account – like stairs to climb in hotels, the food available, the ease of sight-seeing and so on. Somewhere at the bottom of the list is what they want to do, themselves. They have several options and need now to judge which fits their needs best.

Simone is a physics postgraduate student. A journal article has been published that relates to her proposed research. She needs to make judgements as to the validity of the new findings and how they relate to her research.

Jenna is in the process of buying a house. She has seen several, all of which could be suitable but 'don't feel quite right'. She says she needs to 'go back to the drawing board' and think again through her needs and wants.

Abdula is a town planner. He is asked to make an initial report on plans for a new supermarket on the edge of the town.

Jay has just started to sing in a folk club. She is keen to improve her singing and looks back on how it went.

An incident has happened on a guided walking expedition. The leaders are required to reflect on it and write it up as a report.

Moses is an engineering student and is asked to evaluate the design for a footbridge.

Ellen is asked in a tutorial to take a role in a debate on a motion about the prison system.

A significant business decision has been made by Geong International. A meeting is held to ensure that it is a correct decision before action is taken.

Simon has half an hour spare while he waits for a plane. He picks up several newpapers and reads the different views of a current political issue and thinks about his own views on it.

Xu is an architecture student. He and his fellow students are asked to write critically on a new building that has been put up locally.

Françoise is a social worker and has to make a decision about her team's management of a child for whom they have some concern. They are anxious to support the family.

David has an essay to write. The title is 'Critically discuss the role of the Gaslantic writers in the development of the literature of Tarraland'.

Jeremiah has written a poem. He puts it away for a few days and takes it out for a fresh and critical look before he takes it to his writing group.

Samuel is asked, in the context of a personal development planning module, critically to review the modules that he took last year and his general progress in higher education.

Why a book on critical thinking? It's evident, isn't it?

Critical thinking as a topic lurks intriguingly behind and about much of the thinking about higher education and professional development. Now the concept and its relationships to the educational processes seem to have emerged on top and it is time to explore the landscape of this term. If, as many argue, the development of a critical stance could be said to epitomize the aims for the individual of higher education and the professions, it might be reasonable to assume that everyone would know anyway what critical thinking is. After all, the term is used confidently and 'knowingly'. In addition, 'critical thinking' – or words around it – is heavily implied in many descriptions of what should be achieved at higher levels of education (Moon, 2002). This must surely mean that 'critical thinking' is understood. However, with a growing scepticism over many other terms that are commonly used in pedagogy and the various environments of education, this writer has grown more willing to question and then doubt whether commonly used terms like 'critical thinking' are understood in a manner that is appropriate for their use in teaching.

Some of the questions that have prompted the thinking and guided the research for this book might seem to be naïve and it has been interesting to note that the more the delving, the more simplistic have become the questions about it. Below are listed a set of mostly naïve questions that have driven this exploration of 'critical thinking'.

What is critical thinking?

How does critical thinking relate to the process of learning?

Is it one activity or a number of activities?

Are critical evaluation, critical appraisal, critical reflection and similar terms, the same as or different from critical thinking? – that is, of course, if they are understood any better.

How do learners learn the ability to think critically?

Do all learners use the same form of critical thinking from the start or is there a developmental process?

If there is a developmental process, what are the implications for pedagogy?

What are the implications of this for the writing of learning outcomes and assessment criteria?

Are there significant differences in disciplinary 'takes' on critical thinking?

Are there issues about critical thinking that go beyond just sitting and thinking?

What areas of theory might underpin the development and attainment of critical thinking?

Why are there so many books written about critical thinking that tell different stories about it?

Where does logic fit in?

What do teachers need to know about critical thinking in order to support it properly? And what should we be telling learners about critical thinking skills so that they can use them?

And so on . . . and now it is time to start to find some answers. The text of this book is focused on trying to respond to these and other questions both in a theoretical manner and then in terms of classroom and learning practices. As in other books by this writer, there is exploration of the theory and then consideration of the practical implications and the application of the ideas in the classroom with learners. The first part of the book is largely the theory and the latter part is largely practical.

The significance of critical thinking in higher education and the professions

Critical thinking is considered to be central to higher levels of education or a fundamental goal of learning (Kuhn, 1999; Keeley and Shemberg, 1995). It is also a process involved in any research activity. Barnett (1997: 2) calls it a 'defining concept of the Western university' and others pick up the rhetoric and expand this to the attitudes of employers (Phillips and Bond, 2004), or relate the importance of it to their disciplines (e.g. management – Gold, Holman and Thorpe, 2002 or social sciences – Fisher, 2003) or professions (e.g. medicine – Maudsley and

Striven, 2000; social work – Brown and Rutter, 2006); at Master's level (Kaasboll, 1998; Durkin, 2004); and undergraduate level (Phillips and Bond, 2004). A simple search on Google shows that critical thinking has a central role in education and this is evident in mission statement information for higher education, professional bodies and programmes. It is clearly a good and impressive term with some gravitas which is the stuff of missionary zeal. For example, Bradford University, in its mission information cites critical thinking as an 'objective':

> Critical Thinking: To support students and staff in developing a critical, independent and scholarly approach to their discipline which will enable them to apply their knowledge.
>
> (Bradford University Mission Statement, n.d.)

Beyond this, however, and more significantly for the current task, critical thinking is an element in many level and qualification descriptors for education. Level and qualification descriptors describe what we expect students to achieve at the end of a level in (in this case) a higher education programme – or at the point of award of a qualification in higher education (HE) (Moon, 2002, 2005a). For example, the SEEC level descriptors (SEEC, 2001) make the following statements at Level 3:

> Level 3 (last year of the first cycle): 'Evaluation: can critically evaluate evidence to support conclusions/recommendations; reviewing its reliability, validity and significance. Can investigate contradictory information/identify reasons for contradictions.'

The SEEC level descriptors make an advanced statement at Master's level and for Taught Doctorate they say:

> Taught Doctorate (PhD level): 'has a level of conceptual understanding and critical capacities that will allow independent evaluation of research, advanced scholarship and methodologies; can argue alternative approaches'.

The Quality Assurance Agency, in the Framework for Higher Educational Qualifications (England, Wales and Northern Ireland) indicates that those obtaining intermediate qualifications (mid-part of higher education first cycle – or level 2) should be able to demonstrate 'knowledge and critical understanding of the well-established principles of their area(s) of study' and 'be able to initiate and undertake critical analysis of information and to propose solutions to problems arising from that analysis'.

At the Honours level, at the end of the first cycle, they should be able to:

> critically evaluate arguments, assumptions, abstract concepts and data (that might be incomplete) to make judgements and to frame appropriate questions to achieve a solution . . . to a problem.
>
> (QAA, 2001)

Later in the book we imply that these statements about critical thinking processes in level descriptors might sometimes be over-ambitious (Chapter 8). In the Dublin Descriptors which are the basis of the agreements between countries signed up to the Bologna initiatives in European higher education, critical 'analysis' features only at Doctoral level. The descriptors indicate that learners at this level should be capable of 'critical analysis, evaluation and synthesis of new and incomplete ideas' (Dublin Descriptors, 2004). However, these capacities probably do not appear fully formed at this stage!

When critical thinking is clearly expressed in higher education descriptors, it means that students who are achieving those levels or qualifications should be critical thinkers. Brennan and Osbourne (2005) suggest that critical thinking is, indeed, one of the main outcomes of UK higher education, though interestingly it is put in inverted commas – a reflection, perhaps, of the relative lack of clarity as to exactly what we might expect that learners will be able to do to evidence this.

The wider significance of critical thinking

There are plenty of reasons that could be given here to justify the importance of critical thinking in society beyond the educational and professional contexts. Ennis (1996: xvii) says that it is 'critical to the survival of a democratic way of life' because people make their own decisions in the voting process. Similarly, Brookfield (1987: 14) says that critical thinking is 'at the heart of what it means to be a developed person living in a democratic society', though I would add here that there are very 'developed' people who think and act critically and who work towards democracy in societies that are far from democratic – as evidenced by the work done by Amnesty International in their support.

We use a well-known example to demonstrate the importance of the ability to take a critical stance and the consequences of the slip into non-criticality that nearly led to the end of the world as we know it. In 1972, a social psychologist, Irving Janis, was reading about the 'Bay of Pigs events' in America in the 1960s and he considered how 'shrewd men like John F. Kennedy and his advisors [were] taken in by the CIA's stupid patchwork plan'. Janis says, 'I began to wonder whether some kind of psychological contagion, similar to social conformity phenomena observed in studies of small groups, had interfered with their mental alertness' (Janis, 1982: vii). He went on to study several other apparent 'fiascos' (p. 9) of American politics and used them to theorize on a phenomenon that he termed 'groupthink'. Groupthink is, in effect, a lack of engagement in appropriate critical thinking that can occur in a cohesive group where there is a tendency to 'evolve informal norms to preserve friendly intragroup relationships . . . [where] these become part of the hidden agenda of their meetings' (p. 7). Janis summarized the outcome of his research:

> The more amiability and *esprit de corps* among the members of a policy-making in-group, the greater is the danger that independent critical thinking

will be replaced by groupthink which is likely to result in irrational and dehumanizing actions directed against out-groups.

(Janis, 1982: 13)

In the early years of the 21st century, groupthink would still seem to be a characteristic of much political and social thinking. A willingness to be a critical thinker is important – but in situations such as that described above, just sitting and thinking counter thoughts about a group's decision-making is not enough – the thoughts need to be expressed powerfully and possibly acted on. In this book, we recognize that critical thinking is not just a cognitive process – but is linked with expression and action and the various capacities that become relevant. Barnett (1997, 2006) makes this point in a powerful manner which is also political. He refers to the massacre of students in Tienanmen Square in Beijing, saying that those who stood against the tanks were carrying through the outcomes of their critical thinking into significant action. Bowell and Kemp (2002: 4) say, 'those who hold power . . . fear the effects of those who can think critically about moral, social, economic and political issues'. This may be, but it is the step beyond the thinking – the willingness to act – that is really significant. This will be the case in many areas of critical thinking. It is this and other issues that generate academic assertiveness (Chapters 6 and 12).

Routes and roots – the personal origins of thinking that have led to this book

At the beginning of a book, I like to plot out my route into the topic that I cover. Since I theorize about learning – and thinking – from a constructivist stance, I acknowledge that the concept of critical thinking that will emerge is related to the routes that I have taken into the topic – and its roots in the development of my knowledge. This activity in which I engage is part of the process of critical thinking about critical thinking (metacognitive).

Looking back on my track through education, a significant underlying theme has been the development of my conceptualization about the ownership of knowledge and ideas. My initial orientation to this was through the 'A' level route and then in a science first degree and it was about the learning of other people's ideas. The development of knowledge was assumed to be the accumulation of facts. The tasks that were given concerned the identification and reformulation of ideas in order to meet the demands of the task at hand – which was not necessarily of relevance to anything other than the achievement of an educational award. My talent or otherwise as a learner was first the ability to understand the demands of the task, then to be able to gather the appropriate information and ideas that would enable me to respond to it, and lastly to reformulate these resources and to represent them in a manner that was as close as possible to what I thought to be the demands of the task. The parts of that process that expressed my ability were the understanding of the task, the selection of the required and relevant information and the reformulation and representation of it to meet my perception of the demands. There was, for example, in my zoology degree, an undergraduate dissertation involving experimental work on the shell-opening behaviour of mussels in relation to local tidal patterns. The project topic was suggested and the activity of it involved little more than a reformulation of ideas about how to set up the equipment and record the data, and the practical application of this. There was little room for my own thinking or expression of ideas; and relatively little encouragement for critical thinking. Around that time, I found myself in envy of a boyfriend who was studying sociology – and he did seem to have encouragement to work around different views of issues and to express this. He was asked to think and I wanted to be expected to think – I had thought that university was about thinking and I wanted to do this!

The next educational stage for me was postgraduate research on reading and reading difficulties which ended up as a review of the literature on reading and reading difficulties. I went beyond the gathering and integration of ideas and generated a framework to organize the material and to use it as a diagnostic tool, but I remember having doubts about the value of the model. What status did my work have in the greater scheme of things? Who was I to make suggestions as to how the material could be viewed? I was now adept at literature research but somewhat lost and certainly unguided when it came to the legitimacy of the process of the development of new ideas. I had a supervisor who was absorbed with his own work but I doubt if, at that stage, I would have known how to engage in the discussion either from the point of view of personal confidence or understanding of what I needed to explore. These ideas relate to conceptions of 'voice', 'self-authorship' (Belenky, Clinchy, Goldberger and Tarule, 1986; Baxter Magolda, 1999, 2001) and the discussion of the meaning of 'original' and creative or innovatory thinking and academic assertiveness (see Chapters 6, 12). The issues seem to lurk around the edge of the question of 'what is a literature review?' as well (e.g. Bruce, 1994). As a supervisor of PhD students now I wonder how I need to help them to ask these questions about 'voice', their role and the status of their new thinking in their work.

It was not until I was engaged in an MEd that some of these issues of the status of personal thinking and its expression ('voice') settled. There was an overt welcome on that traditional programme for considered and original thought. In particular this was evident in the philosophy of education, which I took as an extra module. Here the essay titles were simple ('What is meant by . . . ? Discuss.'). They invited me to find the questions that were important and relevant as well as my responses to them. While I did relatively little reading of theory for that module (and rightly only scraped through), I revelled in the freedom to think and this had a profound impact on my further development – I could produce 'new' or new-to-me ideas that could be taken seriously. We do not, after all, have most of the knowledge in the world 'taped' and ready just to pass on. There is plenty of worthwhile thinking still to do. This is probably why I write books in which I can further explore.

There was then a very long gap. It is difficult to pinpoint any particular forms of development in my thinking over these years. I did various jobs, at first in teacher education. One memory is of going through the motions of 'teaching' Piaget to 17-year-old Scottish teaching diploma students. Even while I taught Piaget, I was not really sure what they learned. We presented the key elements of his work, but I had serious doubts that the students had the maturity to understand the broader theorizing and its significance. This experience feeds into my later thinking about epistemological development and critical thinking (see Chapter 8).

I also worked in a range of part-time posts in adult education and counselling, alongside looking after children. I was very interested in personal development and the development of self-knowledge, but, away from intellectual challenge my educational confidence waned. This is relevant to Baxter Magolda's work on self authorship and the academic assertiveness that I have mentioned. What excited me intellectually then was creative functioning – drawing, craft and creative writing. I recognize that there is a life balance issue here. Then, the creative functioning predominated and now, at the present time, the intellectual functioning dominates, but the importance of the creative element is not lost. Perhaps a common root is a form of 'mental excitement' (I do not want to use the narrower word 'cognitive') that drives different forms of interest, in this case either creative or intellectual.

Some career moves (plus a Master's degree in health) later and I was back in intellectual mode as a project development officer in a government-funded credit development project. I worked in particular on learning outcomes and on level descriptors (see pp. 7–8). I needed to think with others about what it is in learning that becomes more sophisticated over the period of a programme of higher education. What, for example, makes Master's level learning, 'masterly'? There were many hot and argumentative sessions with academics from a range of disciplines, as we tried to synthesize our different conceptions and vocabularies into a common picture. I can vaguely recall the mention of a few theorists, but there was no common acceptance of any one and the final descriptors were based – as was appropriate – on the generality of perceptions of learner perfor-mance from the disciplines represented, and the individuals present. It was a kind of grounded theory in which we engaged. Later, however, I took a look at the content of the level descriptors that we had generated (Moon, 2005a). In effect, I analysed what we expressed as higher education learning in the level descriptors and what we considered to indicate progression in the learning and educational processes. As I have indicated earlier in this chapter, 'critical thinking' and ideas around it are strongly represented.

Another route into critical thinking for me was the opportunity for a meeting with Mike Riddle and Sally Mitchell who were working then at the University of Middlesex. They were, with Richard Andrews, engaged in a project to explore the process and pedagogy of argument across the disciplines (Mitchell and Andrews, 2000). I remember the feeling that I had at the time that they were study-ing something that was really central to the quality of the higher education process. I set up some staff development workshops through the Society for Research in Higher Education with Mike Riddle, and Ronald Barnett was a speaker at one of the earliest of these. Around that time, Professor Barnett published *Higher*

Education: a Critical Business (Barnett, 1997), a book that I have drawn on considerably over the years, and in particular in this current work.

From there my interests in what I call 'the higher qualities of higher education learning' accelerated in work towards a doctorate and a first book exploring the notion of reflection (Moon, 1999) and another applying the ideas of reflection in learning journals (Moon, 2006). Reflection is clearly related to critical thinking, but I did not explore this directly at that time. I did, however, demonstrate how reflection might be an inherent element in the engaged and interested learning of those who take a deep approach to learning. I suspect that I did not consider the relationship with critical thinking in greater detail because, at the time, I had not considered the 'depth dimension' of reflective learning. 'Depth' came into a further book (Moon, 2004) and now, with the current work on critical thinking as well, I will be able to plot out some of the relationships between critical thinking and reflective learning and the role of depth in both (Chapter 9).

Another key concept in my thinking about critical thinking also emerged from the writing of the two books on reflective learning – that of developmental epistemology (the work of Perry (1970), Belenky et al. (1986), Baxter Magolda (1992), King and Kitchener (1994) and others). Those who have written on epistemological development suggest that there is a progression in the ways in which learners perceive the nature of knowledge. This idea seemed very much to underpin what might be happening in reflective learning – and also in critical thinking. The conception of epistemological development also gave me a framework that enabled me to interpret my own junctures in the pathway of learning. This material is explored in Chapters 8 and 9.

The exploration of reflective learning also gave me an incentive to pull together my ideas of what we do when we engage in the immensely complex process of learning something (Moon, 2004, Chs 1–4). Having thought thus about learning, I now felt ready to think about the relationships between learning and critical thinking. The real incentive to work further on critical thinking emerged from two pieces of work that were connected with ESCalate, the Higher Education Academy Subject Centre for Education. In the first place, I was in receipt of a small award that enabled me to do work on the learning of non-traditional students (in the 'widening access' agenda). I called the project 'Coming from Behind' and worked with students and their tutors who were involved in higher education in further education contexts. In this small project, I was confronted again with the questions about the nature of higher education learning, and what it is that we should be telling these students about it. They are, at the beginning of their programme, just embarking on a journey through the academic jungle, often with very little personal or family experience of anything similar as support for them. In the workshops associated with this project, we explored some of these issues (Moon, 2005b). One of the deep patches of the jungle that these learners will confront is how to deal with learning and with the manipulation of what they have learnt in the processes (or we could sometimes call them 'jargon' words) of analysis, synthesis – and critical thinking. I then wanted to think more about what 'critical thinking' means.

Subsequently in a consultancy for ESCalate, I had the chance to do some focused work on critical thinking. It felt like the chance to think more broadly about the development of academic knowledge. I wrote a short book on critical thinking (Moon, 2005c). With some thoughts about critical thinking now developed, I began to offer workshops both to share these ideas and to engage in a process of further exploration with participants. Over time, the learning I have done as a result of the workshops and the reading for this book have been fed back into the workshop handout. I was in a moving field of knowledge development that did not stop with the writing of the booklet for ESCalate – and that will not stop with this book.

Some matters of vocabulary

There are various matters of vocabulary concerning critical thinking to be dealt with at this stage. Many of the terms that we use appear to relate to situations of formal education but we must stress that the process of critical thinking does not and should not only relate to formal educational situations.

It is not surprising that we have inappropriate or inadequate vocabulary or word use. The language of teaching and learning evolved and was developed centuries ago when ideas about these activities were different. We look first at 'teaching' and 'learning' – words that in many languages are not separated, for example there is one word in Russian for teaching and for learning. To think appropriately about education, we need to see teaching and learning as different processes. Teaching is an activity of a teacher and involves the use of various means of facilitating learning – only one of which is standing in front of a class. A teacher cannot make learning happen in another because learning is the province of the learner. While a teacher is teaching, the learner may be gazing to the far beyond, thinking of her planned bungee jump from the bridge while the teacher is talking about fluid mechanics or George Eliot. This may seem obvious, but we continue to use these educational words in a confusing manner. For example, learning technologies are not about the process of learning but the process of teaching. The learner's brain is likely to be behaving in the same kind of way if the learner is reading a book or sitting in a lecture or working from a screen.

One of the reasons why we tend to behave as if we assume that what is taught is learned is that we do not have a word for what it is that the teacher teaches, and what it is that the learner learns – we use the terms 'material of teaching' and 'material of learning' respectively for these ideas in this book (as in others by the present writer). With these words in place we have a better chance of working out what does and does not go on between a teacher and a learner.

Connected with teaching and learning, there is a word needed for 'bringing off' the curriculum (Barnett and Coate, 2005) and here the term 'pedagogy' is used. Another term that requires to be introduced is 'tools for the manipulation of knowledge'. This was first introduced in Moon (1999) and has proved helpful in exploration of pedagogical ideas. The phrase is used for words that describe techniques for working with knowledge in order to create new knowledge or to communicate it to others in an altered form – such as in the construction of argument. Bloom's taxonomy words would come into this (e.g. explain, analyse, synthesize, evaluate), though I do not subscribe to the implied hierarchy (Bloom, 1956). Critical thinking, and other compound terms such as critical thinking, critical analysis, critical reflection are also involved here. There is further exploration of the word 'thinking' towards the end of Chapter 2.

As with previous books, we will tend to use the term 'learner' in preference to 'student', except where the latter is necessitated by the context. This book is not restricted to formal education contexts. The term 'learner' is more generalized and the outcome of critical thinking will usually be learning. The learners in this book may be students in school or higher education or professionals who are engaged in short courses or in professional development situations or who are making decisions in practice. We will also be using the female pronoun 'she' and possessive 'her' rather than the male equivalents he/him/his or the grammatically incorrect plural 'they' as a 'neutered' singular grammatical construction. As I have said before, half of the population is female and after many centuries it is now our turn for representation of the generic person.

On the subject of vocabulary, it is also worth noting that the term 'critical' in 'critical thinking' does not mean critical in the sense of identifying the negatives in a situation. Its meaning is the subject matter of the whole book, but as a generalization at present it means the examination of an idea thoroughly and in depth rather than taking it at its face value.

The content of the book – and some notes on it

This is not a book in which terms are defined in the first chapter. The main drive of the text is towards the development of a sufficiently comprehensive picture of critical thinking on which to base a pedagogy. Part 6 is on pedagogy, and it is supported by material in the Resources section (Part 7).

It is important to stress that there are no 'right' and 'wrong' ways in which to regard critical thinking and strong advocacy is made in this book for the development of 'local' definitions which apply to a local situation between teachers, or tutors and learners, or those in professional development.

The book is not one that has to be read from start to finish but is suitable for 'dipping into'. Part and chapter headings have been chosen to facilitate this. The second and third parts of the book (Part 2: Mapping the territory of critical thinking and Part 3: The person as a critical thinker) identify and explore issues that might enable us to locate the boundaries of critical thinking. Part 2 concerns elements of the process of critical thinking – approaches to it, cultural issues, standards and so on. The two chapters in Part 3 are concerned with qualities and behaviours of the person that are influential on critical thinking. Chapter 6 breaks new ground in generating a new term – 'academic assertiveness'. This term incorporates the idea that critical thinking and other academic processes are essentially challenging to the person and therefore success in coping with those challenges contributes to ability in critical thinking. It suggests that we should be more explicit in dealing with these issues of challenge.

Parts 1, 2 and 3 build up to Part 4 (Taking stock). Chapter 7 represents a stage to pause and take stock – a summarizing chapter with a defining statement made on the basis of the thinking 'so far'. Part 5 (Epistemological development and depth in critical thinking) deals with two new and linked sets of issues concerning critical thinking – those of epistemological development and depth. These impinge heavily on much of the pedagogy of critical thinking.

Part 6 of the book is on pedagogy (Part 6: Critical thinking and pedagogy). The first chapter in this section reaches the defining statement about critical thinking and introduces issues to consider in pedagogy. Chapters 11 and 12 are practical, discussing a range of activities under headings, which can be used to enable learners to engage better in critical thinking and, in the case of Chapter 12, to become academically more assertive.

The book is supported by a Resources section that can stand alone, but is primarily related to Chapter 11. There is full permission to photocopy this chapter and replicate copies for use by individual learners.

To end this chapter, and, indeed, to end every chapter, we add a 'Thinkpoint,' a short quotation on which to ponder – the kind that might, elsewhere, be at the beginning of the chapter. We recognize, however, that they are, at the beginning of the chapter, rarely read by the impatient reader – like this writer – who is anxious to get on with the content of the chapters.

Thinkpoint

There is one being who cannot think – and cannot have a sense of humour. That being is, of course, God. Thinking involves moving from one state of knowledge to a better one. Since God has perfect knowledge, he is always there already. . . . Nor can God have a sense of humour since there can be no surprise when the punch-lines have always been known. It is only our lack of complete information that makes it necessary for us to think.

(de Bono, 1982)

Writer's note: it depends, of course, what we mean by 'sense of humour' – but that requires critical thinking . . .

Part 2

Mapping the territory of critical thinking

2 Critical thinking as an elusive concept

What critical thinking might be . . .

Introduction

In this chapter we look at the more common conceptions of critical thinking. We need to know how teachers, learners and others regard critical thinking because we need to stay in touch with the common-sense thinking in the processes of theorizing and developing statements of definition, or we will not achieve a good link between learning and teaching. In this case, theory is only of use if it eases forward the everyday thinking. There is little better way to open such a chapter than with a quotation from Bailin, Case, Coombs and Daniels (1999a, 1999b), who, like the current writer, sought a conception of critical thinking for use in pedagogy – but in the narrower context of papers, not a book:

> Any defensible conception [of critical thinking] must construe critical thinking in such a way as to capture most of what people have in mind when they claim that developing critical thinking is an important goal of education. That is to say, it must be true to the core meaning of the educator's basic concept of critical thinking. Should it fail in this regard, it is largely irrelevant to educators concerned with developing critical thinking.
>
> Bailin et al. (1999a)

The first three sections of this chapter concern examples of the views of critical thinking of teachers, of students and a 'common-sense view'. Later in the chapter, we look more closely at words that are associated with critical thinking (e.g. critical analysis) and their relationship to critical thinking. Then we look at the activities of critical thinking – there are different activities that come under the same heading. We close the chapter with a gathering together of ideas on critical thinking 'so far' – in a first version of a defining statement about critical thinking.

Critical thinking – a source of confusion?

Jez is in the second year of an English Literature degree at Siddlewick University. He is required to write a coursework essay comparing and contrasting the approaches to poetry of two 18th century poets. He has received feedback from his tutor that 'There is not sufficient evidence of critical thinking in this essay'. Part of the way through the essay is the comment 'more critical analysis needed here'. He reads the feedback, trying to think what is meant by 'critical thinking' – and then wondering how it differs from critical analysis. He has heard the terms on a number of occasions while at university but he does not really feel that he knows how he would write in order to display them. It must be something to do with 'criticizing' – but he vaguely recalls someone saying that it is not about being critical in the usual sense of being negative – so what is it? He asks some of his mates. They seem somewhat hazy too. Can he risk admitting to his tutor that he does not know the meaning of these terms? His tutor must have expected him to understand because – surely – otherwise she would not have given him this feedback. He goes to see her. She seems a little taken aback by his question and makes several attempts to define 'critical thinking', talking about how it is not only a matter of making negative comments, she mentions something about a concern for assumptions that are made, and then she picks a book from her bookcase and reads a definition from it:

> Critical thinking is 'thoughtful' thinking. It starts with an expectation that the received wisdom may not be correct or the only valid view. It may involve explicit comparisons of possible explanations, theories and models.

She says 'All right, Jez? Do you understand now?' and then she changes the subject. Later Jez mentions to a couple of close friends that he asked the meaning of 'critical thinking' and is still confused. Ellie says that her tutor gave a definition to the tutorial group because several of them had not 'engaged', as the tutor said, 'with the required critical thinking'. Ellie gets out the definition that she wrote down:

> Critical thinking is to challenge an idea. It is being engaged in thinking in an evaluative way by considering the different perspectives and potentially adding value to reach a new level of knowledge – thence adding new and further questioning, finding answers and asking more questions.

Ellie and Jez wonder how these definitions relate to each other, as well as how they help them to write a better essay the next time. How, too, do they relate to critical analysis?

'Surely', Ellie says, 'there is one right definition of critical thinking – I've heard about critical thinking since I came to uni. They always seem to be talking about it. There's got to be a right definition somewhere.'

Ellie and Jez discuss the matter and are further confused when they find that the definitions that they have both seem to assume that there is an idea that is already there on paper – an argument already made – when their task in the essay is to develop an idea or argument.

It is not surprising that Ellie and Jez had difficulties with the definitions given by tutors in their support for learning and their feedback. Chanock (2000) looked at students' understanding of feedback of a simpler nature – involving the words 'description' and 'analysis' – and found that there was considerable confusion among the students, and not always agreement among tutors.

The current writer investigated HE tutors' views of critical thinking in the course of several recent workshops on critical thinking in higher education. They were asked at the beginning of the workshop to write down what they considered critical thinking might be. A selection of these definitions follows. It is worthwhile reading them, as readers of this book, with three points in mind – first, do these communicate to you what this thing is; second, if you were a learner, would you have any better idea of how to go about critical thinking on the basis of the definitions? The third point relates to the implied activity. Most learners come across critical thinking in relation, initially, to one of two activities – either the writing of an essay or the review of an academic paper. Definitions are often written with reference to one or other of these activities but may not apply to both. It is also important to mention that the task was introduced at the workshops with the statement 'there are no "right" and "wrong" definitions'. It is possible that the nature of the discipline may also influence the views given. The definitions were often in note form:

(a) Critical thinking is the ability to consider a range of information derived from many different sources, to process this information in a creative and logical manner, challenging it, analysing it and arriving at considered conclusions which can be defended and justified. Its opposites are prejudice and the risk to judgement. Knowledge has to be constructed – and its meanings change with the context.

(b) Critical thinking is to challenge a theory or an idea.

(c) It is to develop your own argument, deconstructing ideas or synthesizing a range of ideas associated with complex ideas. There may be different routes to the same conclusion or different conclusions to the same issues.

(d) It is a 3-D thinking process – depth, breadth and time; being objective and not subjective; not a personal evaluation but being flexible to apply others' thought or theory.

(e) Critical thinking is the analysis of a situation based on facts – evidence – to be able to make a judgement or come to a conclusion, taking into account empathy, culture and history.

(f) Critical thinking is looking at one's work or situation with value judgement – what did I do right or wrong? It is like criticizing oneself. It can also be applied to other people's work – thinking where they are coming from; whether they are biased, and whether they have a vested interest.

(g) Critical thinking is thinking strategically about something very important like a subject in an exam. We have to critically analyse it and justify our view in order to understand it in detail.

(h) Critical thinking is the thoughtful or meaningful consideration which contrasts with common sense.

(i) Critical thinking is an analysis of one's understanding of the subject from the view which may or may not be positive to the person concerned.

(j) It is the understanding of a problem and how to evaluate the problem in various situations.

(k) It is a way of looking at things from very objective, analytical and differing points of view.

(l) Critical thinking is trying to understand a subject, thinking about it, appreciating it, understanding the strengths and limitations of it and then developing a point of view on the subject.

(m) It is thinking about an issue or problem without allowing conventional limits, boundaries and conventions to restrict the generation of your analysis or solution.

(n) It is the analysis of material, identifying weaknesses and strengths.

(o) It is the examining of evidence which may support or contradict. It is the exploring of contradictions – an active search to find contrary points of view. It is the evaluation of both these contradictions and sources of evidence for their reliability, their validity and their durability, and the making of justifiable conclusions.

(p) Critical thinking is a deep thinking process which helps us to understand what may be right or wrong. It is analysing our past experiences and it helps us to resolve situations.

(q) It is useful to think about what is not critical thinking. Most definitions of it are not coherent – they are bits and pieces that are not joined up. In an essay, students would be expected to join up the thinking. There are lots of 'good' words in the process.

(r) Critical thinking is the questioning and assertion backed up with evidence. It involves not accepting everything as read but it is a process of asking why something is the way it is, working one's way through a problem.

(s) It is the kind of thinking that shows you have engaged in analysis and questioning rather than gut reaction. It requires looking at things from a variety of perspectives – that of either the thinker or others. It should probably be structured.

(t) It is the evaluating of the work of writers of articles, journals or books and the use of serial sources of written information; comparing of ideas from different writings; questioning practice through theory; embedding thinking in the practice.

(u) On both undergrad and postgraduate programmes the ability to think critically shows itself through a deep thought process. Instead of description, we promote analysis. Instead of personal subjective views, we promote evaluation. Critical thinking is an argument which runs like a river through a piece of work and the tributaries join it as elements of evidence.

We identify some of the differences, just pulling out some samples of each.

(b), (t) are about challenging ideas; (c) is about the development of 'one's own argument'.

(f) is initially about the consideration of one's own situation; (l), and many others, relate to 'the work of others'.

(p) talks of analysing what is 'right' or 'wrong' in the presented material; (f) is about 'where did I go right or wrong?'.

(g) talks of critically analysing; others mention the use of analysis (u; n; g). What is meant? – is this part of critical thinking or a different operation?

(f) and (n) see the object with which critical thinking is engaged as material or a problem or situation. (i) talks of critical thinking being applied to 'one's understanding' of a situation or problem.

(k) mentions objectivity, while others mention subjective understandings (e.g. a, f, n, p).

As well as differences, there are many similarities between these statements, of course – but the basic all-important question remains. If you were a learner, like Jez, asking for a definition from a tutor (and probably expecting there to be a clear and absolute definition, Chapter 1) and in reply getting one or more of these responses, would you have any better idea as to how to go about critical thinking? It would appear that we often behave in pedagogy as if terms like critical thinking (and critical analysis, critical reflection and so on) have a set and agreed meaning. This is far from the case, as becomes evident from consideration of these three-minute definitions from groups of experienced teaching staff.

Not only do we behave as if 'critical thinking' and other such terms have agreed definitions, but we use them with learners in this way. In one staff development workshop, there were, by agreement, some postgraduate students present. There was horror in their faces as it dawned on them that there was not an agreed definition for critical thinking among those who were their tutors. There was some embarrassment among the tutors too. The revelation of this simple fact felt like a mischievous move on the part of the workshop facilitator (the writer), but since the rest of the session was devoted to exploration of the meaning of the concept, the situation was aided if not resolved!

The asking of teaching staff for their definitions for 'critical thinking' helped to reveal the range of meanings of the term and valuably informed the writing of this book. A much more comprehensive survey that sought more information from teachers about their thinking and practices on critical thinking is reported in Paul, Elder and Bartell (n.d.). It might be difficult directly to equate the situation for teachers in the USA to that of the UK since there has been a different evolution of the topic of critical thinking in American education.

What do learners think critical thinking is?

We now focus on a piece of work that involved the views of critical thinking of learners. The work analysed the views of the learners and begins to indicate some of the many elements that come into critical thinking – which make its definition so complicated. We would note that the teachers' views of critical thinking that are described above, were spontaneous, but those of the learners below were prompted in a structured manner which would have limited their conceptions – for example they were working on a given problem. Critical thinking will not always be about working with a clearly stated problem. Phillips and Bond (2004) investigated the conceptions of thirteen second-year New Zealand students. Since the students were used to the term 'critical reflection', that term was the focus of the study, though it is reported and titled as a study of 'critical thinking'. The students were interviewed about their conception of critical reflection, and asked to provide an example of 'a recent situation in which they thought they were critically reflective'. They were then given an everyday example of an ill-structured problem with an unclear goal, with different layers of issues, and 'no explicit means for determining appropriate action'. They were asked to talk through their thinking as they worked towards their solution. Analysis of the data indicated four different views of critical reflection. In illustrating these positions, we use the student quotations from Phillips and Bond.

The first categorization of the student thinking saw critical reflection as 'weighing up': students in this group tended to see critical reflection as a matter of making simple comparisons – positive and negative, one or the other, etc. You 'like home in on all the negative aspects as opposed to the positive' (Luke). Mike said 'you want to see both sides . . . you've got to try not to be biased . . . you take it through the pros and cons of the positive and the negative of both sides and try to go in with no opinion and come out . . . with a frame of mind'. As Phillips and Bond say, knowledge is seen as elements of an entity to be shuffled around.

The second categorization was 'looking at it from all the angles'. Students talked about viewing a problem from 'as many different viewpoints as you can and . . . think[ing] what sorts of solution you could come up with' (Cynthia) or 'seeing a situation from a variety of different perspectives and angles in order to come up with what you assume is the correct decision to make' (Theresa). This might include taking on the roles of the people in the given problem. Adam, for example, said 'I can't understand something until I've been in someone else's shoes'. The students talked about the points of view of those involved in the given problem, or 'If I were in that situation . . .' (Adam).

A third categorization involved 'looking back on a situation'. While it could take different points of view of those in the problem, it also allowed a broader judgement which was enabled by standing back from the problem. Such hindsight might allow for noting of personal emotions about the problem as well as those of the actors in the situation.

The last of the categories was 'looking beyond what is there' and this was represented in the engagement of criteria of beliefs and values. These beliefs and values were brought to bear on the problem by the student making their judgement and going beyond the immediate 'givens' of the situation in the problem. The students making these kinds of statements recognized the influences that they themselves brought to their decisions. Sam, for example, talked about 'having a realization of what you bring'. Fenella indicated also that the set of solutions that might be appropriate for a problem in one situation, might not be the same in another – in other words, recognizing the role of context – 'it's kind of looking at . . . the context of the situation, where it is and what sort of people are involved'.

Objectivity is an interesting issue in critical thinking and a word used by some of the teachers above. Phillips and Bond helpfully noted that learners in these four categorizations of critical reflection saw 'objectivity' as represented – or achieved – in different ways. In the first 'weighing up' group, objectivity is obtained by looking at both sides of an issue. In the 'all angles' group, it was obtained by looking more broadly at what was seen as 'all' perspectives. In the third and fourth groups there is a recognition of the influence of one's own patterns of experience, which implies a detachment from the situation, as well as recognition of the role of the variable influence of context and of personal values and beliefs. We discuss objectivity and subjectivity further in Chapter 4.

It is important to reiterate that this was, in effect, a study of critical 'reflection' and some of the findings may be influenced by this. Reflection, for example, might promote a view of 'looking back on something' more than critical thinking (Chapter 10).

Common-sense views of critical thinking

It has been suggested that a 'defining statement' involves the gathering in of boundaries and that we need to gather some ideas that involve 'common sense' considerations of critical thinking. As with other concepts, such as reflective learning, we start by looking at the idea of critical thinking in everyday speech – and what is implied by it.

Critical thinking is clearly something to do with thinking – but, again, it is not all of the process of thinking. Like reflection, it implies more detail than the generic term of 'thinking' (Dewey, 1933). At this stage we will say that some forms of reflection – such as that called 'critical reflection' – might include critical thinking, but when we are engaging in critical thinking, we also reflect in order to achieve the kind of thinking that engages prior experience (see above). We return to this later.

It is clear that critical thinking is something to do with the processes of learning – but it is not all of learning (see Moon, 2004, Ch. 2). It would seem to be a process in which we generate knowledge by bringing to bear a particular way of working with knowledge. The initial knowledge may be what we know already (our 'internal experience'), as when we think critically about our own actions or ideas; and it might involve external material ('external experience') such as someone else's work when we evaluate an academic paper. There will be different focuses, depending on the kind of subject matter. Critical thinking would seem to be a gathering of various processes such as understanding, analysis, synthesis, evaluation and so on (such as those described by Bloom, 1956) and termed 'tools of manipulation of knowledge' (Chapter 1, p. 14). There is implied in the term 'critical thinking' a certain skilled and precise use of these tools of manipulation of knowledge – whether or not they are separately identified by the learner or her teachers.

There is also a sense of direction to critical thinking – a sense that we have some defined reason for engaging in the process. This would often be in distinction from reflective learning, where a sense of open exploration is implied. Generally we reflect in order to find out how something is or to find out more about it. We think critically to find out something more specific – some information that we have in mind when we start. It is an active and deliberate process, again distinguishing it from some processes of reflection. It will usually result in something to do with making a judgement, or judgements. These may be reflexive (judging the quality of one's own judgement and critical thinking processes). There is also an idea that ideas or evidence may be assessed or evaluated in the process – and that the process itself may be subject to evaluation. These latter elements are particularly characteristic of critical thinking, as we indicate later.

In addition to the 'sense of direction', we would not think critically about a simple idea – it would be about something relatively complex (or complex to the thinker) and in engaging in critical thinking, we are taking a deep approach to the learning process, and not a surface approach (Marton, Entwistle and Hounsell, 1997). Critical thinking also implies that there are some potential ramifications of the subject matter, such as alternative viewpoints or opinions, and that it is desirable to take those into account. Critical thinking is therefore not the same as planning, which implies a more straightforward process.

Lastly, in this initial overview of 'critical thinking', we need to consider the connotations that the term carries. Critical thinking has a sense of 'a good thing to be able to do' about it. It would not otherwise be so common in mission statements! It is interesting to note that the similar term 'criticizing' might often be seen to have negative connotations. This is a source again of some confusion for those who are new to the term.

The implications of the word 'thinking'

The content of the sections below leads to the development of a model (Table 2.1) – p. 30.

In the last section, we explored the common sense view of critical thinking, but there are complications in the manner in which we use the term 'thinking' – and we deal with them here and in the next section. Does the action of 'thinking' include or exclude the idea of written work or the oral debate in a seminar?

We need here to distinguish between learning and the representation of learning and thinking and the representation of thinking – as also was necessary with reflecting and its representation (Moon, 2004). Representation for any of these cognitive activities can take place in writing, drawing, drama, sign languages, speaking in an oral recording and so on. Thinking, learning and reflecting go on inside the learner's head. No one beyond the learner can know about the content of these processes. Perhaps through the notions of intuition or of un- or sub-conscious activity, the learner herself may be unaware. As soon as the learner writes, or speaks or represents her cognition in another manner, she is enacting a further process – that of representation. However, the act of representation is a means of further learning as the material is organized, categorized and censored in the process of representation. We also learn differently from different forms of representation (Eisner, 1991). For example, if we write about a difficult interview and then talk about it or draw it in a cartoon, different ideas will emerge in the processes of representation. Most of what we discuss as 'critical thinking' in this book is going to be about the representation of critical thinking – which is most often written – but we should not ignore other forms of representation. Cartoons and drawing have their place in critical thinking.

The fact that we are often going to be talking about critical writing rather than thinking has been an issue of consideration in the development of this book. We could, from now on, take a hard line and adopt the term 'critical activity' to include thinking and writing and other forms of representation. The difficulty with such a policy is that much of the literature uses the term 'critical thinking', and the introduction of a different term might be confusing. We will therefore, alongside the term 'critical activity', largely continue to refer also to 'critical thinking', which may often mean the thinking and the representation of the thinking – however, we will be clearer as to the meaning in the local context. In the final development of the defining statement, we will reconsider future uses of terminology (Chapter 10).

Representational vocabulary associated with critical activities

The use of the term 'critical activity' enables us to pull together the idea of the thinking and the representation of that thinking and to develop a model which can act as a framework into which we can now slot in terms that are associated with critical thinking and its representation.

There is a range of other 'critical' words which need to be located in relation to critical thinking and its representation. It is a list that seems ever to expand at the present time – and we would sceptically suggest that it expands because the notion of something being 'critical' provides a 'good' higher education or academic connotation. 'Critical' adds the idea of the application of academic rigour to a subject without necessarily doing anything. All of the following words, for example, may be prefixed with the word critical:

understanding	reflection
appraisal	review
analysis	interpretation
evaluation	appreciation
management	awareness
care	being
action	practice

There are similar words like 'criticality', 'critical incident' (Brookfield, 1990), 'critically reflective learning' (Brockbank and McGill, 1998), and some words not associated with higher education such as 'critical situation', 'critical state', 'critical mass' and others which serve to confuse things further.

How do these words relate to critical thinking? There is no 'right' answer to this any more than there is a single response to 'what is critical thinking?'. However, for the purposes of this book and for the purposes of thinking about the pedagogical implications of critical activity in higher and other areas of education, we can make some suggestions within the model. It would seem that the word 'thinking' can broadly encompass most of these words (above). They are forms of mental processing that might well come into the notion of thinking and into the actual process, as we have so far described it, of critical thinking. They all have their particular emphases, though – critical reflection is akin to the definition of reflection, but probably what is described as deeper forms of reflection (Moon, 2004). Critical evaluation and possibly appraisal too, emphasise the judgement of quality of something and so on. We shall therefore see critical thinking as a term that encompasses these words, but the words put emphases on particular areas of critical thinking activity or on the kinds of outcomes that are expected from critical thinking. There are a number of articles in the literature that seem to concur with this organization of the vocabulary of critical thinking by referring to these subset words within the broader context of critical thinking (e.g. Phillips and Bond, 2004; Clegg and Bradley, 2006).

There is also the notion of acting in a critical manner (Barnett, 1997) and a specialized form of critical action is 'critical practice' – usually a term used in professional education and development (e.g. Adams, Dominelli and Payne, 2002; Ford, Johnston, Brumfit, Mitchell and Myles, 2005; Brown and Rutter, 2006). The action may be an outcome of initial representation of the critical thinking in written or other forms. As such the action will be a secondary form of representation and we should remember that each transformation into a new representation will involve a change of the original thinking – and may well involve more learning. The written representation that precedes the action may, for example, be in the form of a learning journal (a tool to support the learner's reflections on her own learning – see Moon, 2006). Critical practice may then be recorded in the journal, and may yield further learning.

In the recognition of the distinction of the mental component from the representation component of critical thinking, we can reiterate Barnett's important idea that it is not just critical thinking that we want – or indeed, just the writing, but it is the critical action that we want. We do not want learners who can sit around just thinking effectively (and being able, thereby, to put in successful assignments and examinations, but learners who are active in their criticality, who have a habitually critical stance in the world, who question and challenge and seek for meanings and their proper justifications. Barnett makes this point in seeing reflection as the mental process on which critical action is based. In the model we would distinguish between the non-represented forms of critical thinking, the represented forms with some secondary representation and the action-based activity, which also may be another form of secondary representation.

It is further worth noting that some of the representations of critical thinking are recordings or reports of the thinking, but others are designed to stimulate others into critical thinking activities. Representations such as cartoons, satire, critiques, some jokes and humour and so on may be designed to have this effect.

There are other somewhat obtuse methods by which one finds out about the breadth of terminology around subject matter. One is to go to a library and look at books with possibly related titles or those in related sections and determine whether or not they are talking about the same or a different concept. The writer's library visits led to a number of different shelves and related queries. Were the psychology studies of cognitive activities (e.g. studies of thinking and learning) relevant and what of the business-studies problem-solving and decision-making? What of de Bono and his books on practical techniques of thinking (de Bono, 1976, 1982, 1983 etc.)? There are study skills books on critical thinking which focus on the elements of it (see Chapter 4). There are also books on the pedagogy of the subject. What about practice in social work and nursing – and those that focus on philosophy in discussions of logic or on 'philosophizing' – (e.g. Emmet, 1968). The psychology books might have seemed to be relevant, but much of the study of thinking in psychology is laboratory-based, and relates to the processing of relatively simpler or isolated concepts – far from the complexity of the processes to which we refer here. Critical thinking probably accords a construct that is many sets of behaviours. It seems to be the individual components that are of interest to the psychologist. Indeed, a widely used textbook – *Thinking and Reasoning* by Garnham and Oakhill (1994) – has no reference to critical thinking as such. Janis (1982) seems to have had a similar problem in his work on 'groupthink'. It is complex to research, he says, because it is 'at the intersection of three disciplines' (p. x). We would argue that critical thinking is at the intersection of a few more than three disciplines! The breadth of disciplines that can contribute to critical thinking do, however, increase its richness as a subject of study, but also increase the need to clarify its concept. We gather material from many of these sources in later chapters of the book.

Perhaps the most direct challenge in relation to the terminology of critical thinking is in the practices of problem-solving and decision-making (e.g. Ranyard, Crozier and Svenson, 1997). Most of the books on these topics are business-related and they are therefore very much based in the 'real world' or the swamps of professional practice (Schon, 1982, 1987). They mostly relate to situations that are complex and in which judgements must be made on the basis of evidence that is appropriate at the time. We would see these situations as applications of processes that would usually accord with critical thinking. Where the problem-solving is towards a single solution that could be construed as 'right' or 'not right', we would not use the word 'critical thinking'.

The basis of the model (Table 2.1) is, as we have said, the separation of thinking from the representation of thinking, and thence the appropriate allocation of different terms that are associated ·with critical thinking (in its common and broader meaning). The 'representation' column contains activities that may be primary representation or may be re- or secondary representation of some form. Thus, for example, a result of thinking may be writing – and it is as a result of critical writing that there is some form of action. Some forms, such as the cartoon, satire or literary critique may be art forms in themselves.

Table 2.1 Critical thinking and its subsets

Critical thinking and subsets of it – tools for the manipulation of knowledge	*Forms of primary and secondary representation*

Critical thinking – which includes critical:
    appraisal
    evaluation
    reflection
    understanding
    analysis
    review
    appreciation
    management
    awareness
    care
	oral representation –
	    debate, discussion and other
	    oral representation
	
	written representation –
	    critical reports, reviews, critique,
	    satire, essays, metaphor –
	
	graphic depiction – cartoon, pastiche,
	    sketch

Critical incident analysis	forms of action –
	    assertive action; critical or professional
	    practice, reflective practice, dramatic
	    or theatrical representation, etc.

Problem-solving and decision-making are forms that can be broadly similar to critical thinking when there is no one fixed solution to be sought	Various forms of representation

The activities of critical thinking

The idea that there might be a range of activities described as 'critical thinking' became evident in the definitions of critical thinking that were provided by the teaching staff (pp. 21–3). Different teachers had different frames of reference for critical thinking based on different activities in which the thinking was employed. For example, in the definitions (a) and (c):

> Critical thinking is the ability to consider a range of information derived from many different sources, to process this information in a creative and logical manner, challenging it, analysing it and arriving at considered conclusions which can be defended and justified. Its opposites are prejudice and the risk to judgement. Knowledge has to be constructed – and its meanings change with the context.

and

> It is to develop your own argument, deconstructing ideas or synthesizing a range of ideas associated with complex ideas. There may be different routes to the same conclusion or different conclusions to the same issues.

The context suggests the development of an argument, as would be done in an essay, for example. These contrast with the first phrase of (m), which is about thinking about the work of others – for example an academic paper.

> It is the evaluating of the work of writers of articles, journals, or books . . .

On the other hand, (d) relates critical thinking to the review of personal situations:

> Critical thinking is looking at one's work or situation with value judgement – what did I do right or wrong? It is like criticizing oneself. It can also be applied to other people's work – thinking where they are coming from; whether they are biased – do they have a vested interest?

(n), however, could be applied to the appraisal of an object – and that would be a form of critical thinking that is used in practical subjects where a product is produced (e.g. engineering or art and design, etc.).

> It is the analysis of material, identifying weaknesses and strengths.

In contrast, (h) is more generalized and implies a habit of thinking and being that might be expected in higher education or the professions or in other situations that require thoughtful processes.

> On both undergraduate and postgraduate programmes the ability to think critically shows itself through a deep thought process. Instead of description, we promote analysis. Instead of personal subjective views, we promote evaluation. Critical thinking is an argument which runs like a river through a piece of work and the tributaries join it as elements of evidence.

Through noticing the different activities implied in these definitions and the development of this thinking in further conversations, the categorization of the activities of critical thinking was developed. The categorization below is of the activities of critical thinking as it stands as the book is written. We use the term 'learner' for convenience, but clearly these processes are not always concerned with intentional formal learning.

Review of someone else's argument. In this case the argument is given and consists of the presentation of a series of ideas that lead to a conclusion. This could be in an essay, a research paper or a dissertation. It may involve the description of actual research. The task of the critical thinker here is to review the components and process of the argument, the quality of the conclusion and the process of reaching it. Learners review others' arguments when they read research papers for review *per se* or when they decide whether or not to refer to the work of others in their own reviews – a decision that will be based on the relevance and quality of the others' work.

Evaluation of an object. We think critically in making an evaluative judgement of an object – such as a work of art, a piece of writing (e.g. a book), or another construction (e.g. in architecture or engineering). There may be elements in common with the review of someone else's arguments here, but the real focus is on the object that has been developed, itself, and there may be interest in, and/or critical concern about the process of construction. This form of critical thinking may entail creative thinking that is beyond that engaged in by the developer of the object. It is the form of thinking of those called 'crits' in art, design or media work (etc.). The judgements may be on aesthetic grounds.

Development of an argument. In this case the argument is constructed by the critical thinker, working with her own presentation of evidence and reasoning and drawing her own conclusion. Again, the concerns should be the content and the process of reasoning, but often there are issues about the presentation of argument in terms of the structure of the writing (or speech). Learners would use this process in writing essays or the writing up of research in reports or in larger project work like dissertations and theses.

Critical thinking about self. This form of critical thinking might often be called reflective learning or critical reflection (Brockbank and McGill, 1998; Fisher, 2003), though it could be construed to be more focused on a particular characteristic or activity with the idea of improvement. Since the self is relevant to any other form of critical thinking, the issues involved in critical thinking about self can be a part of other forms of critical thinking. If these aspects of the self are seen in an objective manner, then this form could coincide with the evaluation of an object. The difficulty in this form of critical thinking is that the chooser of the evidence or criteria on which the thinking is based, is the subject and object of the thinking.

The review of an incident. Critical thinking about an incident will often be in the context of professional education or professional development and may be termed 'critical reflection'. It is likely to entail the reviewing of an event (which may be called a 'critical incident') in which the thinker has been involved and the objective will be to review her performance and consider how the incident may have been handled differently. In this respect, it may coincide with critical thinking about the self. It is possible that the 'incident' could be a scenario (e.g. a natural disaster) in which the thinker has not been directly involved, but usually the concern will be practice with respect to the incident.

Engage in constructive response to the arguments of others. The addition of this category follows the work of Bailin et al. (1999a, 1999b) who suggest that the engagements with others in argument is a further activity of critical thinking because, within it, the thinker has to consider the context of the argument and the response. The response could be represented orally or in writing and other ways of representation.

Habit of engagement with the world. We have already talked of critical thinking as a disposition and a way of engaging with the world. In this respect it could be said to be a habit of listening and processing that listening – in other words, thinking about it, evaluating or reflecting on the ideas. The 'habits' come into the manner in which people process experiences, write and speak or express themselves in other ways, and they flow over from academic or thoughtful activity into the everyday world.

This last category is not an 'activity' in the same way as the others, being an ongoing disposition. We return to the notion of critical thinking as a habit of engagement with the world in the next chapter.

It would seem, therefore, that the idea of critical thinking is applied to a range of different but specific activities and not just one. All of these activities include the making of judgements on the basis of assessing different kinds of evidence from different kinds of sources and we begin to see this as the central activity of critical thinking. The habit of engagement suggests the adoption of a habit of broad assessment of ideas before judgements are made in all areas of life.

Towards a defining statement about critical thinking – a first version

We can now pull together some of the ideas from the chapter as an initial statement about critical thinking. At this stage, we present what is literally a collection of ideas.

The central activity of critical thinking is the assessment of what might be called evidence, in order to make a judgement.

We treat critical activity as one aspect of a generic word that includes the idea of critical thinking and its various representations, including action, speech, writing and so on. We would see the various terms such as critical appraisal, evaluation, reflection, understanding, as elements of critical thinking where there is an emphasis on particular kinds of mental activity. There are many forms of representation.

Critical thinking is an aspect of the activity of thinking. It is a form of learning in that it is a means of generating new knowledge by processing existing knowledge and ideas using what we have called the 'tools of manipulation of knowledge' (e.g. analysis, understanding, synthesis). We might call critical thinking itself a 'multiple' tool for the manipulation of knowledge.

There is a sense of precision and skill in the use of critical thinking. When we engage in critical thinking, we are usually working towards an anticipated form of outcome, which is likely to be a 'judgement'. Critical thinking would usually relate to subject matter that is complex and about which there might be some alternative viewpoints, and it involves deep engagement with that subject matter. Reflexivity is usually implied in the process.

For the learner, critical thinking can be involved in a variety of activities with different intended outcomes that are still judgements (e.g. evaluation of an object, development of an argument). It is not, as may be assumed, just engaged in situations in which an argument of another person (e.g. in an academic paper) is reviewed.

Thinkpoint

Choosing wisely is a skill that can be learnt.

(Hastie and Davies, 2001: 2)

People abhor uncertainty. A common way of dealing with our experience of the uncertainty in life is to ignore it completely or to invent some 'higher rationale' to explain it. . . .

(Hastie and Davies, 2001: 313)

3   Approaches to critical thinking in the literature

Introduction

In the last chapter, we began to map the territory of critical thinking by looking at a common-sense view of it, and words that are associated with it, and by the listing of activities which form the contexts for the engagement of critical thinking. There were some references to literature but the emphasis was on language and the opinion of practitioners and learners. In this chapter we focus on what others have written about critical thinking in the formal literature. We begin by taking a broad overview of the range of variations in the literature and then consider ways in which critical thinking has been introduced or treated, usually educational contexts. We have called these 'approaches'. The approaches have been generated when there has been work to do with critical thinking – such as teaching it or enhancing its functioning in learners – or making sense of it (e.g. Bailin, Case, Coombs and Daniels, 1999a, 1999b). Approaches represent frames of reference that writers have used, consciously or not consciously in order to work with the complexities of critical thinking for the purpose in hand. They are not necessarily 'fixed' – it is possible for the same person to adopt different approaches at different times or for the same model to fit several 'approaches'. Study of the different approaches furthers the development of a defining statement about critical thinking.

An overview of the literature of critical thinking

We go back to Jez, our enquiring student from the last chapter. Not only might he have been given any one or two of the teachers' interpretations of critical thinking, but he and his peers might have started out with a conception of critical thinking that matched one or more of the interpretations of critical thinking that are represented by Phillips and Bond's sample (2004) see p. 24 in this volume. He – or his teachers – might have been given a definition of critical thinking that emphasized the skills, such as:

> [critical thinking involves] working out whether we believe what we see or hear; taking steps to find out whether something is likely to be true; arguing our own case if someone doesn't believe us.
>
> (Cottrell, 2005: viii)

They may have been given a definition that emphasized the quality of reasoning:

> Critical thinking is a kind of evaluative thinking which involves both criticism and creative thinking and which is particularly concerned with the quality of reasoning or argument which is presented in support of a belief or a course of action.
>
> (Fisher, 2001: 13)

Or they might have been told that:

> critical thinking is the intellectual discipline process of actively and skillfully conceptualizing, synthesizing and/or evaluating information gathered from, or generated by observation, experience, reflection, reasoning or communication, as a guide to belief and action.
>
> (Scriven and Paul, n.d.: 1)

Alternatively they might have been shown some sort of statement of what it is to be a critical thinker:

> Being a critical thinker involves more than cognitive activities such as logical reasoning or scrutinizing arguments for assertions unsupported by logical evidence. Thinking critically involves our recognizing the assumptions underlying our beliefs and behaviours. It means we can give justifications for our ideas and actions. More importantly, perhaps, it means we try to judge the rationality of these justifications. We can do this by comparing them to a range of varying interpretations and perspectives . . . we can test the accuracy and rationality of these justifications against some kind of objective analysis of the 'real' world as we understand it.
>
> (Brookfield, 1987: 13–14)

Jez probably would find critical thinking easier to understand if he was given the 'skills' definition that is commonly the 'study skills' approach to critical thinking because it is designed to be easy to understand. However, those involved in academic thinking have commented on the skills approach as being simplistic. Barnett (1997) talks of 'the critical thinking industry' that is 'so swept along . . . by the belief that there is a single set of actions, skills, propensities or dispositions that can be labelled "critical thinking" that they lose sight of the end of critical thinking' (Barnett, 1997: 3). Similarly, Bailin et al. (1999a), say:

> It is our view that much of the theoretical work and many of the pedagogical endeavours in this area [of critical thinking] are misdirected because they are based on faulty conceptions. . . . Critical thinking is frequently conceptualized in terms of skills, processes, procedures and practice.

So what is Jez to believe when his teachers and the literature itself propound different views of critical thinking? Ironically his teachers might not allow Jez the intellectual space in which to engage in critical thinking about critical thinking because – as an undergraduate – they will give him marks according to whether he has critically thought according to their own conception of the process.

So it is not only the views of practitioners that differ on what critical thinking might be, but the literature itself. That makes it difficult to summarize the literature – because in the end there simply are different views of critical thinking because we have constructed our views differently (though see the section 'Critical thinking and the brain' in Chapter 4).

Before we look at approaches to critical thinking and towards the end of providing a general review of literature, we take an overview of some of the variations in the views of critical thinking that cut across the approaches. It may be helpful to see the literature of critical thinking as having a number of what we might call 'dimensions'. Some are as follows:

- A breadth dimension. There are narrow views of critical thinking which focus primarily on the language of argument and reasoning and others that are very broad, viewing the characteristics of the critical thinker as leading to a way of operating in the world. There are many other examples in between.
- A longitudinal dimension. Some study critical thinking at a particular educational stage. They see it as a developed or less developed capacity and they study it as it is. Others, who teach critical thinking skills or who nurture it in facilitative classroom atmospheres, clearly base their conceptions on the notion of a longitudinal dimension of critical thinking, in which there is capacity for development however they actually define the capacity itself. There are others (and this will apply in the later chapters of this book), who see the very nature of what we observe as critical thinking to be related to developmental processes (Chapter 8).
- There is a dimension that relates to the way in which critical thinking is viewed in relation to the discipline of the learners – either as a capacity that is developed in close association with the nature of knowledge within a discipline or as a generic ability that can be applied to any matter (Fisher, 2001). The position adopted on this dimension is often not spelled out, but is implied in any pedagogical processes.
- There is a dimension that relates to the origins of the researcher or writer. Cognitive psychologists are likely to have a different view of critical thinking (often as a form of problem solving) from the philosophers (who may see it as a form of logic – see next chapter) from the educationalists.
- Another dimension is 'technical' as opposed to what might be called 'softer' views. The technical views of critical thinking (as this chapter will indicate) are often characterized by lists of skills or procedures (which may even be expected to occur in a particular order). Soft views acknowledge that learners may become good critical thinkers without resort to the learning or practice of a list of skills or procedures.
- And the view of the activities of critical thinking (see last chapter) also influences the manner in which critical thinking is described. We have seen that

many writers view critical thinking as engaged when a learner is reviewing the argument made in an academic paper. Others see it in a much broader manner that may encompass a range of activities.

The approaches to presenting critical thinking

There is no particular sequence to the approaches to critical thinking and, as we have seen, this is largely a manner of reviewing some of the more important literature and making sense of a complex field of ideas. Approaches that are described below are the following:

- logic
- listing of components – skills and abilities
- pedagogy
- 'ways of being'
- developmental approaches
- and approaches that take an overview.

The consideration of the approaches to critical thinking is similar to the work of Bailin et al. (1999a), though the actual categorization differs. Bailin et al. describe three 'conceptions' of critical thinking – thinking skills, procedures and collections of mental processes such as analysis, synthesis and so on. In the current consideration we have not included the generic thinking skills as a particular category. As Bailin et al. say, the separation of generic thinking skills from the material of the thinking – the knowledge – creates difficulties. The first approach that we consider is logic.

Approaches to critical thinking through logic

For thinkers in the past, logic was the main method associated with critical thinking. We must acknowledge that there are many forms of logic, and that we therefore generalize here. The application of logic was seen to maximize the 'objectivity' of critique and argument – a point about which we might disagree (see Chapter 4). Logic deals with the quality of the reasoning and the argument. In terms of the activities of critical thinking (Chapter 2), logic largely focuses on the analysis of the arguments of others and the construction of argument – though often the assumption in some of the introductory texts is that the subject matter is represented by problems with some kind of 'correct answer' which will be detected through the appropriate techniques of logical analysis.

We further the discussion of logic in critical thinking with a story – because the experience of this story to the writer is not a unique one. The place of logic in critical thinking became a particular challenge during research for this book. Initially a general definition of critical thinking seemed to accept logic as part of, but not as the whole story about critical thinking. But then there was a run of books that suggested that they were definitive texts on critical thinking and where the content was confined to a discussion of logic. Bowell and Kemp (2002) is an example – with the title *Critical Thinking: a concise guide*. It is introduced on the cover as 'essential reading for students and professionals . . . seeking to improve their reasoning and arguing skills'. A writer on critical thinking, finding a book with such a title might feel that the work has been done – why write another book? So it was with this writer, who set out with Bowell and Kemp on a long train journey – with an aim of finding out if there was anything more to write about critical thinking. Bowell and Kemp focus on the quality of reasoning and take a hard line on 'objective truth'. The subject matter looked complex and formulaic and there are (in this 'essential reading for students') over fifty technical definitions in the eleven page glossary. Was this really the only way to go about critical thinking? The idea of writing a book on critical thinking nearly sank at this point.

Other books on logic also said that they described critical thinking but most did not seem to take such a hard line about 'objective truth' (e.g. Ennis, 1996; Van Den Brink-Budgen, 2000 (*Critical Thinking for Students*); Fisher, 2001). The situation was further confused – and redeemed – by publications like one called *The Miniature Guide to Critical Thinking* (Paul and Elder, 2004) which contained no reference to logic. It seemed that writers on critical thinking came either from the 'logic' camp or from approaches that were more variable and which did not work primarily on the basis of objective truth. There were a few 'middle lines' such as Toulmin (1988).

The writer was not unique among writers in meeting this difficulty with logic and its role in thinking. Edward de Bono, in his many books about thinking and its development, energetically confronts the divide between those who equate logic with thinking and those who see logic as a discipline that deals with a specific element in the process of reasoning. He acknowledges that 'Most schools equate thinking with logic' [cover], but goes on to say that logic is a tool that shows 'what is implicit in the concepts used [in argument] and to expose contradiction' (de Bono, 1982: 77). He implies that logic may have held its popularity because, while it was considered that students should be taught how to think, other than logic there seemed to be little to grasp hold of and to then teach – what set of rules for thinking was there, apart from logic? De Bono's popularity and the range of different approaches he has developed as means of 'grasping hold of' thinking, stand as contrary evidence to this.

Other writers have found their different ways around the issues of logic and critical thinking. Flew (1975) acknowledges the confusions about the role of logic – and indicates that his book which is 'intended to help people to improve their thinking' is 'an exercise in logical coaching'. This exercise, he says, 'may be beneficial even though neither the coach nor the coached have or acquire any familiarity with the calculi of Logic' (p. 21). Paul and Elder (2004) incorporate logic in their definition of a 'universal intellectual standard' and ask thinkers to question:

> Does this really make sense? Does that follow from what you said? How does that follow? But before you implied this and now you are saying that. I don't

see how both can be true. When we think, we bring a variety of thoughts together into some order. When the combination of thoughts are mutually supporting and make sense in combination, the thinking is 'logical'. When the combination is not mutually supporting, is contradictory in some sense, or does not 'make sense', the combination is 'not logical'.

(Paul and Elder, 2004: 8)

In terms of the role of the study of logic, we also note Meyers's (1986) evidence that learning logic does not seem to contribute to critical thinking ability. Bernstein (1995) tried the use of informal logic to teaching critical thinking and found that it provided 'a powerful guide for critiquing arguments [but] it provides no grammar for fashioning a rapprochement between competing arguments. Rather it depends on the "fitter" argument to survive. The non-surviving one receives little attention.' It is important to note that a 'logical' argument does not need to be 'right' (de Bono, 1983) – something can be very 'logical', but not at all in keeping with the principles of critical thinking.

While there may be some value in teaching formal logic because it helps the learner to become sharper in her processes and construction of argumentation, issues that concern the quality of argument seem to be a relatively small corner of the much broader picture of critical thinking. Nor does it seem necessary to be fully acquainted with the fifty-plus definitions in the glossary of Bowell and Kemp in order to think effectively and critically. We would suggest, therefore, that there is a division between those whose concern is the process of argument, and those whose concern is the management of complex and constructed interrelationships between learning, knowledge, epistemology, values, beliefs and the quest for ideas to live by.

This book, therefore, has little to do with formal logic. It does not seem essential, as Flew said, to be familiar with the terminology or exercises of logic; however, there are important principles in the discipline of logic. There is the idea, for example, that we should be aware of the **quality of the language used** in the construction or analysis of argument, and the meanings and assumptions that can be present in words used. We would see the quality of thinking and awareness that is covered in depth by study of logic as a component of critical thinking, but one which can be covered by ensuring that learners are aware of the issues. This does not need to be taught through the use of the terminology and disciplinary structures of logic itself. Some more of the valuable qualities of thinking stressed in logic are the **systematic approach** to a problem, the **stress on persistence** and the **requirement for clarity and precision** – ideas that we carry forward.

A concern that is inspired by the logic approaches to critical thinking, is the place of 'rules' to the learning processes of critical thinking. We have indicated, and will further be demonstrating, that an important aspect of critical thinking in its more sophisticated forms is the willingness and confidence to challenge rules. The idea that critical thinking is to be taught by way of a set of rules that should be followed, seems to present a strange contradiction. We return to this idea later.

Approaches concerned with component processes, skills and abilities of critical thinking

Other approaches to critical thinking are either less rule-bound than formal logic or utilize a different set of rules. A common approach is to identify the component processes, skills and abilities in critical thinking usually in order to make the idea seem more comprehensible, more usable and to relate it to practice. In this section we have not tried to distinguish skills from processes, because the difference between what might be called a skill and what might be called a process may be little – and is it a skill or a process to review a piece of text for the assumptions that are made in it? There are many different studies that fit into this approach. Most cover similar kinds of material, but they differ in the detail to which they go in breaking down the processes, skills and abilities. We present them in two groups below – those that suggest a sequence of processes to be followed and those that simply list the components.

In any comparisons of skills or processes in critical thinking, we need to be aware of the contexts, noticing the discipline or professional practice context of the work which may determine emphasis on particular elements of the critical thinking. For example, personal and professional values are an issue in social work (Brown and Rutter, 2006) – but this is not so emphasized in a generic study skills approach to critical thinking like that of Cottrell (2005). The aim of most of the literature in this section is to facilitate the learner's engagement with critical thinking, whether or not the activity is mediated by a teaching process. It is also important to note that there are differences in the kinds of activities of critical thinking (Chapter 2) that are implied. In most cases, it would seem that the writers have in mind the activity of reviewing somebody else's argument – but occasionally there is some attention paid to the development of one's own argument.

Sequence approaches (which are treated as a separate group in Moon, 2005c) can look a little like cookbooks. Earlier work of Cottrell (1999 – see also 2005 work described below) provides the first example of the sequenced view. She starts by saying that critical thinking 'means weighing up the arguments for and against' (p. 188). She then describes a series of 'steps' of critical thinking in reading. The steps are 'identify the line of reasoning', 'critically evaluate the line of reasoning', 'question surface appearances', 'identify evidence in the text', 'evaluate the evidence', 'identify the writer's conclusions' and 'evaluate whether the evidence supports the conclusions'. These are good thinking activities, though the learner may have no more understanding of 'critically evaluate' than 'critically think'! We also note that the steps listed may not seem to lead the reader towards what she might expect to find from the initial definition – a 'weighed up' argument that is either 'for' or 'against'. It does not seem unusual for recommended processes to add up to an apparently different end point than is initially implied – such as finding the 'correct' solution to a specific problem – which we would not normally call critical thinking. We should note also the simplicity of conception of 'for or against' views of critical thinking (see Phillips and Bond's work described in Chapter 2).

Another example of a sequence approach is that of Bell (1995) – writing in the context of psychology. It is worth noting that much of the discipline-specific material on critical thinking arises in the discipline of psychology. Bell's book, written for a student audience, is short, focused and specifically directed towards the activity of evaluating a secondary source. Below we paraphrase the six stages given by Bell (who also provides exercises and examples). The quotations below are from p. 72 except where otherwise stated.

'Stage 1. Identify the Source' – written by whom, where and when?

'Stage 2. Read to understand' – looking for the central idea of the text, and the key points.

'Stage 3. Analyze the definitions of important terms' – looking for concepts that are un- or ill-defined. Bell says that any 'propaganda techniques' should be listed. Earlier in the book (p. 26), he elaborates the meaning of propaganda techniques as labelling devices which appeal to hatred (e.g. 'manipulator'); generalities such as 'conclusive', 'the best'; 'testimonial' statements such as 'X is an expert' and 'bandwagon' suggestions where 'the reader is asked to uncritically accept something since everyone else has'.

'Stage 4. Analyze the research evidence' – identifying the evidence and noting any that is not complete.

'Stage 5. Evaluate the research evidence' – looking for deficiencies in reasoning, looking at the dates of the study, subjects involved in experiments, research methods used, the results, the statement of outcomes, and given explanations, their explanations, the conclusions drawn and their relationship to the key points.

'Stage 6. Evaluate the rest of the source' – looking at the supporting content of the other parts of the article (e.g. literature reviews) and finally 'Describe what you believe about the article's central idea based on your critical thinking about the evidence and reasoning in the source'.

(Bell, 1995: 72)

We can compare Fisher's approach to critical thinking (Fisher, 2001) with that of Bell. It also indicates a sequence which includes the following components (described as 'some of the fundamental critical thinking skills' (p. 8), each elaborated in the context of the subsequent chapters). Like Bell, he is clearly thinking here of the review of someone else's argument:

identify the elements in a reasoned case, especially reasons and conclusions;
identify and evaluate assumptions;
clarify and interpret expressions and ideas;
judge the acceptability, especially the credibility of claims;
evaluate arguments of different kinds;
analyse, evaluate and produce explanations;
draw inferences;
produce arguments.

(Fisher, 2001: 8)

Within the chapters, the headings are broken down into checklist form in 'thinking maps'. The 'thinking map' for 'Skillful analysis . . . of arguments' says:

1. What is/are the main Conclusion(s)? (may be stated or unstated; may be recommendations, explanations, and so on. Conclusion indicator words and 'therefore' test may help.)
2. What are the Reasons (data, evidence) and their Structure?
3. What is Assumed? (that is implicit or taken for granted, perhaps in the Context.)
4. Clarify the Meaning (by the terms, claim or arguments).

(Fisher, 2001: 56)

While it is not entirely fair to take material out of its context, the complexity and detail in the 'thinking map' is evident! While Fisher's sequence broadly matches that of Bell, and would engage the student in fairly similar activities, it is noted that in these two books for students, very different language is used. The work of Fisher uses some of the simpler terminology of logic – that of Bell uses language that is closer to that used in study skills books. In both cases it is the writer's view that abstract instructional language such as this is difficult to 'get a grip of'. It needs to be exemplified. We return to this issue later.

While still identifying a number of points that need attention in critical thinking, Plath, English, Connors and Beveridge (1999) also take a less technical approach to the identification of the processes. Their work was in the context of under-graduate social work. They provide 'an outline of the skills needed for critical thinking in social work practice' that were 'developed as expected outcomes in the teaching of critical thinking in the social work degree'. However, the activity that is implied is more generalized.

Take an issue/problem/proposition and state it in clear and not too limited terms.

Come to an understanding of the meanings of the major terms used.

Think through the implications at various levels, e.g. individual and group, emotional and cognitive.

Identify the major models, theories, paradigms that inform your thinking and the nature of the evidence used.

Determine the gaps in the theory or evidence, values and assumptions.

See the issue from the different points of view of the various stakeholders, direct and indirect.

Arrive at a 'proper' solution, knowing that all the evidence will never be available and that you will never be aware of all the possible models or theories that could be applied.

Make a statement on where you sit with this issue/problem/proposition and any assumptions you make because of where you are personally coming from.

(Plath, et al. 1999)

The list of skills above provided a structure for the teaching of critical thinking skills to undergraduate students via a series of exercises. In this account of critical thinking there is much more effort to stress that critical thinking is often dealing with uncertainties and the writer's attempt to support the appropriate management of this uncertainty.

The second group of approaches under this heading of component processes and skills puts emphasis on the listing of components and they are less specific about the sequence. In a study skill book for geography students, Kneale (2003) suggests that critical thinking is 'working through for oneself, afresh, a problem' (p. 3). She identifies some processes that might be involved, such as 'critically evaluating', making judgements, awareness of bias, 'commenting in a thoughtful way'. We mentioned, above, the use of terminology that there again is no clearer than 'critical thinking'. Fairly similarly, Marshall and Rowland (1998) talk of the 'fundamental elements' of critical thinking as 'the presentation of arguments to persuade', debate and negotiating position, reflection, the communication aspects of it, and the outcome in making a decision and 'acting on what you have come to think and believe'. They say that critical thinking involves 'emotion as well as reason and rationality' (p. 34). Marshall and Rowland's approach differs, however, from that of Kneale in the kinds of critical thinking activities implied (see Chapter 2). The approach of Mumm and Kersting (1997) – writing about social work undergraduate studies – seems to relate to the general evaluation of social work theories and it provides a contrast with Plath et al. (1999) (see above) which was about dealing with a specific dilemma. The 'five interrelated skills that promote critical thinking for social workers' here are:

1. The ability to understand social work theories.
2. The ability to divide a theory into its components (assumptions, concepts, propositions, hypotheses).
3. The ability to assess the practice implications of a theory.
4. The ability to develop and apply criteria for evaluating a theory.
5. The ability to identify common errors in reasoning.

We now come to a comprehensive approach to the skills of critical thinking – that of Cottrell (2005). Her book *Critical Thinking Skills* is wholly devoted to identification and discussion of critical thinking skill components with a great many exercises for learners (in 200-plus pages). The book is described as taking 'an easy step-by-step approach to developing a range of critical thinking skills' (back cover). It is designed for the student or the general reader. It takes the stance that 'skills in reasoning can be developed through a better understanding of what critical thinking entails and through practice' (p. 1). It includes chapters on the following (based on the contents pages):

The identification of arguments and non-arguments
Recognizing the quality of the author of the argument's statement of her case
Recognizing assumptions and implicit arguments

The identification of flaws in the arguments

Finding and evaluating sources of evidence

The processes of critical reading and note-making, 'critical selection, inter-
    pretation, and noting of source material'

Critical thinking in the context of writing

The evaluation of critical writing.

(Cottrell, 2005)

Cottrell's book covers the activity of evaluating the arguments of others as well as the skills that underlie the development of one's own written representation. It provides self-assessment charts, exercises and activities as well as descriptive text. The interesting question that arises now is whether the ability to think critically is vastly enhanced by an engagement with such material. Is this all there is to critical thinking, and can the ability to think critically be gained just by such a skills approach, or is there more to it? If there is more to it, might there be other ways of learning? How did I – the writer – learn to think critically if I have never engaged in any material of this sort? Could I have come to what I know more quickly – a little voice also adds, what is it that I 'know' about critical thinking anyway? Does it matter that the exercises in such a general book as Cottrell's are not usually going to match the issues of the particular discipline? We return to these questions later.

While the booklet written by Paul and Elder (2004) in some parts provides a sequence of stages for the learner, there are more generalized aspects as well. The definition of critical thinking in the booklet is 'a process by which the thinker improves the quality of his or her thinking by skilfully taking charge of the struc-tures inherent in thinking and imposing intellectual standards upon them' (p. 1). This seems to be a reasonably simple definition, but the booklet expands into a range of other factors such as 'universal intellectual standards' (p. 7) – see above; clarity; accuracy; precision; relevance; depth; breadth and logic; and 'structures'; and by the end of the booklet it is difficult to see how all of these factors are interrelated. The guide stresses the use of a systematic approach, the expectation of a judgement as an outcome, with evaluation as an ongoing process with the sense that there are standards to meet in making the judgement. The booklet approach seems attractive as a means of supporting students, but may be too complex for its size and too much condensed for use as a 'simple' guide.

What do we take from these approaches to critical thinking that emphasize the components or skills? Below, we will consider whether the listing of the com-ponents of the critical thinking process of an adept critical thinker and the giving of that list to learners, can help to improve the thinking of the learners – or is there something missing here? We can say that **there are identifiable skills and processes that may be part of critical thinking**. This does not mean that listing them and teaching them separately is necessarily the way in which we learn the activities of critical thinking. Some of these lists follow a sequence and this may seem sensible, though, as we have said for logic, the process then becomes like rule-following and there is an anomaly that rule-following is just what critical thinking is not!

Pedagogical approaches to critical thinking

A group of influential writers and educators describe critical thinking in relation to pedagogical issues and, in so doing, adopt a less structured approach to its identity. They are more concerned about how to guide learners into being critical thinkers rather than treating the process as an entity in itself. One could say that their definitions emerge through the ways in which critical thinking is facilitated (usually by teachers). We consider this group here in more general terms, but draw on the detail of their work in the chapters that focus on pedagogy later in the book. They wrote, mainly, at a time when critical thinking was promoted widely in American college education.

Brookfield (1987) seems to typify this 'pedagogical approach' to critical thinking. He says that 'Phrases such as critical thinking . . . are exhortatory, heady and conveniently vague' (p. 11) and that 'trying to force people to analyze critically the assumptions under which they have been thinking and living is likely to serve no function other than intimidating them to the point where resistance builds up against this process' (p. 11). He advocates processes of 'trying to awaken, prompt, nurture and encourage this process' (p. 11). Meyers (1986) also focuses on how to enable learners to think critically, though his focus was on young college students while Brookfield was concerned with adults. Like Brookfield, Meyers suggests that critical thinking should be fostered through engagement of students' interest and motivation in a facilitatory environment. Lipman (1991) is another of this group, who argued that the best manner of developing critical thinking in learners was to teach forms of philosophy early on. To some extent the use of 'Theory of Knowledge' sessions in the International Baccalaureate was based on a similar idea – and seems to be valued by most learners once they have engaged with it (International Baccalaureate, 2005 – www.ibo.org/diploma/curriculum).

A more recent example of a pedagogical approach to critical thinking that also emphasizes the educational conditions under which critical thinking is developed is that of Kaasboll (1998) who worked with computer students. The interest was in improvement of the critical thinking and the problem-defining skills of undergraduate computer science students. The approaches to this included pedagogical methods, for example a reduction in the volume of course material, improvement in the preparation of the teachers to encourage greater interaction with learners, and the use of a more effective project-based and inductive approach. There was a general improvement in learning and critical thinking.

Another example of this approach is that of Bernstein (1995). Bernstein does advocate the need for the teacher to identify the model of critical thinking to which she adheres, since the model will support a particular method of working with the learners. Bernstein describes the development of three 'complementary models' of critical thinking – the informal reasoning model (logic), the problem-solving model and the negotiation model. We considered Bernstein's dissatisfaction with the informal reasoning model earlier. The problem-solving 'takes its contemporary form from the analogy of the mind to a computer [and therefore] it is not surprising that it provides poor guidance for the social and highly conflicted problem solving of everyday life'. Bernstein later developed the 'negotiation model' which is largely the subject of his paper. He describes as 'most attractive . . . its insistence on treating all parties in the debate with respect and on the importance of being genuinely empathetic with all their interests'. This indicates a similar attitude to that of Meyers and Brookfield but it is achieved in a different manner.

Those who advocate the pedagogical approaches to critical thinking tend to be a group who are concerned with the conditions which support critical thinking rather than creating tight definitions. They demonstrate the **influence of emotion** and of **a nurturing environment**, the **negative influence of threat** and the need for an appropriate challenge to thinking as means of facilitating the development of critical thinking.

Critical thinking as characterizing a way of being

This approach is obviously associated with the 'activity' of critical thinking as a 'habit of engagement with the world' (Chapter 2). Some take this approach to critical thinking in order to emphasize the personal attributes that are important in the process of critical thinking. In these cases, the 'way of being' may be one component among others that are mentioned. For example, Coles and Robinson (1991) use the notion of critical thinking as a disposition in order to emphasize some positive characteristics of what they see as the effective critical person – a 'respect for persons, readiness to consider alternative explanations, care for the procedures of inquiry, readiness to listen to others, a habit of judicious suspension of assent and a habit of self-appraisal' (p. 13).

Brown and Rutter (2006) use the notion of critical thinking as a 'way of being' in the context of work with social work students on a post-qualifying programme. They associate with it the notion of appropriate 'habits of mind', which they describe (p. 9) as commitments, attitudes or habits (e.g. respect for reason and truth, an open rather than a defensive attitude), which are 'closely tied up with our ethics and values'. The work of Brown and Rutter draws from that of Ford, Johnston, Brumfit, Mitchell and Myles (2005) who discuss the development of students as critical practitioners, which implies the development of a critical disposition. Ford et al. include the following issues in discussion of a critical disposition:

- the 'territory of criticality' which they base on the model of Barnett (1997) (see below);
- 'the relationships between formal knowledge, the self and action' in which they see reflective practice to be a 'strong element';
- 'the nature of professionalism' in which they list traits that 'the profession should aspire to';
- the 'micro-practice' environment of the individual;
- and the knowledge, abilities and skills required.

Values are not overtly associated with these issues. There is no assumption that the critical thinker, by her nature, is one who respects persons, for example.

Significantly for our later arguments, Ford et al. put these ideas into a developmental context (see the next section) and they view disposition or 'way of being' as a complex notion which is related to the nature and context of the learner, her development and her activity, which is, in this case, professional social work.

Barnett's (1997) work underlies that of Ford et al., Brown and Rutter and many others – and is the main example in this section on critical thinking as a 'way of being'. To explain how he sees critical thinking as a way of being or a disposition, it is necessary to look at the whole of his framework, which involves a comparison of critical thinking with other forms of thinking, and to touch into political reasoning. The essence of Barnett's (1997) argument is that more comprehensive meanings of critical thinking as a central activity in higher education have been lost and that academic criticism is being replaced by the activity of reflection. He says that it is understandable that reflection, in the form of self-monitoring, is emerging but he sees it to be at the service of 'an instrumental agenda' (p. 91) which is about the creation of a useful workforce, not about self-development and growth. Barnett (p. 103) argues that there is a hierarchy of criticality with the 'discipline-specific critical thinking skills' that are geared towards problem-solving at the lower end of the scale of 'critical being', rising in the scale through levels of reflexivity ('reflection on one's understanding'), to the refashioning of traditions to the highest level of 'transformatory critique' in which the self is reconstructed and there is 'critique in action'. He argues that the lowlier forms of critical thinking go no further than local thinking within the discipline, and do not address the wider concerns of society. The sophisticated transformatory agenda involves the willingness to act as a result of the thinking, in a manner that is emancipatory. He argues that higher education should work towards the development of people who can critically reason, are critically self-reflective, and who can act on their reasoning (critical action). In this way they attain a state of critical being. In this sense, the state of criticality is a disposition – a way of viewing, feeling and working in and with the world.

Through his arguments about the hierarchy of critical thinking and the current limitations of the valuing of it only as an intradisciplinary problem-solving skill, Barnett makes a substantial political point, suggesting that critical thinking has become a form of control that avoids the challenges of the truly critical learner. While pointing out the potential for emancipatory criticality, he counters some of the comments in the first chapter that imply that critical thinking is a counteraction of those who would take power in an undemocratic manner. The taking of action as an element in critical activity is discussed in other areas of this book under the heading of 'academic assertiveness' (Chapter 6).

The approaches to critical thinking that include the notion of ways of being or dispositions can add much to the idea of critical thinking. They suggest that it is **more than skills, more than component activities, more than being good at argument or logic**, that are switched into operation – **but a general set of habits and attitudes towards everything and a recognition that emotion is involved in different ways**. There are implications from some of this work that critical thinking undergoes a **developmental progression** and that its expression as a 'way of being' is when it is at its highest form of development. We continue with this theme in the next section.

Developmental approaches to critical thinking

Barnett's work on critical thinking could be seen to take a developmental approach but there is no suggestion that there is a fundamental cognitive or affective process of development that underlies it. It appears that the progression is subject to the influences of a carefully managed facilitation of learning in an educational context. In this same sense, anyone who considers how to teach critical thinking and starts with simple ideas and shifts towards the more complex, could be said to be acknowledging a developmental trend in critical thinking. In this section, however, we focus on those who seem to recognize qualitative differences in the nature of the thinking at different stages and this, as we have seen, anticipates some of the later content of this book, so we do not go into detail at present (see Chapter 8).

We start by looking again at Ford et al. (2005), who take a dispositional view of critical thinking but also consider that there is a developmental dimension with the kinds of qualitative changes to which we refer. They describe it as follows:

- 'precriticality – learning about the basic values, theories and cultures of social work;
- criticality within the agenda of others' – in which the thinker operates in a critical manner but 'without much challenge to given frameworks';
- 'criticality to one's own agenda' – which is realistically described as 'operating according to the kinds of professional standards outlined by Barnett' (see above) . . . 'within the usual standards of how far we can ever work on our own agendas'.

Kuhn (1999) focuses a whole paper on the developmental aspect of critical thinking. She suggests that the educational movement in critical thinking ('that shows no sign of waning'), would do well to take a 'developmental conceptualisation' of its subject matter'. She describes three second-order cognitive operations that are both directly relevant to critical thinking processes and that are subject to developmental changes. These are metacognition (the recognition of our own knowledge and our processes of knowing); metastrategic processes (the effective management of our strategies of working with knowledge); and the epistemological aspects of knowledge (which concern a person's 'broader understanding' of the nature of knowledge and knowing). She argues, as does this book, that true critical thinking cannot occur while the learner is in the more naïve belief state about the nature of knowledge.

Phillips and Bond (2004), whose research was mentioned on page 24 in relation to the views of students on critical thinking, indicated a series of conceptions of critical thinking that match developmental progression, at least in epistemological terms. Mingers's classification of critical thinking would also fit into this section as a developmental approach, though he does not acknowledge that feature of his work himself but presents it as the outcome of an overview – so it is into that section that we put it (Mingers, 2000).

While relatively few writers make the direct suggestion that **learners progress in their ability to think critically** and that the progression may be represented by a **developmental sequence**, the implications are substantial. For example, the view could fundamentally reshape the manner in which we view critical thinking and its pedagogy. It might be – and several writers hint at this – that the apparent differences in the quality of critical thinking in learners are related to the changes that occur in a developmental sequence. In response to this same view, we develop a conception of depth in critical thinking (Chapter 9).

Approaches that take an overview

There are some who have more obviously stood back from critical thinking in order to take an overview of it and we place them into a section of their own, though there is not necessarily much in common between them. The taxonomy of critical thinking of Ennis (1987) can hardly fit anywhere other than as an overview – it is so comprehensive. The chapter within which this listing occurs is called 'A taxonomy of critical thinking dispositions and abilities' and within this chapter nearly four pages are devoted to a very detailed listing of 'The goals for a critical thinking/reasoning curriculum' (pp. 12–15). The list seems to be an account of what Ennis would see as needing to be covered in a very comprehensive curriculum, down to such great detail as:

> Asking and answering questions of clarification and/or challenge, for example:
>
> a)   Why?
> b)   What is your main point?
> c)   What do you mean by . . .?
> d)   What would be an example?
> e)   What would not be an example (though close to being one)?
> f)   How does that apply to this case (describe a counterexample)?
> g)   What difference does it make?
> h)   What are the facts?
> i)   Is this what you are saying ————?
> j)   Would you say some more about that?
>
> (Ennis, 1987: 12–15)

And so on. Whether this is a list of what people learn to do when they learn to think critically, or whether it is just a list of what people can do when they are effective critical thinkers, is a question that we have asked before.

Halonen (1995) overviewed critical thinking in relation to her experiences in the well-known Alverno College (USA). She talks of her process of 'demystifying critical thinking' through a framework that lists various parameters, qualities and dimensions of critical thinking 'that provide a foundation for identifying important dimensions of critical thinking scholarship' in order that the critical thinking may be evaluated effectively. The context of the paper (and the journal in which it is published) is the teaching of psychology, and the framework assumes a considerable degree of initial knowledge of critical thinking as a process. We pick out a few of the headings below:

'Nature of critical thinking and access concerns – how is the origin of critical thinking ability conceptualized? Trait, emergent or state;'
'Contexts of critical thinking – in what contexts or settings does critical thinking occur – academic, interpersonal, workplace and citizenship;'
'Propensity components – affect, attitude, physical readiness and metacognition.'

While there is some discussion in the text on these aspects of critical thinking, it is hard to see how they really 'demystify critical thinking' – even for one with a psychology background.

Mingers's paper (2000) is also related to the teaching of undergraduate students on a management degree programme in a business school and Mingers's work is directed towards the need to sort out a meaningful response to the question 'What is it to be critical?' Mingers notes the tensions that are inherent in the facilitation of a 'critical approach' among learners who are working in a relatively positivist environment and subject area. From the deliberations, his first conclusion was that a 'fairly simplistic framework would need to be developed'. The framework is as follows. It is based on the language of a series of 'levels' – which we question later.

'Critical thinking as the critique of rhetoric' – the 'simplest level' where the concerns are the technical 'soundness' of the language of the argument, the ability to use appropriate language and the awareness of the purpose of the process of being critical.
'Being sceptical of conventional wisdom – the critique of tradition.' This level includes the development of a critical attitude towards actions in organizations, cultures and traditions and the assumptions that underpin these beliefs.
'Being sceptical of one dominant view – the critique of authority.' It is interesting that the positioning of this level suggests that there is more challenge to the student in the criticism of a 'local' authority – such as the education system within which the learner is working, than in the more distant critique of tradition. In this 'level', too, Mingers suggests that there also resides a recognition of the 'multiplicity of perspectives'.
'Being sceptical of information and knowledge – the critique of objectivity.' In this – the most sophisticated level that is described by Mingers, there is a recognition that knowledge and information is never 'value-free' and that they are continually reshaped by the 'structures of power within a situation'. It implies the metacognitive processes of critical thinking.

This framework is valuable because it recognizes the range of thinking about critical thinking, and the number of dimensions of critical thinking and it encapsulates these into a simple descriptive framework that can underpin the management of teaching and of student learning. We might question the notion that these categories are called 'level'. The term 'level' implies a qualitative similarity which may not be most appropriate in a philosophical view of the framework – for example, we would suggest that the technicalities of language use in argument is a different process from the learner's understanding of the shaping effects of power structures. However, in the manner in which the framework is used to organize teaching, the word 'level' may well have been adopted for pragmatic reasons. It is interesting to note that Gold, Holman and Thorpe (2002), who cite Mingers's work, describe the framework as providing the 'four most significant elements of critical thinking' and recognize that these are not mutually exclusive.

Mingers's framework is valuable also because it is sufficiently generalized to apply to any of the activities of critical thinking, rather than the usual models that apply largely to the critique of another's argument. Significantly too, it is also an overview that makes sense of both the mechanical and the 'depth' characteristics of critical thinking. The idea of depth relates also to the epistemological development which is discussed in the section on developmental approaches. It might be taken to suggest that the same idea can be subjected to critique at different 'levels'. When we look at most of the examples in this chapter (e.g. Cottrell, 2005), it is evident that many match mainly the 'critique of rhetoric' level. In recognizing the 'depth dimension' explicitly, Mingers's work (notably with that of Barnett, 1997) anticipates issues that we pick up in Part 5. It is interesting to note also that the management students in the work of Phillips and Bond (2004) (Chapter 2) themselves categorized critical thinking in a similar continuum to that devised by Mingers. There were no references to Mingers's work in the latter.

The last section in Mingers (2000) is an evaluation of the module that was developed after the first year of its operation. There were some difficulties. Mingers notes that 'the unthinking acceptance of the course objectives is a sign that, at a deeper level, the course was not wholly successful'. Perhaps we could argue that if the framework is only introduced in the final year of a programme, it is hardly surprising that learners found it difficult. In some senses, it was asking them to question all that they had learnt and to suffer confusion at a time when it was presumably their view that they were coming to the end of their degree course with appropriate knowledge! Perhaps an error in the view that Mingers puts forward is that this framework should underpin the whole of a degree – or all of higher education teaching – and not just one module at this late stage in a degree. It should underpin more than just work on management subjects too.

We mentioned earlier Barnett (1997), whose work is perhaps the most alike to that of Mingers, though it is not referenced in Mingers's work either. We have described Barnett's framework earlier in this chapter (critical thinking as characterizing a way of being). It is interesting to note that the issue of 'critical action' might also be relevant to Mingers's thinking. There is a difference between critical awareness and being able to argue on paper or in a debate in an educational setting.

What really counts for management students – or any other students – is their ability to be appropriately assertive about their thought-through point of view in an environment of narrower thinking or direct opposition (Chapter 8).

Lastly, in looking at approaches that represent overviews of critical thinking, we turn to the work of Bailin et al. (1999b). This work clearly must have a place among overviews and yet it is different from those above in that the writers set out to pull the idea of critical thinking into some kind of order ('conceptualization'), as is the activity of the current writer. In the discussion about the concept, they stress the following:

- that critical thinking is the making of a judgement about what to do or to believe;
- that there are standards that the critical thinker wishes to acknowledge in her thinking;
- that there are minimum thresholds for the standards that the thinker would require herself to meet.

Bailin et al. recognize the range of kinds of judgement, the range of standards, the range of activities that are involved in the thinking process (but not using the same meaning as our use of 'activities' above). They say that it is the quality of the thinking and not the process of thinking that distinguishes critical thinking from other thinking. This last point distinguishes their view from those of many others – in particular those who propound skills approaches or taxonomies. Bailin et al. include the notion that some creativity is involved in critical thinking in that the generation of broad thinking on a topic is, in essence, imaginative. They go on to list the intellectual resources needed by the effective critical thinker. The first of these is the material of critical thinking – the knowledge – and the second group concerns four elements – the operational standards of critical thinking, the knowledge of key concepts (such as the ideas of value, conceptual or empirical statements), strategies and procedures for critical thinking, and habits of mind.

The overview of critical thinking of Bailin et al. indicates many issues in critical thinking that are in common with those of the current writer, but there are differences as well, primarily in the issues of depth and the possibility of a developmental sequence, which we have introduced above and both of which the current writer would see as important and which are elaborated later in Chapter 9.

Overviews of critical thinking are useful because they represent an intention to stand back from the topic and look at it in a wide context that is not necessarily directly related to a specific task (though this is not the case for Mingers). The overviews generally confirm the writer's view that **logic does not need to play a central part**, though there are **issues about standards** to be taken into account in a conception of critical thinking. Most hint at a **developmental sequence** for critical thinking; and their broader perspective enables them to note some less commonly expressed ideas, such as **a role for creativity and imagination within critical thinking**. We also need to take into account **the level of knowledge**, the content of critical thinking.

What do we learn from a review of approaches to critical thinking?

There is no tight conclusion to this chapter because the review of approaches to critical thinking was partly a mechanism for reviewing the literature in a structured manner. It was a means of drawing down useful ideas from the various approaches for the development of the defining statements since the different approaches generally emphasize particular characteristics of critical thinking. We can, however, pull together the ideas that have emerged from the various approaches (taking here the liberty of expanding the ideas a little to make them comprehensible). In critical thinking:

There is a need to be reasonably adept with language;

- a need for clarity and precision in language and ideas;
- a need for persistence;
- the need to be relatively systematic;

Critical thinking is more than a set of skills and processes and there are many different skills and actions that *may be* involved in critical thinking;

Emotion and emotional climate (two different things) are relevant and may need to be taken into account;

Critical thinking is 'nurtured' in its development. Nurturing might imply that it is best developed in a challenging environment which is relatively free of threat;

There are issues about the standards of thinking and the outcomes (not necessarily a coherent picture of standards). The standards may be external or may be the personal standards and level of satisfaction of the learner;

What we might be willing to call proficient critical thinking (at least in higher education or the professions) is likely to have a generally questioning habit of mind – a particular way of being in the world;

Learners may progress in their developing ability to think critically and there may be a developmental progression in critical thinking;

There may be issues about the critical thinker's ability to be sufficiently confident or assertive (Chapter 8);

There is a role for creativity and imagination in critical thinking.

There are important general points to have emerged from the broad study of the approaches. We provide them with words emphasized in order to be able to relate back to them, but the points sometimes relate to each other.

Perhaps the most important point that accords with the views of the writer is that **good-quality critical thinking is not demarcated by the quality of the processes involved in the thinking, but by the quality of the thinking itself** (Bailin et al. 1999b). In other words, 'critical thinking' may be just the same as any other thinking, but at an enhanced level of competence. Have the great philosophers of past centuries needed a specialized term or a specialized delineation of a technique in order to engage in what amounts to critical thinking? This point also has consequences for pedagogy.

The next point arises from the approaches that involve logic or other rule-bound approaches to critical thinking. It is a concern about **the place of 'rules of operation'** for critical thinking (and logic). It could be argued that the general picture of the good critical thinker is of a person who is autonomous. The whole point of thinking critically is to find an appropriate response or a decision in a judgement. The following of something presented as rules does not match this conception. Rules interpreted as 'rules of thumb', heuristics or personal 'ways of doing things' can be different.

This third point is relevant to approaches in which there are long lists of skills or components associated with learning to operate as a critical thinker. How it is that many **adept thinkers can manage without such detailed learning of all the critical thinking skills** or acquisition of all of the concepts. How is it that teachers work successfully with learners to facilitate effective critical thinking without the aid of such lists (Meyers, 1986)? Lists of skills of critical thinking are presumably written by those who can think critically – so a list is essentially written in retrospect. In effect, they are lists of what a critical thinker does to think critically, and it may be that we learn in a more organic manner, not by an accumulation of a set of skills. We may later make sense of our learning – if we wish – by looking at a list. We conclude that critical thinking can be engendered without the following of detailed lists of processes. Indeed, if we add into the picture the attributes and outlooks of a critical thinker, the need for confidence and the possibility of a developmental aspect to it, we also conclude that simply learning lists of skills, or following lists of processes or procedures, will not necessarily create critical thinkers because there is more to proper critical thinking than could be captured in a list. Having declared this as a position, however, we need to know more about what it is that might facilitate critical thinking (see Part 6 on pedagogy).

There is an important **difference in view implied in the contrast between the highly detailed approaches to critical thinking and those that are more generally described**. In highly detailed approaches, the implied view is of a mechanical process, each essential part of which is operated separately, as we have said of the skills approach, above. In the more generalized views there is a sense of a more holistic approach wherein there is implied trust of the effective learner to operate her critical approach in a more instinctive manner without specifically engaging separate skills. Again we ask what are the implications of this for pedagogy? Which is the desirable state for learners and how do we reach it?

We have suggested the **existence of a developmental sequence** in critical thinking. This may mean that what are taken as individual differences in the ability to think critically may be representations or consequences of developmental stages (Chapter 9). We have introduced the term 'depth' to deal with this. The concept of depth may not just apply to the thinking of the individual, but also to the concepts of critical thinking that have been developed. For example, the skills or component approaches to critical thinking are mostly working with a relatively 'surface' conception of critical thinking as an operation. Those that concern critical thinking as a way of being, as involving metacognitive activities, or as the review of any assumptions and so on, are conceptions that are 'deeper'.

The next point is more specific. Behind the building picture of the person who is able to be a critical thinker, is the sense that there are personal attributes that are needed to be effective. One of these, which links to other areas of academic literature, is **the need to be relatively assertive in an academic context**. We pick up this point later (Chapter 6).

Some sceptical observations

Finally, we add some sceptical notes which quite definitely reflect critically on the writer's own activities. First, for many of these schemas as they are presented in the academic literature, that are re-presented in this book, and this book itself, it is reasonable to ask 'what is the problem to which these processes are the solution?' What are we trying to do with all this writing and thinking about critical thinking? Are we trying to sort out something in our minds, to entertain our minds with this as subject matter? Do we actually need to know all this to improve pedagogy?

Second, perhaps the academic study of critical thinking does much to construct a conception of critical thinking – which we then need to deconstruct in order to understand it and in order to facilitate the reconstruction of it in learners. All of these activities take up a lot of academic hours and brain-time.

The third and fourth points here can be made no better than their expression by Nickerson (1987). He asks, 'How do we promote an attitude of critical inquiry on the one hand and a healthy respect for valued tradition and legitimate authority on the other?' On the same page he asks, 'How do we teach students to think independently and to arrive at their own conclusions when we are not indifferent to the conclusions that they draw?' (p. 35).

> ## Thinkpoint
>
> No-one can tell another person . . . how he should think any more than how he ought to breathe – but the various ways in which men do think can be told. . . . Some of these ways are better than others. The person who understands what the better ways of thinking are – can, if he will, change his own personal ways until they become more effective.
>
> (Dewey, 1933: 3)

4 Some of the broader issues of critical thinking

Standards, objectivity and the cultural basis

Introduction

Looking at the approaches to critical thinking does not bring us into contact with all the issues that need consideration in this exploration of critical thinking. Some of these further issues are reviewed in this chapter – and some are the subject matter of later chapters. The issues considered in this chapter are the quality and references to 'standards' of critical thinking; issues such as truth, objectivity and subjectivity, the degree to which critical thinking is subject to cultural influences; and there are a few comments about the degree to which it may be shaped by the manner in which human brains are constructed. Some of these points develop from issues raised in earlier chapters.

The quality and 'standards' of critical thinking

We suggested in the previous chapter that critical thinking is more than an activity that simply exists or does not exist – for it varies in quality and perhaps depth. Certainly, a number of research projects on critical thinking, by their use of techniques of evaluation of the critical thinking, imply that there is a 'quality dimension' to be taken into account (for example, Bailin, Case, Coombs and Daniels, 1999b; Plath, English, Connors and Beveridge, 1999; Fisher, 2003; Phillips and Bond, 2004). Plath et al. used a number of critical thinking scales in order to evaluate the outcomes of intensive critical thinking instruction with social work students. The nature of the scales used implied a conception of varying quality. In the last chapter we cited Bailin et al. who go further – 'It is the quality of the thinking, not the processes of thinking which distinguishes critical thinking from uncritical thinking' (p. 288). A question that follows is as to whether or not there is a matching conception of 'quality' among these different writers.

In addition to discussion of quality, some have associated the notion of 'standards' with critical thinking (e.g. Bailin et al. 1999b; Paul and Elder, 2004; Ford, Johnston, Brumfit, Mitchell and Myles, 2005; Brown and Rutter, 2006). But what do we mean by standards and how does this meaning relate to quality? Brown and Rutter, in their work on the professional education of social workers, derive some of their standards from the principles and language of logic (e.g. in the evaluation of deductive argument). They ask questions such as: 'When viewed together, do the premises constitute sufficient grounds for the truth of the conclusion?' – p. 6). They also provide standards that are derived from the questioning of research results (e.g. 'Have the authors clearly explained the purposes of the study, how it was carried out and the results?' – p. 7). On this conception of 'standards' of critical thinking, the standards are those issues that the critical thinker should have addressed in the process of her thinking.

In contrast, the conception of 'standards' of Paul and Elder is much more generalized and is described as 'universal intellectual standards'. These comprise ideas such as 'clarity', 'precision', 'depth' and 'relevance'. Bailin et al. cite a list of a similar nature as 'attitudes and habits of mind', and include:

> 'an inquiring attitude (inclination to assess the support for judgements one is asked to accept)';
> 'fair-mindedness (. . . giving fair consideration to alternative points of view . . .)';
> 'independent-mindedness ([which includes] the personal strength to stand up for one's firmly grounded beliefs)';
> 'respect for legitimate intellectual authority (appreciation of the importance of giving due weight to the views of persons who satisfy the criteria for being an authority in a relevant area of study or practice)'.
>
> (Bailin et al., 1999b)

All these conceptions of standards and quality have their place. A critical thinker needs to address the appropriate issues about a topic wherein bias may creep and a good critical thinker will be aware and be able to discuss the processes and rigour of her own critical thinking process. Bailin et al. acknowledge the variation in the viewing of 'standards' (and 'principles') and the manner in which they tend to be 'embedded in complex practices' (1999b: 297). They indicate that what is important is that the good critical thinker should have the 'good judge-ment in determining what critical thinking principles require in particular contexts'. This could be taken to suggest that, beyond a certain point, the spelling out of standards is a curtailing of the bounds of thinking of a proficient critical thinker.

Before moving on from the issue of standards, we return again to the notion of depth which was mentioned in the last chapter – and which is also mentioned by Paul and Elder. Most of the various standards that are discussed above are a matter of being sufficiently taken into account in a person's critical thinking – or not. Depth, as a quality, is not like that. It begs many more questions: What do we mean by 'depth' of critical thinking? What does 'surface critical thinking' look like? How would we recognize it and what changes would be needed to make it 'deeper'? – and so on. We will argue later that the concept of depth of critical thinking, with further development, can include many of the other qualities and standards mentioned – and we attempt to illustrate that there are criteria that can clarify it, and ways of supporting the development of students' conceptions of it (Chapter 9).

Truth, objectivity and subjectivity

We now come to one of the most confusing issues in critical thinking – a cluster of issues around what we understand by the terms **truth, objectivity and subjectivity**. We start with a quotation from Bowell and Kemp (2002): 'All arguments can be understood as attempting to provide reasons for thinking that some claim is true' (p. 7), and later (p. 257): 'It is crucial for critical thinkers to recognise that truth is objective and not relative. Otherwise the critical thinker's objective of analysing and assessing arguments with the aim of getting at the truth of a matter is deeply undermined.' The notion that critical thinking is all about the seeking of an objective truth seems alien to the conceptions of critical thinking that underpin the thinking for this book and the general language of higher education itself. In level descriptors (Chapter 1), we talk of enabling learners to work in situations of new knowledge, to manage uncertainty and to deal with unpredictability and to recognize the constructed nature of knowledge. This is far from the matter of seeking the one truth about a matter. Bowell and Kemp do acknowledge relativism in a much later chapter in their book but the focus for their target audience of students and professionals is the description of methods of working towards 'objective truth'.

Paul (1987) provides terminology for the different approaches to truth. He describes the kind of problem in which thinking seeks a single, 'monological' response – 'This implies that they are settled within one frame of reference, with a definite set of logical moves. When the right set of moves is generated, the problem is settled' (p. 128). The other kind of problem is 'multilogical'. Here, 'because more than one frame of reference is contending for their construal and settlement, we must somehow "test" the frames of reference themselves' (p. 128). He goes on to say:

> Most important issues of everyday life are multilogical and human. We do not live in a disembodied world of objects and physical laws. Instead we live in a humanly contrived and constructed world. And there is more than one way to contrive and construct the world. Not only our social relations, but our inner cognitive and affective lives are inferential in nature. We do not deal with the world-in-itself, but with the world-as-we-define-it in relation to our interests, perspective and point of view. We shape our interests and point of view in the light of what significant others think, and, as a result, live in a world that is exceedingly narrow, static and closed. For purposes of self-protection we assume our view to be moral and objective. For the most part, our viewpoints are in fact amoral and subjective.
>
> Paul, 1987: 131)

Paul goes on to argue that schooling is mostly based on working in a monological system of thinking – 'there is a truth that you need to know'. As a result, he suggests, when learners leave school, they 'do not understand how to read, write, think, listen or speak in such a way as to organize and express what they believe' (p. 136).

Sweet and Swanson (2000) argue a similar case to Paul's, but take their thinking into a (real) class on critical thinking at Stanford University. The students are led to work with monological problems, seeking to work in an objective manner. The teacher of this class stresses that critical thinking is about questioning, and constructs a picture of critical thinking that consists of creating 'oppositional structures which are, quite clearly, binary constructs' and that they will need to 'look equally and intently on both sides'. 'In fact', he says, 'if you're predisposed towards one side, what you really have to do is look harder at the other side because your mind is not going to want to do that' (p. 43). The 'objectivity' of this process is stressed. Subjectivity must not come into the decision-making process. Sweet and Swanson comment on the written work of a student, following the critical thinking class. 'In this essay, [the student] seems to be engaged in a mental ping-pong game, bouncing from side to side on every issue he raises, to demonstrate his objectivity, his willingness to look at both sides of the basic critical question he is supposedly asking' (pp. 49–50). Sweet and Swanson sum up their chapter by saying that the kind of instruction about argument or critical thinking that they have demonstrated in their case study they would see as typical of the kind of instruction that most students get in critical thinking and argument – 'one based on a western metaphysical dualism that implicitly proscribes and delimits the kinds of thinking we accredit or accept as valid. From such positions, students effect their own erasure of the "political" from their thinking' (pp. 51–2). This view of critical thinking accords with the 'weighing up' conception of some of the students in Phillips and Bond's study (2004) – Chapter 2.

Through the use of these three contributions to the literature on critical thinking, we have covered much ground and explained a number of the differences in thinking and writing about critical thinking. Scattered in the examples above, we find the words 'objectivity' and 'subjectivity', not always used in a consistent manner. It may be possible to talk more easily about objectivity where there is one truth to be sought in a monological problem. The objectivity then is in the accuracy of the reasoning and argument. In a multilogical problem, objectivity is played out differently according to the different frames of reference that are engaged in dealing with the issue. In the work of Phillips and Bond (2004), in their study of students' conceptions of critical thinking, this is neatly illustrated. Their research demonstrated a range of views of critical thinking – and the different views were defined to an extent by the way in which 'objectivity' was evidenced. Where students saw critical thinking as 'weighing up', objectivity was demonstrated in the 'comparison of pros and cons'. Where students saw critical thinking as looking at a situation from all angles, objectivity was assured by the examination of the multiple perspectives. Objectivity in the 'looking back' view of critical thinking was gained from the multiple perspectives and in the action of extraction of the self from the event, and the act then of looking on from the outside. The last conception was 'objective' in the setting of the issue in a wider perspective, seeing beyond the situation and the consideration from the point of view of the person within the problem situation. This research indicates that in multilogical problems there is no one form of objectivity to be sought.

But what of subjectivity? It could be said that the more sophisticated the critical thinker is, the more she will be aware of and will bring into the open, the essential subjectivity of her reasoning, her emotional reactions and the knowledge, language and situation of the problem (Kuhn, 1999). She will counter subjectivity as much as possible by using the kinds of 'objective' tools described in Phillips and Bond's work above. She will, however, recognize that knowledge is a human and personal construction, and ultimately is subjective. It is not only the thinkers themselves who cannot be objective, but their teachers too. Meyers points out (1986: 93): 'Teachers can no more teach "objectively" than scientists can pursue their research devoid of personal values and interests . . . the more openly teachers acknowledge more subjective elements in their teaching, the more . . . objective they can show themselves to be.'

For these reasons, it would seem to be difficult to apply the term 'objective' to critical thinking – but then to call it purely subjective would seem to counter many of the processes designed to support critical thinking. We need to work with our ideas of objectivity and subjectivity – overtly bringing them explicitly into the processes of critical thinking.

We come back to this area of thinking in the recognition – towards the end of this chapter – that humans think critically the way that they do, to some extent because of the structure of their brains. But maybe critical thinking is related to culture too. This is another form of subjectivity.

Cultural issues in critical thinking

We begin this section by returning to Barnett's widely quoted phrase that critical thinking is a 'defining concept of the Western university' (1987: 2), for we did not examine it in full in the earlier chapter but ignored the significance of the word 'Western'. Is critical thinking particularly 'Western' – and if it is, what does this mean for international students? Durkin worked on this issue in a study which involved East Asian students. On the basis of intensive interviewing with 67 East Asian students, some English students and some lecturers, she concluded that the majority of East Asian students 'reject full academic acculturation into Western norms of argumentation, which is characterized by rigorous "strong" critical thinking, polarized linear logic and "wrestling debate"'. Instead they will tend to opt for what Durkin calls 'the Middle Way', which is characterized by 'more holistic, empathetic "constructive reasoning"' (Durkin, 2004: abstract). They are more concerned than in the Western patterns, to value the other and prevent 'loss of face'. There is also more of a tendency to follow the ideas, and revere the 'expert'. With this as the case, there are problems when critical thinking is taken to mean the comparison of a number of different views on a topic.

Durkin's work shows that there are multiple sources of difference in the viewing of academic process between the students whom she studied and Western practices. She demonstrates the difficulties that students might often experience in working with Western notions of critical thinking. The following example indicates a number of issues, in particular referencing and the notion of ownership of ideas, which is a separate but overlapping issue with referencing. The student is a Master's level East Asian student, being interviewed. He says: 'If I reference from someone that means it is not in my mind, that the assignment is not my own work'. When the student was prompted by the interviewer, 'But if you copied it word for word, is it your own work?', the student said, 'I find these ideas in books. It is my effort. If I show that someone has already said it, that is not valuable' (Durkin, 2004: 170).

Another student in Durkin's study related referencing directly to plagiarism, saying: 'At first I thought that if I think about plagiarism a lot then my essay becomes full of authors' names. All the ideas come from the authors and nothing from my mind. But now I realize it shows you have read a lot' (p. 170). This statement begins to acknowledge the value of referencing, but it could be said to demonstrate a weak understanding of the use of the work of others (it 'shows you have read a lot'). The following statement shows greater understanding of Western ways of working: 'When you try to read a Korean journal or article, it is very difficult to find where the information comes from. So I found referencing very logical and it helps us to develop academically' (p. 170).

There may also be differences in habits of precision of meaning. Durkin comments that such precision and explicitness may be seen as unsophisticated in some East Asian cultures. A Chinese lecturer explained that the language of Chinese is designed more for literary work than the argumentation style of the West – 'Chinese poets are always trying to imply things rather than telling things directly . . . Asian culture believes that a higher level of communication is communication without language' (p. 164). Along similar lines, a Japanese student explains that 'In Japan we are not required to follow arguments through. We can write more randomly' (p. 164). Durkin comments further that the language skills that are required to demonstrate critical thinking are relatively sophisticated – paraphrasing is an example. These students have the further disadvantage of the challenge of work in a second language.

The cultural differences that are suggested to lie between East Asian and Western patterns of thinking will be significant for those supporting learners where both patterns exist, however there may be other cultural differences of a more subtle nature. Alexander and Dochy (1995) studied the conceptions of knowledge and belief in 54 adults from the United States and 66 from Holland. They concluded that there were significant differences between the two groups in the manner in which the groups viewed the nature of what a belief is and of what knowledge is and the kinds of relationship between them. The Dutch subjects tended to see knowledge as within the realm of beliefs, whereas the Americans were more likely to see belief as overlapping knowledge, but separate from it in some areas. It may be significant that 'beliefs' were more strongly characterized by their religious content in the American sample. The way in which one conceives the nature of knowledge and beliefs can be fundamental to the processes of critical thinking (see also Chapter 8).

Critical thinking and the brain

In terms of the study of the context of critical thinking, it is important to acknowledge that the nature of the critical thinking of humans is determined by the structure of our brains. We have no means of determining whether there could be other forms of critical thinking beyond what we can perceive, though the fact that there are cultural differences in the perception of the process shows that different forms may be possible. There are some particular points to make about this. For example, our making of judgements is related to brain structure. Hastie and Davies (2001) point out how, with regard to our ability to make judgements,

> we have several truly fundamental, virtually automatic cognitive abilities; the ability to estimate frequencies; the ability to judge similarities between objects and events; the ability to recognize a previously experienced situation or individual and the ability to infer causal relationships. These processes are 'wired' into our brains so deeply that they do not change much across the healthy adult life span.
>
> (Hastie and Davies, 2001: 73)

Using a similar argument, Laming (2004) confirms this through many interesting descriptions of his laboratory studies and very persuasively demonstrates the inadequacies of human judgement processes, and the power and diversity of social suggestion. We cannot make absolute judgements. 'All judgements are comparisons of one thing with another' (p. 9). 'No one is unbiased . . . we simply judge other peoples' biases against our own' (p. 141). These factors inevitably influence our capacities to be critical. On this basis, it is not too much of a step to say that the mental processing of critical thinking is limited by the structure of our brains and the manner in which they function. The notion of 'related' may be taken to mean that the brain structure favours the methods we use, or that it is limited by the methods that we use. It may explain why it is difficult to explain terms such as critical thinking to others – including to students; there are no reference points with which to compare it. On the same basis, we have observed that learners are happy to think about what is and what is not critical thinking when they have an example with which to work. This has been borne out in experiences of working with the concept of reflective learning (Moon, 2004) and the same principle is applied in this book in the attempt to explain the concept and qualities of critical thinking (Chapter 10). The giving of an example provides a reference point, a point for comparison.

A conclusion to this chapter?

It can be useful to use a conclusion to pull ideas together to round off neatly and tidily – but this is again not to be the case for this chapter. The message of this chapter, as much as for the last, is that critical thinking is a 'messy' concept with many ideas about it presented in forceful but conflicting ways that do not lead us easily to a coherent conclusion. But then there is a powerful idea behind the very messiness of it – because critical thinking itself is about the management of knowledge and beliefs in uncertain situations in such a way as to allow what we might call productive progress – or in more colloquial language – 'so that we can move on'. In this chapter we have continued to map out some of the messiness of the idea. In the next chapter we look at some aspects of critical thinking that many would ignore. We pursue the notion that the person constructs her own knowledge and her ways of operating as a thinker, and therefore the person herself is a relevant topic for coverage in a book on critical thinking. We look at the personal aspects of critical thinking.

Thinkpoint

The main purpose of thinking is to abolish thinking. The mind works to make sense out of confusion and uncertainty. The mind works to recognise in the outside world familiar patterns. As soon as such a pattern is recognised, the mind switches into it and follows it along.

(de Bono, 1982: 39)

Part 3

The person as a critical thinker

5 The role of emotion, language and curiosity in critical thinking

Introduction

When the content of this book was planned, material on the person as a critical thinker was not given a chapter. However, in the research process things have changed and there are now two chapters devoted to this topic. This first chapter concerns the roles of emotion in critical thinking, issues around the knowledge and use of language; and there are a few words in what must be an important section – on the intellectual curiosity of the learner. We also mention the need for time. It takes longer to think critically than to just leap to conclusions. The next chapter covers a range of personal orientations and attributes that seem to warrant an overall heading – and for this we have introduced the term 'academic assertiveness'. Academic assertiveness is about the thinker's personal confidence and ability to process and express critical ideas and to act on them. So, these two chapters are closely linked in their content.

There is still not a large volume of literature on the person as a critical thinker and it is dispersed. Most references are 'fringe' comments alongside more 'hardline' or 'objective' material on the thinking processes or the skills. Perhaps it is because the personal topics are complex and difficult to 'pull together' that they are often treated as relatively insignificant. A literary vicious circle could be operating here. Another explanation might be because there are not thought to be many pedagogical concomitants of this personal material. With this we would now disagree, having looked into the notion of academic assertiveness.

Meyers (1986) and Brookfield are clear examples of writers who would also support the importance of concerns with the person. With regard to the personality and cultural background of critical thinkers, Brookfield says: 'Information about these two factors is the most important I can obtain before I try to make a person think critically about some aspect of life' (1987: 231).

Emotion and critical thinking

Personal emotion is important in – or 'central' to – critical thinking (Brookfield, 1987), but it is a 'neglected issue' (Blom Kemdal and Montgomery, 1997: 74). The literature is scant, and complex. Hastie and Davies (2001: 206) comment that 'everyone knows that emotions play a significant role in decision-making and choice', but, as they say, it is difficult to determine the role of emotion because there is no useful consensus on what emotion is. We would suggest that we are dealing with more than one role. De Bono (1982: 99) says something similar:

> In the end all thinking is emotional. . . . In the end our decisions, choices and courses of action are all determined by emotions, feelings and values. The purpose of thinking is to serve us as human beings and feelings are the best judge of the effectiveness of that service. . . . There is, however an important point. Do we use our emotions first and allow these to determine our perception and our thinking? Or do we use our perception first and allow emotions to determine our final decision?

A vivid illustration of the roles played by emotion (in this case, termed 'affect') in the processes of scientific thinking is provided in quotations from research scientists by Shaw. Shaw and Runco (1994) interviewed scientists about the processes of their academic work, looking at the flows, the blocks, the periods of incubation, the illumination and so on. There is a great richness in the emotional experiences that are cited and the language that is used to describe them but that never, of course, finds its way into the formal writing up, even though the emotions cannot fail to have influenced the thinking process, as well as being generated by it:

> On getting stuck: 'You stop. You can't get anywhere. Everything stops. You feel that you are ready to come apart. There is a sense of agitation. Frustration starts to appear, along with some anger.'
>
> (p. 15)

> On intuition: 'You know, it just feels right' – and: 'It's what makes you go off in a particular direction to begin with. It's a feeling, a sense. I've got cognitive answers . . . it's going to come from everything you are and know' – and: 'You have some sense that there's an answer.'
>
> (p. 11)

> On the requirements for becoming immersed: 'There is a warmth in the stomach that begins when you know something is correct, some data are important. I had that warmth.'
>
> (p. 11)

If we need any more evidence of the importance of emotion in critical thinking, then we can return to the introductory words of Janis (1982: 13): 'the more amiability and *esprit de corps* among the members of a policy-making in-group, the greater is the danger that independent critical thinking will be replaced by groupthink'.

Many definitions of critical thinking do not mention the involvement of emotion in critical thinking. For example, Paul and Elder (2004), who address the 'elements of thought' in their booklet, do not take into account the degree to which thought can be swayed by emotion. Ironically, though, it is Paul who, in earlier writing, said 'emotions and beliefs are always inseparably welded together' (Paul, 1987: 142) and then wrote that he had no space in which to expand on that matter.

So if emotion is of vital or central importance to the activity of critical thinking, how do we further our understanding of this relationship? We start by taking the issue seriously and not dismissing it as 'touchy-feely' and take the position that all human activity is influenced by and influences emotion (Damasio, 2000). From this position, we can explore the forms of relationship that there might be between emotion and an activity like critical thinking. We adapt work done previously on the roles of emotion in reflective learning (Moon, 2004). This model was used to make sense of the literature on emotion and learning and in order to facilitate thinking on this topic. It was a grounded model that emerged from the process of reading the work of others and from the experiences of the writer in teaching and counselling and other academic work. The model has been in the public domain for three years – in print and in many workshop presentations. It suggests that one of the reasons why we have such difficulty in conceiving of the relationships of emotion and mental activity is that there is not just one relationship, but there are many and they are different. In any one situation, emotion is likely to be involved in several of these different ways. We will use the critical thinking literature to illustrate some of these relationships.

The development of the model of emotional processes and learning (Moon, 2004) started with an examination of the literature on 'emotional intelligence' on the assumption that this well-publicized conception might elucidate difficulties of understanding emotion and learning. However, while the emotional intelligence literature has done much to point out the important role of emotion in learning and teaching (e.g. Goleman, 1995, 1998; Mortiboys, 2005), it is too broad as a concept to apply to specific activities like reflection or critical thinking. For example, it is possible to find that emotional intelligence in the same person might enable the person to be better at the emotional management of others, and at the same time, good at the management of her own emotions. Human, indeed personal experience, would suggest that this is not the case. In the earlier work, the writer used 'emotional intelligence' as a term to account for the management of or the ability to work with the emotions of others (see below). Below we produce the model, illustrated by reference to critical thinking literature.

A framework of observed relationships between emotion and critical thinking (based on Moon, 2004)

- **'Emotional intelligence' – the ability to relate to the emotional states of others**. In terms of critical thinking, this is illustrated in situations where learners work together. Underwood and Wald (1995) talk about setting up 'conference teaching' as a means of engendering critical thinking among (psychology) students. They say that their learners need to respect the impact 'of one's own intuitions and those of others', they need the 'sensitivity to recognize and evaluate the goals of others from diverse backgrounds', and they need to 'consider the connection between what they and others care about and what they are studying'. Similarly, Brookfield (1987) talks of an important element of critical thinking being the ability to listen and respond to another. In essence critical thinking is often a direct social activity, and the emotional awareness is required in order properly to communicate in a clear and precise manner.

• **Emotion is involved in critical thinking where emotions, or topics with emotional associations are the subject matter of the critical thinking – or where relevant emotion is a conscious influence on the nature of the knowledge**. For example, issues concerning a particular war may be associated with feelings of fear for one person, or excitement or anger for others. Another example concerns critical thinking activities when the activity is the reflection on oneself or one's behaviours. Brookfield (1987: 231–2) says 'challenging unquestioned assumptions, looking sceptically at givens we have lived by, and trying to shake off habitual ideas and behaviors so that we can try out alternatives, are emotionally potent activities'. In the same context, Nelson-Jones (1994) talks about the process of critical self appraisal (an activity of critical thinking – Chapter 2), about the emotional influence of one's own feelings, the letting go of defensiveness, the perceptions of oneself and others more positively and realistically.

• **Emotion can have an influence on the process of critical thinking** – it can 'tangle up the process': it can influence the manner in which we work with the ideas and material of learning. We illustrate this point by reference to the pedagogical literature that indicates the need to create 'safe' or risk-free environments in which learners can learn to express the outcomes of their critical thinking (e.g. Meyers, 1986; Underwood and Wald, 1995; Mortiboys, 2005). Read, Francis and Robson (2001) in their research on 'the student voice' in writing found that learners often lacked confidence to express themselves, both because of the power relations with the tutor and because of their position in the academic hierarchy – 'Denise felt that she could not criticize 'leading' historians. She commented, 'You can't just turn around to someone like that and say "sorry, I think your saying is rubbish!"'. In this category we include situations in which the emotions are relevant to the process (e.g. the fear or lacking in self-esteem that relates to power relationships in critical thinking situations). We return to this issue also when we consider academic assertiveness in the next chapter.

• **Emotion – relevant to the subject matter – may arise from the process of critical thinking or learning**. Emotion can arise in the flux between the material or memories involved and the present purposes for the thinking activities. As an illustration, Brookfield says that the engagement in questioning our beliefs and behaviours (about others and ourselves) 'may well produce anxiety, fear, resentment, and feelings of being threatened or intimidated. They may lead to emotional outbursts against the person who is prompting others to think critically' (Brookfield, 1987: 232). In another example, Gold,

Holman and Thorpe (2002) used argument analysis and story-telling to facilitate critical thinking in management students. They observed that 'almost all managers found that the process of story-telling and argument analysis evoked a range of feelings and emotions'. They provide the example of Ruth, who found emotions of fear, anxiety and worry emerged again as she revisited a particular event in work on story-telling. In this case the emotions that were aroused related to the memories described. Strong-Wilson (2006) reports similar experiences from work with teachers that was designed to facilitate critical reflection on their practice. Excitement and satisfaction can be strong experiences when particularly good evidence for the upholding of an argument is found. A vivid example of how relevant emotion can interfere with critical thinking comes from the work of Shaw (1994: 15 – see above) in the form of a quotation from one of the scientists he studied. The scientist talks of finding contradictions of his understanding in the literature by 'legitimate people . . . and I get to a point where I'm so damned confused that I don't know where to go'. It is interesting to note that the emotion 'spills' into the language used to describe the situation.

- **Emotions that are not obviously relevant to a given situation, may inhibit, facilitate or modify cognitive processes such as critical thinking**. For example, there is a literature on accelerated learning (Beard and Wilson, 2002) and 'flow states' (Csikszentmihalyi, 1990; Claxton, 2000), in which cognition is enhanced. There is also the notion that there may be 'blocks to learning', which may be distractions from the task, and the process of critical thinking may be easier or more difficult because of the emotional state or the emotional 'atmosphere'. For the current writer, there is something about the quiet of the early morning that facilitates deeper thinking. Anger or upset about a completely irrelevant matter can disrupt thought. From the literature of creativity, Shaw (1994) provides another example of how critical thinking can be facilitated by a new situation. One of the scientists said, 'I'll be working on another problem and I'll sit back and I'll be tired of the other problem . . . and I'll start thinking about something [else], and it will just come to me, "Oh, now I know how to get round that road block"' (p. 18).

The manner in which emotion can distort critical thinking is important. De Bono (1983) talks about the general need that people feel to 'be right', which might often be translated into 'winning the argument'. The need to be 'right' will often be associated with the maintenance of self-esteem (see section below on self confidence) or the place of a person in a hierarchy. As de Bono says, 'In practice, being right has nothing to do with reality. Being right means believing that you are right at the time of thinking' (p. 100). We would add that sometimes it is a crucial issue that the other believes you to be right. The need to be right may be reflected in the manner in which the evidence for a case is selected or the manner in which reasoning is distorted, or it may affect the manner in which language is used (see below on language).

- **Emotion as a trigger to thinking or in the process of thinking**. This new category (from Moon, 2004) is inspired by a statement made by Brockbank and McGill (1998: 55) – 'Emotion is often the lever or source of energy that can yield shifts in ways of seeing the world, impacting on knowledge, self and (recognizing social context) agency in action.' It would be in the same realm of thinking to note that the first indicator of an idea is a connection with the emotions experienced (Damasio, 2000). In this way it directs attention (de Bono, 1976).

- **Emotional insight**. Moon (2004) suggested that there might be another link between emotion and learning or reflection and she coined the term 'emotional insight' for this. This hypothesized link may be more relevant to critical thinking activities that involve self-appraisal (Chapter 3). 'Emotional insight' would seem to be a form of learning where there is a fairly sudden and (to the individual at least) noticeable shift in personal outlook (belief or opinion, or as reflected in behaviour), but where the processing that led to that change is not evident or conscious and appears to have occurred rapidly. A shift of this kind can result from counselling interventions, but they also occur in everyday life. Hastie and Davies (2001: 207) talk about research on emotion and choice and make the point that 'the precursors of many emotional responses are unconscious, and these emotions are often mysterious to the person experiencing them'. Donaldson (1992), in her work on the nature of mind, suggests that Western ways of thinking have not always recognized the range of experience and learning, particularly those of an emotional nature. An example of emotional insight in critical thinking involves a student teacher's reflection on a painful incident that occurred when she was at school. It is an incident that has always bothered her – and is very much around as she works in schools. One evening she is watching a 'soap' and suddenly the incident comes to mind and she sees it in a different light. This influences the whole of her orientation to teaching – worries fall away and she feels 'different', though she cannot describe the feeling or the process. Brookfield (1987) seems to be talking of this kind of change when he refers to 'feelings of liberation' that can result from some forms of critical thinking (p. 232).

Based on the framework above and in particular the examples from the critical thinking literature, we suggest that there are different ways in which emotion relates to learning and it would seem likely that the different kinds of critical thinking activities (Chapter 2) might be more or less affected. For example, there may be more effects of emotion on critical thinking that relates to the self or personal relationships than that which is about academic topics. However, we would say that this is a generalization, and that emotion can be unexpected in its influences. Cartoon depictions of Archimedes leaping with excitement from his bath in his 'ah-ha' moment of discovery in physics can remind us of this.

Like so much more of this topic of critical thinking, there can be no easy and straightforward conclusion about the role of emotion in the process of critical thinking. There is an important relationship – the process of critical thinking is related to emotion but not in a simple way. There seem to be a number of different relationships as we have indicated in the framework above – and there may be some principles to discover, but perhaps we can only do this if we can fathom the unconscious and preconscious activities of the brain.

Language and critical thinking

Language becomes important when critical thinking is represented in written or spoken form. The topic is vast and here we pick out a few pertinent issues that will help to fill out the emerging picture of critical thinking and the ways in which it can best be supported in teaching and development processes. The emphasis on the role of language in critical thinking varies between the different approaches to critical activities (Chapter 3) – it is, for example, central in logic, and less obviously emphasized in most of the approaches that focus on components or skills. Regardless of its emphasis, it must be seen as extremely important in any critical thinking in the manner that the communication of the thinking is conveyed, distorted, precise or not precise, clear or not clear, subject to manipulation, filled with assumptions, and so on. This section is also a prelude to the next chapter on academic assertiveness and critical thinking.

Emmet (1964), in a helpful section entitled 'Language and bewitchment' provides ideas that should be background awareness for the critical thinker. Most of the ideas are self-evident – but that does not mean that we always take due account of them. He points out that language has been constructed by human beings and we should be willing to change it. It was largely constructed many centuries ago and it was based then on the conceptual structures of that time. These may not always translate into the variety of ideas that we need in current times. We have provided illustrations of that point in the discussion earlier about the language of learning and teaching – and have suggested that there are frequent misuses of that area of language in discussions about the natures of learning and teaching (Chapter 1). It has been suggested that more and new vocabulary is required to overcome the deficit. The words of education were developed in times when what was learnt was conceived to be directly related to what was taught.

The title of Emmet's chapter ('Bewitchment') is taken from Wittgenstein (see Emmet, 1964) and it refers to the role of language as a 'holder' for meaning. Emmet explains: 'If, as a result of language and the way in which it is used, we are misled about the nature of reality . . . then our intelligences may be said to have been bewitched by language' (p. 36). On that basis, we live in a state of bewitchment – an idea propounded by the philosophy of postmodernism. Elements of, or the whole of, an act of critical thinking may be the act of making sense for the reader or writer of the bewitchment that she confronts in the ideas that she uses, studies or conveys. We are culturally 'bewitched' in the sense that the reality which is conveyed by our language relates to the cultures which we experience. We have shown how the nature of critical thinking itself seems to be born out of a Western way of thinking (Chapter 4).

Most critical thinking is ultimately a social activity and this brings in another aspect of language – that of communication. The manner in which we think in personal thinking does not matter so long as it meets the needs of any task (visually, in word, in images . . ., in Ancient Greek or English). However, when we transmit an idea in order that another may endeavour to meet our perception of reality at that moment, we need to find a way in which the idea is transmitted in the best manner possible. Clarity and precision come into play again here. So also do our abilities to understand the reality of the other – so that we can mould our meanings to hers and enable her to understand the communication in the most effective manner possible. As Emmet says, 'It is no good saying that a word means such-and-such if people do not in fact use it this way or understand it this way' (p. 33). Sometimes there are culturally specific ways of using words. There is a 'language' of academia and of specific disciplines that may differ from common usage. It is one that learners probably need to acquire. Academics are not always good at recognizing their specialized words, or when their words are specialized and require introduction to learners. The word 'critical', itself, is a particular example of this.

The ambiguity of words is a central issue to critical thinking, whether reference is made directly, or is taken as implicit understanding. Words need to be examined for the meaning that they convey – whether as part of the structure of reasoning or as the subject matter of that reasoning. In different ways, for different people, they carry assumptions, connotations, or values. Words can be collected up into sentences or into concepts, where these units may carry different assumptions, connotations and values for different listeners.

Values can be described as systems of consistent beliefs that guide or influence the manner in which we think, communicate and (often) behave. Examples are personal values (e.g. self-esteem, self-confidence), relationships to a social group (e.g. the degree programme), moral values and those which relate to humanity (ecological concerns, etc.). We may not be aware of the manner in which our values determine the manner in which we function. De Bono (1982) talks about 'value-laden' words such as 'informer' or 'sneak' and 'goodie' and 'baddie' words such as 'human rights', or 'popularizer', 'superficial'. Indeed, we have suggested that some educational words seem to have connotations of 'goodness' such as 'experiential learning' (Moon, 2004) – and indeed, critical thinking is also generally a 'good' intellectual activity and hence, as we have suggested, it often appears in mission statements. Some areas of political critical thinking have focused very much on the language used in society and by the followers of the movement. 'Consciousness raising' (Hart, 1990) in the feminist movement is an example.

These issues about language are often not conveyed explicitly in the context of work on critical thinking – and are revealed in the examination of the nature of assumptions. Good attention to and good use of language are like underpinnings to critical thinking, and provide a basis for the way in which a good critical thinker will operate. We suggest that these simple ideas about language need to be brought into the open in discussion when learners are helped in their critical thinking – and hence we return to this material in the section on pedagogy.

Interest and intellectual curiosity

We add one more element to the list of personal attributes for critical thinking – interest or intellectual curiosity. There is not much to say about this except that for many it is the driving force behind critical activity – the whole reason why a person might question and 'worry at' an issue. Some people are intellectually curious and are apt to think critically while others tend to accept ideas (Kneale, 2003). How likely it is that we can generate intellectual curiosity where there was little, it is hard to say – except that the words 'foster' and 'nurture' seem important – as do features that are associated with relationships such as mentoring. There are emotional connotations – intellectual curiosity is a form of motivation. There is also something about the need for learners to have freedom to explore and have some control over their learning situations in order to allow their intellectual curiosity to thrive. Nor should we necessarily associate intellectual curiosity directly with academic achievement – because the latter may be measured in assessment by methods that do not best suit the intellectually curious, such as examinations. Meyers (1986) builds his pedagogy of critical thinking partly on the basis of stimulating curiosity and interest. The curiosity inspired by 'disequilibrium' in thoughts is related to this.

Time

We add the notion of time here because Meyers (1986) links it to the nurturing of curiosity and it needs to be added into the picture somewhere. Meyers says: 'it is difficult to nurture natural interests and to encourage attitudes of reflection when students are never given enough time to become fully involved with a subject' (p. 42). He is largely talking of the 'giving of time' by those who facilitate critical thinking. Barnett (1997) talks of the need for 'intellectual space' which seems to be a slightly broader concept in which the learner is in control of her time, but is stimulated to take more time by the very nature of the task set or suggested (for example, a learning journal – Moon, 2006).

Another kind of time that is important to critical thinking is 'wait time' (Tobin, 1987) – this is the time needed for the brain to engage in thinking in, for example, a lecture, or in debate or sustained conversation. Wait time is the pause for breath, the rhetorical question (needing no answer), the time to wander back to the laptop buttons when PowerPoint is used. The principle of wait time reminds us that the brain does take time to process ideas, and that a pause for thought in a conversation or a presentation would mean that the listeners – and maybe the speaker too – can better work the contingent thinking processes.

Thinkpoint

Knowledge does not investigate society as much as confirm the key beliefs of hegemonic political interests. This circularity is the product of a dominant paradigm which defines what are acceptable concepts and theories through the medium of the conventional wisdom, but which tends to present itself as apolitical and timeless. It reinforces this power by appeals to a universal rationality that may be expressed by such means of legitimation as religion, nature or the market. In this way it can obliterate social alternatives by undermining their assumptions without recourse to reason. It is precisely the existence of this power that underlines the importance of developing paradigmatic argument.

(Eisenschitz, 2000: 17)

6 Academic assertiveness

Being appropriately assertive as a thinker

Introduction

As this book has taken shape through the research and workshops, it has appeared that an area of thinking might be missing in many considerations of critical thinking – or more generally missing from higher education. The concept of 'academic assertiveness' came to being first as the writer sat at a conference in London, somewhat frustrated at what was being said about student learning. The view of the student was of a passive being, manipulated in a system in order that appropriate responses could be elicited. Is this what we really want? How do we elicit more active approaches to learning? Since then the idea of academic assertiveness has been explored in a couple of 'think tanks' and thrown around in discussions at a subsequent conference – and it seems to be seen to have some value. Academic assertiveness is about the thinker's personal confidence, her 'voice' in academia and her ability to process, work with and express critical ideas and action. The use of the word 'assertiveness' is as it is used in assertiveness training – it is not to be confused with aggression. It is positive behaviour that is characteristic of successful people in their self presentation. The intention is that academic assertiveness should only be a theoretical notion of something that is missing, but pedagogical practice and hence its description in this chapter is written in terms of the behaviour of learners. This chapter describes the concept in preparation for later discussion of the pedagogy (Chapter 12).

Academic assertiveness in relationship to critical thinking

In general terms, the ideas we express are similar to those in a small section of Barnett and Coate (2005) entitled 'Student voice' where they combine the ideas of self-critique and self-drive (p. 113). Barnett and Coate say, 'There is a sense here of personal autonomy, of determinedness not to be boxed in by dogma or fashion but to find a way forward that maintains one's integrity' (p. 113). They ask where these ideas are to be found in the curriculum. They sum up the section in a question: 'How might curricula be so fashioned to nurture the student voice, to give students the powers of human expression in appropriate and telling ways in different contexts with different listeners?' (p. 114). Directly relating these ideas to critical thinking, Meyers (1986) says that the full process of critical thinking 'is not a dispassionate learning process in which students need only to be shown new ways of perceiving things in order to follow it, but a threatening encounter that challenges one's very selfhood' (p. 96).

We illustrate our more specific and practical view of academic assertiveness with some scenarios in which the assertiveness is either clearly lacking, or is displayed:

- Jez and his colleagues (Chapter 2 onwards) are unsure what comments that imply insufficiency of critical thinking in their essays mean, but it is a risk to demonstrate ignorance about the meaning of the idea and ask a tutor. Jez did ask his tutor – he was assertive – but then did not take the further risk of indicating that he still did not understand when she gave him some definitions that did not make sense to him. His tutor hid behind definitions and it seems probable that she did not actually understand critical thinking either. The admission of not knowing something is part of being assertive.
- The next scenario is represented in a collection of examples of what students said about the process of essay writing (usually forms of critical thinking). This material comes from Read, Francis and Robson (2001):
  - Kate says: 'I think [in a first class essay], they're just looking for maybe something more from yourself, and I don't really have the confidence to . . . gamble. I tend to . . . play safe.'
  - Vanessa says: 'I felt that at my stage of knowledge, I hadn't the right to 'lay down the law' . . . I might say [that there was] a tiny bit [of] feeling that who am I to question all these established writers'.
  - Fatima says: 'The thing is that if you argue the opposite view to what they [the tutors] believe, it's that much harder to get a first, 'cause you really have to back it up with evidence, and you're sort of against someone who's at a much higher academic level than you'.
- In another scenario, Gold, Holman and Thorpe (2002) talk about Ruth. Ruth is a mature student on a management education programme and she reflects on the value of learning Toulmin's model of argumentation (1988). She says, 'I was always scared that I would be put down' and she relates this to growing up with dominant males and being told that she was 'average'. She says, 'I think, well, I have a voice, I can say things'. She says, 'Before it was just like this is how I am'. Being taught the model enabled her to question this state – 'if I don't want to be like that it's up to me to change'.
- We then have a more general example from Belenky, Clinchy, Goldberger and Tarule (1986). Inez (p. 52) was a woman who grew up with a sense of worthlessness because she had inadequate parents and 'had come to equate authority with physical power', with a continually reinforced sense that:

> women were supposed to remain in a position of silence and servitude . . . she did not trust her own judgment nor did she believe that any woman could 'think and be smart'. Inez has changed though, she no longer listens

to the external 'authorities', but listens to herself. She has become independent, with a job and a motorcycle, and openly can say of herself 'I am just getting to the point that everybody else starts'.

(p. 53)

Many of the writers on critical thinking insert a word or two into their descriptions of critical thinking that imply that learners need to have some of the capacities that we are terming 'academic assertiveness', but few go far in exploring the range of these capacities – or, like Barnett (1997) and Barnett and Coate (2005), they maintain the description at a theoretical level.

Identifying academic assertiveness

The development of the ideas of academic assertiveness that we present below have been derived from several situations, most of which are based in actual behaviour rather than theory. Sources have included direct observation of issues that students face (including those faced by the writer's own children in higher education), literature on critical thinking and student learning, ideas derived from work with and research on non-traditional students (widening participation) and from work in assertiveness training, again from theory (Moon, 1993) and practice in running courses.

Below we propose a general defining statement on academic assertiveness and then summarize the behaviours that it might incorporate. We then elaborate the behaviours, particularly as they relate to critical thinking. A working definitional statement about academic assertiveness follows:

Academic assertiveness is a set of emotional and psychological orientations and behaviours that enables a learner to manage the challenges to the self in progressing in learning and critical thinking.

It might include the following behaviours. These are behaviours in academic work and in the general experience of being a learner (they are in no particular order and there are overlaps):

- the finding of an appropriate 'voice' or form of expression through which to engage in critical thinking or debate;
- the willingness to challenge, to disagree and to seek or accept a challenge;
- the ability to cope with the reality or the likelihood of not being 'right' sometimes; making an error or failing; effective recovery from these situations; the willingness to change one's mind if necessary; the openness to feedback on one's performance (academic or otherwise);
- willingness to listen and take account of the viewpoint of others, awareness that others can make mistakes and reasonable tolerance of their failings;
- autonomy – a willingness to be proactive; to make and justify independent judgements and to act on them;
- an appropriate level of academic self-esteem.

We expand each of these groups of behaviours in order to link them in the tasks that learners face, and with relevant literature on critical thinking.

The factors in academic assertiveness

The finding of an appropriate 'voice' or form of expression through which to engage in critical thinking or debate

The word 'voice' arises frequently in the literature and it may have different meanings. It is used, for example, as a very general term by Barnett and Coate (2005) and Vanessa, Ruth and Inez (above) illustrate further uses. The interview with Inez was part of a widely read study of the developmental epistemology of women (Belenky, Clinchy, Goldberger and Tarule, 1986). In this work, the word 'voice' was taken to mean the sense that one could possess and express a point of view and is related to 'development of a sense of voice, mind and self' (p. 18). This is a broad view of the term which is used to describe the general ability to feel recognized and comfortable as a person with opinions and the ability and will to express them (also Gilligan, 1998). The work of Belenky et al. and of Gilligan were based on the exploration of gender issues, and it is important to recognize the role that gender issues can play in academic assertiveness and the lack of it. Gender is, however, only one 'divide'. Learners from non-dominant cultures (Chapter 4), or from non-traditional backgrounds can have similar difficulties with their 'voice' in educational situations (Moon, 2005b).

The Belenky et al. broad notion of 'voice' would actually cover most of the definition of academic assertiveness, so we explore the notion of voice here in the more specific context of learning and critical thinking. In this narrower context, 'voice' is what Vanessa (above) is lacking – the confidence to express herself in the academic environment, where she feels very much a novice (in her final year in a Bachelor's degree). Read et al. (2001) suggest that, apart from a lack of general confidence, the 'holding back' is due to unequal power relationship between academics and students and 'through a belief that lecturers will penalize views with which they do not agree'.

However, there is something more implied by 'voice' in the context of critical thinking – it involves an appropriate sensitivity within the process of critical thinking. Those who talk of 'nurturing' critical thinking (e.g. Meyers, 1986) or fostering it (Young, 1980a) seem to have in mind a similar idea to this development of appropriate sensitivity to the learners with whom they work. Baxter Magolda (1992) similarly recognizes that learners find this aspect of their voice in situations where there is not a 'monologue' but a 'dialogue of authority' in the working teaching process. She says that as teachers, 'We need to be silent and suspend the authority automatically ceded to us by the students, the classroom structure and the academic system' (p. 276). It is often the process of assessment that is so much the upholder of power – and in effect is the dominating authority in academia (Hinett, 2002). We perhaps do not always utilize that form of power most effectively to support learning.

In the context of critical thinking and its written expression there is another relevant meaning of 'voice' – and that relates to the nature of the expression of the writer in the text. It is the sort of meaning that is implied in the comment on an essay – 'Where is your voice in all this?' (Giltrow (2000: 137). It concerns the state of personhood of the writer as she expresses herself in essay or other form. This kind of 'voice' may also imply influences of the discourse of the discipline. An example of this is the student of Ford, Johnston, Brumfitt, Mitchell and Myles (2005) who described herself as 'feeling like a social worker' after her placement experience. She has the 'confidence, know-how and nascent professional identity' – the 'voice' of a social worker.

We summarize some of the meanings of 'voice' that are relevant to the development of appropriate expression of critical thinking:

- voice as an expression of the whole writer as a person with her personal life experiences which may include her disciplinary origins and her status;
- voice as a shorthand for the development of the person's expression, her understanding of knowledge, and her self;
- voice as meaning confidence in speaking out in situations where, for example, there may be issues with the authority of another;
- voice as implying an appropriate sensitivity in the expression of critique to the object of that critique which may be a learner learning to express critical thinking.

In connection with these ideas, academic assertiveness will be to do with 'voice building' (Gleaves and Walker, 2006).

The willingness to challenge, to disagree and to seek or accept a challenge

We refer, here, to the need to enable learners to shift towards the more active, challenging mode of being that is described by Barnett (1997). There are, however, surprisingly few references to the willingness of critical thinkers to challenge, seek challenge and disagree, three activities that one might have thought were very relevant to critical thinking. There is more discussion about an opposite occurrence to the acceptance of challenge – the 'spoon-feeding' of students. McKay and Kember (1997), working in Hong Kong, expressed surprise at the results of their research on the self-fulfilling myth that students want to be 'spoon-fed' with an unchallenging 'transmission' mode of didactic teaching. They interviewed students on a programme that had been didactic, and then modified it to facilitate independent learning. The students preferred the modified course and adopted a deep approach to their learning. One student said that it meant that there was 'more thinking and active learning', that 'we need to pay more effort to think', and 'sometimes we need to think differently from the books or reference texts. We need to pay more logical thinking on this.' The student implied that when they were challenged to think critically, they liked it.

Meyers (1986) mentions the creation of challenge in a number of places in his book about the pedagogy of critical thinking. He introduces the idea of challenging by the creation of 'disequilibrium' (or 'constructive disorder' – Yinger, 1980) – 'Teaching critical thinking involves intentionally creating an atmosphere of disequilibrium, so that students can change, rework or reconstruct their thinking' (p. 14), but he suggests that this must be done carefully – 'gauging sensitively the amount of disequilibrium that will do the most good' (p. 15). This is an important point. In any one class, some learners will be challenged just by being there (Peelo, 2002) while others will be ready and able to manage more challenge. As we will indicate later, there are likely to be learners interpreting ideas in different ways according to their level of epistemological development (Chapter 8).

The challenge in critical thinking is by definition of sophisticated thinkers, a 'challenge to oneself'. Paul and Elder talk of 'having intellectual courage' (Paul and Elder, 2004: 13). They describe intellectual courage in critical thinking as 'having consciousness of the need to face and fairly address ideas, beliefs, or viewpoints towards which we have strong negative emotions and to which we have not given a serious hearing'. While this statement is clear, it may not provide the full picture of 'challenge'. There is an emotional element. When we challenge the thinking of someone else – as for example, in the thinking of Vanessa (above) – the challenge is to our feelings about the other, and not necessarily to the idea. This brings us to the notion of 'disagreement'. It is an inevitable part of critical thinking sometimes to disagree with another's viewpoint. There is an inherent logical difficulty in the fostering of disagreement because, in the process, we foster the challenge to the very system itself, especially one with a structured system of assessment! Brookfield (1987) talks of developing critical thinking as a 'learning conversation' (p. 238), which entails work to encourage a 'diversity of opinion [and] disagreement over "correct" interpretations of an idea, rule or behavior and challenges to existing ways of thinking and acting'. He suggests that the essence of understanding is that there is 'a multiplicity of interpretations of practically every idea or action', which in turn forces learners to contemplate alternatives in . . . [their] own thoughts and actions' (pp. 240–1).

Coping with the reality or the likelihood of not being 'right' sometimes; making an error or failing; effective recovery from these situations; the willingness to change one's mind if necessary; the openness to feedback on one's performance (academic or otherwise)

A specialized area of coping with risk or challenge in critical thinking is coping with not 'being right', coping with failure, and with the admission that one wants to change one's mind. These all require emotional management of the self and they can all seriously affect the self-esteem (see later) and thereby the effectiveness of further critical thinking. These experiences are part of life for many learners but there is little in the literature to help them or to help their teachers to support them – other than when the matter comes into the realm of counselling.

We need to distinguish 'being right' from the evaluative processes of judgement-making. De Bono (1983), for example, talks of four ways of being right (p. 100), but these are ways of making an evaluative judgement (emotional, logical, a form of intuitive rightness and a rightness based on evaluation), and not the sense of producing the 'right or most appropriate response in a particular situation', which is the reference here. 'Being right' here is also linked to the notion of 'winning an argument' or being judged 'right' by others – or the corresponding experiences of failure.

These issues relate to the practices of academic assessment. For learners in formal education, 'rightness', in effect, is usually that judged 'right' by the tutors who grade the learners' work. The deliberations of the students cited in examples above with reference to their final-year essays illustrate this. A comment from another, Jo, illustrates this further: 'in the first year I started off writing essays on how I felt about whatever the subject was, and by the third year, I was writing more on what I thought the lecturer wanted to read . . . you write what they want you to read . . . if . . . you echo their teachings, you'll get a higher mark'. Jo presumably wanted a higher mark and did not want to risk failure – but the cost may be a personal loss of her capacity to think critically (Read et al. 2001).

There is much in the American literature of the 1980s and 1990s that skirts around the idea that critical thinking is a potentially risky and potentially threatening process for the learners because of the failure that they may experience (e.g. Young, 1980b). There is talk of the manner in which students 'stubbornly resist' critical thinking (Kinney, 1980). Keeley and Shemberg (1995) take these ideas further by relating the resistance to critical thinking to situations in psychotherapy. They introduce their paper through a hypothetical discussion between a student and her tutor:

Student: 'I want you [the expert] to give me the answers to the questions: I want to know the right answer.'

Teacher: 'I want you to become critical thinkers, which means I want you to challenge the experts' answers and pursue your own answers through active questioning. This means a lot of hard work.'

Keeley and Shemberg then analyse the situation as if students are clients and teachers are psychotherapists and they apply counselling and therapy principles to the management of resistance. The points are much the same as those that emerge in pedagogical literature elsewhere (rapport building, nurturing, fostering growth, etc.); however, they do acknowledge 'that students are often unresponsive because critical thinking involves new, and complex activities, and, in particular, "because they are afraid"'. They suggest that we should 'calmly state that we understand our students' fear and help them to overcome it; accept all student efforts . . . encourage risk and not punish mistakes . . . [We should] model criticism of ideas, not persons'.

This last point in the previous paragraph relates to a common problem for many learners who receive critical comments on their work. Regardless of how any comment about failure or error has been made, they can find it difficult to recognize that the issue is with the task or the conduct of it, and not of their whole person. A learner might interpret 'This piece of work . . .' as 'I cannot do critical writing'. Sometimes tutors are not sufficiently careful to direct feedback to the task as opposed to the learner as a person.

In a completely different area of literature (that on concerns about student retention), Cannon (2002) talks of failure and the recovery from failure (e.g. on a module or assignment) and of the difficulties of generalizing about the effects of failure because of the different individual reactions to it. The literature on assertiveness training deals with making errors, failure and recovery from failure as an acceptance that humans simply do fail sometimes and need constructive thinking to recover (e.g. Back and Back, 1982; Gillen, 1992). Within the critical thinking literature, Mingers (2000) gives his students a 'health warning' about the expression of critical thinking. He tells them that in the critique of powerful bodies that the latter can bite back. He talks about how critical comment 'can very easily be negative and destructive', that receiving it can be 'threatening and demoralizing'. He stresses the important of a constructive approach to coping.

Another difficult action that is integral to good critical thinking is the ability to change one's mind or position in an argument. It can be a hard process personally when the original position has many other justifications associated with it. It can involve a sense of being unsettled, in 'disequilibrium', as Meyers calls it (1986: 15). Changing one's mind may invoke negative or even abusive comment from others and it takes some emotional effort that is rarely acknowledged in discussion of critical thinking.

The willingness to listen and take account of the viewpoint of others, awareness that others can make mistakes and the need to have reasonable tolerance of their failings

Critical thinking is usually a social activity and hence the actions of others impinge on those of the thinker. It involves the good reading of others' work, good listening when they speak and an awareness of what lies 'between' the lines – the agendas, the insinuations, the assumptions and the context of the information.

In terms of paying appropriate attention to the viewpoints of others, Paul and Elder (2004) introduce the term 'intellectual fairmindedness' (as opposed to what they call 'intellectual unfairness'). They see it as 'having a consciousness of the need to treat all viewpoints alike, without reference to one's own feelings or vested interests, or the feelings or vested interests of one's friends, community or nation'. Bailin, Case, Coombs and Daniels, (1999b), following their review of the literature on critical thinking, use the term 'fairmindedness' in a similar manner, saying that there should be 'respect for others in group inquiry'. This implies the giving of a fair hearing to others, but also recognizing the role of their feelings. They add a point that suggests the recognition of the authority of those who could be deemed to have greater expertise on a particular matter.

The ability to be autonomous; a willingness to be proactive; to make and justify independent judgements and to act on them

More than in most of the behavioural representations of academic assertiveness above, we need to see this as a group of ideas that epitomize good critical thinking, but also act as a personal basis for the development of critical thinking. Bailin et al. (1999b) use the term 'independent mindedness', which, among other characteristics such as courage and 'intellectual honesty', implies the ability 'to stand up for one's firmly grounded beliefs'. There would be many times when honesty would demand that one uses courage to say 'I do not know' or 'There is not enough evidence to go on'. Independent judgement here is therefore not necessarily just about the judgement made, but about the process of making a judgement.

We have discussed Ronald Barnett's stance on the need for higher education to produce people who are willing to engage actively with the communities within which they are located, instead of just being good at thinking and reflecting (Barnett, 1997). Barnett and Coate (2005) talk of the need for a curriculum that demands 'critical engagement' from the learner – 'Critical engagement calls for courage to take a stand, to declare oneself, to be clear about one's point of view, one's argument, one's position' (p. 148), to be willing to take a lone stand if necessary. Others make a similar point (e.g. Lipman, 1991; Marshall and Rowland, 1998; Brockbank and McGill; 1998; Kneale, 2003). From the dates of these writings, it is evident that this is not a new idea. In 1980, Robert Young edited *Fostering Critical Thinking* (Young, 1980a), which was a text that was intended directly to respond to the idea that teaching in the USA had become too didactic. The last chapter in the book is entitled 'The next agenda, practical reasoning and action' (Young, 1980b). In it Young said, 'Critical thinking encourages the student to act as a practitioner rather than as an observer . . . most curricula and programs neither teach the skills and dispositions necessary for effective action, nor encourage students to try out their understandings, analyses and solutions in any real way' (pp. 93–4).

The development of learners who are proactive and willing to make independent judgements is being addressed in the UK to some extent in the employability agenda, which has encouraged the development of work placements for learners (e.g., Watton, Collings and Moon, 2002; Duignan, 2003; Yorke and Knight, 2006). There are much greater and more coherently promoted and managed schemes of experience in service learning in the United Stages (and increasingly elsewhere) (Service learning, n.d.). It is interesting to note that such experiences seem often to have a positive influence on the academic performance of learners when they are back in their academic settings (Lucas and Tan, 2006). This observation is also borne out by research – in a report of a survey of over 22,000 students engaged in service learning in the USA (Astin, Vogelgesang, Ikeda and Yee, 2000).

So we are saying both that the opportunities for work or placement situations support the development of vocational skills and that critical thinking may be improved as a result of learners being confronted with situations in which they have to make independent judgements. Baxter Magolda, following the work of

Kegan (1994), studied the development of the capacity to make independent judge-ments in relation to learners' other abilities to process knowledge, and suggests that both capacities are linked to the increasing epistemological sophistication that is fostered within and demanded by higher education. We explore these ideas in more detail later in this chapter and in Chapter 8 (Baxter Magolda, 1992, 1996, 1999, 2001; Baxter Magolda and King, 2004) and return to the work of Baxter Magolda in the context of the concept of 'self-authorship' in the next section.

An appropriate level of academic self-esteem

Self-esteem lies behind most of the elements of academic assertiveness above – we said that these sections are interrelated. It has been shown to relate to the manner in which a learner approaches a learning task, those with greater self esteem tending to take a deep approach (Abouserie, 1995). However, it may not be as simple as that in critical thinking. The learner with high academic self-esteem may feel that she has easy access to the 'right' answer in critical thinking. On the other hand, the encounter of situations in which one cannot find an acceptable outcome to a process of thinking also requires a certain level of self-esteem. Self-esteem needs to be appropriate to the reality of the occasion. Jacobs, a mature student whose piece about dissertation work on argument appeared as an intro-duction in Mitchell and Andrews (2000) (Jacobs, 2000), comments on the role of self-esteem for herself and her colleagues and the issues it presented for them as 'returners':

> there appeared to be a strong connection between early personal experi-ences of verbal argument, methods of negotiation at this stage and resulting self-esteem. Almost without exception, participants [in higher education programmes] needed encouragement to challenge ideas they encountered in their academic writing – to feel they had a right to do so. They needed the confidence that they were worthy of holding an opinion and that the opinion itself would have worth.
>
> (Jacobs, 2000: x)

There are different aspects of self-esteem, and most are relevant to the processes of critical thinking and often would underpin other aspects of academic assertive-ness that we have identified above. Self-esteem may also affect the manner in which a learner handles a critical thinking task with which she has difficulties. Those with low self-esteem may see the whole of the learning self as the problem, whereas those with higher self-esteem are more able to see the learning issue to be the problem, and isolate it from the feelings about the whole self. Changing the approach to the problem is probably easier than changing the self.

Academic assertiveness: some related ideas

In this section we will briefly consider several more general conceptions of personal functioning that come close to what we have termed 'academic assertiveness' – assertiveness training, self- or personal efficacy, and self-authorship.

Assertiveness training has been common in business and community situations since the mid twentieth century at least, having a powerful boost in the rise of the women's movement (e.g. Alberti and Emmons, 1970). Assertiveness courses cover a series of practical steps that aim to enable participants to feel more in control of their lives and more effectively to stand up for themselves. Some of the elements that are covered on such a course are: the nature of assertive, non-assertive and aggressive behaviours; the role of thoughts in behaviour; dealing with fears and 'put-downs'; a person's rights as a person; making mistakes; changing one's mind; dealing with the giving and receipt of criticism (in the negative sense) or critique; constructive criticism and so on. It is not unusual for higher education students to be offered assertiveness courses, but usually they are in the context of student unions (e.g. Hinton, 2006) and not within or applied to their academic courses or their learning processes. These ideas have been influential in the manner in which we have framed the notion of academic assertiveness and organized the subsections above.

The second conception that is close to academic assertiveness is a set of ideas around self- or personal efficacy. Barrell (1995) said that personal efficacy is 'the power to achieve a desired goal. Students with personal efficacy know that they, as individuals control what is being learned based on a belief in their abilities to apply effort and achieve a goal.' Dweck's work on self theories (1999) has been influential in the development of this thinking, and a recent redevelopment of the idea is that of Yorke and Knight (2004). The latter have constructed a model for the enhancement of the employability capacities of students which includes 'efficacy beliefs (and self theories generally)' (Knight and Yorke, 2002). Efficacy is included in the model alongside understanding, skills and metacognition (including reflection) and it describes a 'synergistic blend of personal qualities, skills of various sorts . . . and disciplinary understanding'. Efficacy beliefs and related personal qualities are seen to 'colour everything the student (and subsequently the graduate) does'. The concept of self-efficacy is a valuable guiding principle to teaching and the facilitation of learning and critical thinking with a focus on the general development of the learner's sense of control and her potential for new learning, change and achievement (Yorke and Knight, 2006). However, academic assertiveness is at the practical and classroom end of this guiding principle in which the concern is with actual behaviours – on what it is that the learner needs to do in order to gain the sense of self and control.

Another general concept that is related to academic assertiveness is self-authorship. Kegan explains this as:

> a system for organizing experience – not the mental operations themselves. This system is a 'new whole', which '. . . is an ideology, an internal identity, a self authorship that can coordinate, integrate, act upon, or invent values,

beliefs, convictions, generalizations, ideals, abstractions, interpersonal loyalties and intrapersonal states. It is no longer authored by them, it authors them and thereby achieves a personal authority.

(Kegan 1994: 185)

To achieve this organization role, the system that Kegan describes relies on the recognition of the person that she is 'in charge' of constructing the knowledge systems of her life. She recognizes that knowledge itself is constructed, and she will have the ability to understand the full and deep processes of critical thinking that involve the questioning of every element of thought, including the thought itself and the mediating language systems. The state of self-authorship could be said, therefore, to lie at the heart of proper or good critical thinking and academic assertiveness, but in the latter the focus is on behaviour. In the manner in which Kegan defines the idea, there could be a situation in which a learner, though fully understanding that she has constructed her own knowledge and is fully conversant with the processes of critical thinking, is too unsure of her social position in a particular context to express her ideas, and hence remains silent. She lacks academic assertiveness – and no one would know about the level of her critical thinking because it is unexpressed.

Baxter Magolda has done much to develop the concept of self-authorship (1992, 1996, 1999, 2001; Baxter Magolda and King, 2004) and to look at its components. In her hands, the concept comes to acquire more of the active and behavioural elements that are a feature of academic assertiveness. Baxter Magolda suggests that self-authorship comprises epistemological development (Chapter 8), an intra-personal foundation which is the self element as described by Kegan, and an interpersonal foundation which is described as a 'capacity to engage in authentic interdependent relationships with diverse others in situations wherein the self is not overshadowed by a need for others' approval etc.' (Baxter Magolda, 2004: 8)

Academic assertiveness – a conclusion

We suggested that academic assertiveness is a set of emotional and psychological orientations and behaviours that enables a learner to manage the challenges to the self in progressing in learning and critical thinking. We have identified six factors that seem to make up this capacity. As we have demonstrated, the ideas that support academic assertiveness as it relates to critical thinking, are all well supported by the literature, but the references are 'dotted about' and they tend not to be discussed in relation to classroom practice. There are some other concepts that overlap with academic assertiveness. Self-efficacy and self-authorship are conceptions that are more theoretical also. Assertiveness training is generic and does not address directly the particular issues of academic learning. We would argue that there is a potential means of improving critical activity by doing more work with learners in their development of academic assertiveness. We explore this in Chapter 12.

Thinkpoint

When Edward Glaser published his famous work *Experiment in the Development of Critical Thinking* in 1941 he listed over 340 scholarly books and articles, all of them either documenting that thinking can be taught or explaining how and why to teach it. The studies quoted [in the chapter written by the author of the quotation] are part of a huge corpus of work that has grown in the five decades since Glaser's book and extended our knowledge of the possibilities of teaching thinking.

The problem now is not whether we can teach thinking. The evidence suggests we can. The problem continues to be whether we are willing to make the pedagogical changes necessary to do so, and if we are, which changes might be the most effective.

(Coles and Robinson, 1991: 22)

Part 4

Taking stock

7 Critical thinking

A pause to take stock

Introduction

It has taken six chapters to lay out most of the basic ideas on critical thinking. We have pulled the ideas together only once so far – at the end of the second chapter. It is now time to gather ideas again – to take stock – before the next stage in the thinking about critical thinking. We do this by building on the first version of the defining statement in Chapter 2 on the basis of the various topics that have been covered in subsequent chapters. We include some details – such as the identification of the activities of critical thinking and the approaches in order that this material can act as a brief summary, particularly for those who have not read the earlier detail.

Towards a defining statement about critical thinking (second version)

We treat critical thinking as one aspect of a generic term, critical activity, which includes the idea of critical thinking and its various representations, including action, speech, writing and so on. We would see the various terms such as critical appraisal, evaluation, reflection, understanding etc. as elements of the critical thinking processes where there is an emphasis on particular kinds of mental activity.

(Chapter 1)

The central activity of critical thinking is the assessment of what might be called evidence, in order to make a judgement.

(Chapter 2)

Critical thinking is, itself, an aspect of the activity of thinking. It is a form of learning, in that it is a means of generating new knowledge by processing existing knowledge and ideas using what we have called the tools of manipulation of knowledge (e.g. analysis, understanding, synthesis). We might call critical thinking, itself, a 'multiple' tool for the manipulation of knowledge.

(Chapter 2)

There is an employment of precision and skill in the use of good critical thinking. When we engage in critical thinking, we are usually working towards an anticipated form of outcome which will usually be in some form of 'judgement'. Critical thinking involves the taking of a deep approach and would usually relate to subject matter that is complex and about which there might be some alternative viewpoints. Reflexivity is usually implied in the process.

(Chapter 2)

For the learner, critical thinking can be involved in a variety of activities with different intended outcomes. It is not, as may be assumed, just engaged in situations in which an argument of another person (e.g. in an academic paper) is reviewed. The activities of critical thinking that we have earlier identified are:

    Review of someone else's argument.
    Evaluation of an object.
    Development of an argument.
    Critical thinking about the self.
    Review of an incident.
    Constructive response to the arguments of others.
    Critical thinking as a habit of engagement with the world.

(Chapter 2)

There are different approaches to the teaching or presentation of the idea of critical thinking. While they enrich the general conception of critical thinking, they also serve to contribute to the confusion about it in working from different conceptions of critical thinking, some broader and some narrower:

    Approaches that involve logic.
    Approaches concerned with component processes, skills and abilities of
        critical thinking
    Pedagogical approaches to critical thinking
    Critical thinking as characterizing 'a way being'
    Developmental approaches to critical thinking
    Overviews of what critical thinking is or involves.

(Chapter 3)

There are issues in critical thinking about standards. 'Standards' can relate to the standard or quality of the thinking, or the sufficiency of the quality of the outcome or conclusion to the thinking. The notion of depth of thinking is useful and may be related to a developmental sequence and epistemological development. (This is yet to be explored.)

(Chapter 4)

While the words 'objectivity' and 'subjectivity' appear often in the literature of critical thinking, they tend to be confusing since they are interpreted differently.

Good quality critical thinking can sometimes be said to be 'objective', but equally, the sophisticated thinker recognizes the constructed nature of knowledge and its relation to a context and to the human minds that process it, and therefore becomes more able to recognize its essential subjectivity.

(Chapter 4)

Critical thinking is a culturally influenced process. There is evidence to suggest that the picture of critical thinking that we are developing is essentially a Western way of processing ideas. Learners from other cultures may confront difficulties in understanding it because they work and value other ways of thinking and representing the thinking.

(Chapter 4)

In addition to sitting in a cultural milieu, critical thinking is also formed and limited by the structure and functioning of the brains that engage in it. This applies particularly to the manner in which we can only make judgements of one thing in relation to another. We work on the making of comparisons.

(Chapter 4)

Critical activity is affected by the personal characteristics of the thinker. Emotional factors seem to interact with thinking in many ways and it is difficult, therefore, to identify direct relationships between the two. For example, emotion may be the subject matter of thinking, it may facilitate or inhibit thinking or be produced in the process of thinking, and so on.

(Chapter 5)

A person's ability to use language skilfully is relevant to critical thinking where it involves language, and the thinker needs to be sensitive to different usages, connotations and understandings of words and ideas.

(Chapter 5)

Intellectual curiosity and interest are relevant to the willingness to pursue critical thinking and these dispositions are therefore important. It is also important to note that critical thinking requires time and intellectual space.

(Chapter 5)

We suggested that a collection of capacities and dispositions that are relevant to the ability to think and act critically could be summarized as 'academic assertiveness'. This set of capacities relates to the thinker's ability to find an appropriate 'voice' for expressing critical thinking, the willingness to challenge others' expressions, the acceptance and capacity to cope with errors and mistakes, and so on. It is linked with self esteem and it has pedagogical implications.

(Chapter 6)

The effective provision of evidence as a central theme of critical thinking

The element of critical thinking that emerges as central to all of these further issues is the ability of a person to make effective provision of evidence to justify a reasonable judgement. This conclusion is much the same as that reached in the earlier publication on critical thinking (Moon, 2005a). We would reiterate, therefore, as a central idea in critical thinking:

> Critical thinking is a capacity to work with and express complex ideas, whereby a person can make effective provision of evidence to justify a reasonable judgement. The evidence, and therefore the judgement, will pay appropriate attention to context.
>
> (p. 12)

As we have demonstrated, this statement is very much 'shorthand' for a far greater area of consideration.

Is the critical thinking jigsaw complete? Introducing the issues of depth and epistemology

Does this interpretation of critical thinking give us the whole picture so that we can turn to the pedagogy of critical thinking?

There have been indications above that there are still some pieces of the jigsaw missing. There are, for example, a number of hints of an underlying developmental progression in critical thinking – and also issues of the depth of critical thinking that may well be related to developmental progressions. Depth of critical thinking is a quality issue and we therefore have more to say about quality in pursuing this further thinking. We have held back from adding the material on the possible developmental progression and the matter of depth in critical thinking, because these important ideas are better applied now that many of the earlier issues have been worked through.

In order to cover the issues of developmental progression and depth in critical thinking, we need to take account of an important area of thinking that is only recently having an impact on the literature of higher education and which the current writer considers to be of extreme importance to the underpinning, particularly of higher and (UK) further education. We consider the literature of epistemological development. We will show that epistemology and the work on critical thinking are closely related and that epistemological issues need to be taken into account in a definition of critical thinking and its pedagogy. In broadening our approach to critical thinking in this way, we add two elements to our thinking – the influence of the student's conception of knowledge in her ability to think critically and the implication from this that the capacity for critical thinking should be seen as a developmental process.

The term 'epistemology' is used here to relate to the learner's view of the nature of knowledge – we talk of a learner's 'conception of knowledge' or 'epistemological belief' synonymously. Epistemological development has been the subject of a number of studies over the last half-century that indicate that there is a developmental sequence in learners' conceptualization of the nature of knowledge and that this influences the manner in which learners function – particularly affecting their capacity for critical thinking. We suggest that the notions of depth (and thereby 'quality') of critical thinking are related in that better 'depth' in critical thinking closely relates to what we might conceive of as further developed critical thinking that in turn is based on the learner's greater development on a continuum of increasing sophistication in the learner's conception of knowledge. There are important concomitants for pedagogy too (Chapter 11).

The measure of significance that we assign to developmental epistemology is indicated by the allocation of a whole chapter and a part title to it. For the casual reader of this book, particularly one whose interest is primarily pedagogical, the close reading of Chapter 8 is not essential. We therefore include a summary at the end of it. The chapter on depth (Chapter 9), however, is important for pedagogy.

Thinkpoint

I keep coming back to how elusive this thing called critical thinking is. It is caught up in the middle of a web of words and meanings – the more I think that I am approaching a meaning of it, the more 'sticky other things' tug for my attention and pull me off course.

(Jenny Moon, extract from journal maintained during the writing of this book, 20 April 2006)

Part 5

Epistemological development and depth in critical thinking

8   Critical thinking and learners' conceptions of knowledge

Introduction

This chapter could be seen as a diversion from the journey through the ramifications of critical thinking. Other chapters have largely started from critical thinking and explored associated literature and theorizing. In contrast, this chapter starts from another area of thinking and will be applied to critical thinking. Few writers, other than Meyers (1986), Kuhn, (1999), Kember (2001) and the present writer have directly made the connection between developmental epistemology and critical thinking.

We have arranged the ideas on epistemological development in a particular order. We describe the four main studies as a means of indicating the main ideas and then look at other relevant studies that elaborate aspects of the main idea. We draw a tentative conclusion from both sections as a basis for then relating these ideas to those developed in earlier chapters on critical thinking and furthering the latter. From this point, we are using two terms – epistemological development (as a process) and epistemological beliefs (of the individual) – to imply the developing understanding by the individual of the nature of knowledge.

As we indicated at the end of the last chapter, there will be a summary of the main points of this chapter for those who do not feel that they need the detail of this work, or for those who are familiar with it. It is covered in less detail in Chapter 2 of Moon (2004).

Epistemological development – brief description of four of the main studies

Perhaps best known of these studies is that of William Perry (1970). Perry published his main work on an interview study of intellectual and ethical development in male Harvard students. He reported that he could detect nine progressive 'positions' from the least to the most sophisticated. He suggested that learners in higher education initially interpret the world in absolute terms – black and white, them and us, right and wrong, and so on. They look for certainty and tend to see facts as largely indisputable and either right or wrong. This is described as a 'dualistic state'. Correspondingly, the learners view teachers as experts – as the holders of the knowledge or facts that they pass over to their students while the latter 'absorb' the knowledge. On Perry's view, learners progress to a state where they recognize that it is possible for experts to hold justified but opposing views. They see that there can be multiple perspectives on a topic. They then shift toward a view of developing and justifying an opinion in situations of uncertainty in which they recognize that others have a 'right' to an opposing opinion, and later they adopt a relativistic view in which they can see that knowledge is relative to the frame of reference that is applied to it by the learner, and that this needs to be taken into account when working with knowledge. Correspondingly now, they see the role of a teacher as one of partner and facilitator in the development of knowledge. Perry's students seem not to have displayed the full development of epistemological belief in which learners see knowledge as constructed and justified by evidence that is related to the context (King and Kitchener, 1994).

Perry's work was published on male students. Belenky, Clinchy, Goldberger and Tarule (1986) therefore suggested that females might develop their conceptions of knowledge in a different manner. They interviewed a sample of female college students and women from family agencies (i.e. not all in education) and within the interview were embedded questions that enabled them to locate the subjects within Perry's 'positions'. As a result of their work, Belenky et al. identified five 'episte-mological perspectives'. These deal with a wider span of personal development, since their sample had in it some women who had received very little formal education. The first of these perspectives is termed 'silence'. Silent women saw themselves as incapable of having a voice of their own and they felt themselves to be at the whim of authority (i.e. further back on the continuum than Perry's first position). The most sophisticated stage consisted of those who recognized knowledge as constructed and related to its context, as we have described above. We referred to some of the Belenky et al. sample in Chapter 6 in the context of academic assertiveness and the importance of 'voice' to critical thinking.

King and Kitchener (1994) worked on what they called 'reflective judgment' which, in its definition, relates closely to the view of critical thinking in this book. They adopted a broader remit than the two projects described above, work-ing with both genders and a wide representation of the population. They used many empirical studies and the work that they reported in 1994 had been pursued then for over fifteen years. They used subjects' capacity to work on ill-structured problems as an indicator of subjects' frame of reference for knowledge. Ill-structured problems are those which have no right or wrong 'answer', but that require reasoning and personal judgement – such as ethical issues. After working on such a problem, subjects were interviewed on the intellectual processes in which they had engaged, and the sequences of their thinking. King and Kitchener iden-tified seven stages of development, which broadly accord with the sequence identified by the writers described above, though they considered that their subjects demonstrated development beyond the students in Perry's study.

Baxter Magolda (1992) was initially interested in the gender issues that she suggested might distinguish between the kinds of thinking in men and women. She studied a mixed population of around a hundred college students, using semi-structured interviewing, and she identified four domains of knowing and reasoning which again demonstrated a similar developmental sequence to those described above. We use Baxter Magolda's sequence to illustrate in more detail the continuum of development of conceptions of knowledge that is relevant to higher education, because her work is simpler (with only four 'domains') and because it is well illustrated by quotations from the students whom she interviewed. (For more detailed description of these domains and illustrations of them by quotations from the learners at the relevant stages, see Resource 8: An exercise in the recognition and understanding of epistemological beliefs for staff or more advanced students.)

Baxter Magolda's first 'domain' is 'absolute knowing' and is similar to Perry's dualist stage. Knowledge is seen as certain or absolute and formal learning is a matter of absorption of the knowledge of the experts (e.g. teachers). She describes as 'transitional knowing', a second stage in which the learner begins to have doubts about the certainty of knowledge – and gains a position where she acknowledges that there is both partial certainty and partial uncertainty. The third domain is 'independent knowing' – when learners recognize the uncertainty of knowledge, and cope with this by taking the position that everyone has a right to her own opinion or beliefs. This seems to be an embryonic form of the most sophisticated domain – that of 'contextual knowing' – in which knowledge is seen as constructed, and is understood in relation to the effective deployment of evidence that best fits a given context. Teachers are, at this stage, seen as facilitators and partners in the process of the development of knowledge.

It is important to note that very few of Baxter Magolda's subjects were at the stage of contextual knowing at graduation from their undergraduate studies. In separate studies (1994, 1996) Baxter Magolda found that two influences seemed particularly to facilitate their progression into this stage – either experience of postgraduate education or situations when they were required to make significant independent decisions (Chapter 6). In subsequent work Baxter Magolda (1999) confirmed and expanded the latter finding.

We have, therefore, four pieces of work described in this section that broadly provide evidence of a continuum of development of epistemological beliefs that may coincide with the period of higher education. There are, identified in this work, nine, seven, five and four points or stages identified on the continuum that are said to have distinctive characteristics that are in accord with the trends in the continuum. The end points of the continua are very similar. The multiple stages could be seen as providing the detail of the transitions between the stages; on the other hand, it is interesting to note Baxter Magolda's observation that students shifted between domains and might work on different conceptions for different topics at the same time. This seems to support the adoption of the simpler system that she used. Latterly other researchers have argued that the only important stages that we mainly need to work with are the dualist and relativist stages (e.g. Kember, 2001). We review some of these considerations about the stages and the nature of the continuum in the next section.

Other work on developmental epistemology

Schommer started from considerations of the continuum that had been observed (as described above) but queried whether the schemes of 'epistemological beliefs' should be seen as one trait or as a 'system of more or less independent beliefs' (1994: 300). A series of studies (Schommer, 1990, 1993, 1994; Schommer and Walker, 1995) suggested that five relatively independent continua might account for the construct of 'epistemological beliefs'. The constituent beliefs in the form of continua that she identified were: certainty (from 'knowledge is absolute to knowledge is constantly evolving'); organization of knowledge (from 'knowledge is compartmentalized to knowledge is highly integrated and interwoven'); control of learning (from predetermination of learning ability to learning ability is 'acquired from experience'); and lastly speed of learning (learning is 'quick or not-at-all to learning is a gradual process') (all quotations from Schommer, 1994: 301). All of these constituents would, of course, be relevant independently to critical thinking and other learning activities. Schommer said that they largely affected learners' willingness to persist with difficult tasks, their comprehension of written tasks and their ability to cope with ill-structured material. Schommer said that she found evidence of these five continua, but in a review of her work Hofer and Pintrich (1997) indicate concern about the reasoning and methodology that underpins the research. However, they did see as useful the initiative to seek alternative views of epistemological belief from a single continuum to a complex system of independent variables. We return to this notion later.

The link between epistemological beliefs and learning is, of course, crucial. It is, perhaps epitomized in the title of one of Perry's publications, 'Different worlds in the same classroom' (Perry, 1985), suggesting that the same material of teaching can be perceived and conceived of very differently among individuals in a group of students in the same classroom who are at different stages of epistemological development. This is well illustrated in the quotations in Baxter Magolda's books (1992, 2003) and it is discussed further in the next chapter on depth in critical thinking.

Others have studied this relationship between epistemological development and learning. Ryan (1984), basing his work on Perry's findings only, demonstrated that the epistemological orientation of a group of students at a number of stages of their college education related to different standards in their comprehension of a text and to different levels of academic performance. He suggests that 'one's epistemological beliefs . . . form the psychological context within which [the student] develops standards for evaluating the degree to which knowledge has been extracted from a text'. In other words, the reader's satisfaction with the nature of knowledge gained from reading a text is related to the stage of her epistemological beliefs. It seems reasonable to assume that the same 'standard' relates also to the reader's reading of her own writing, her monitoring of her standard of, for example, critical thinking, and the construction of written work in which that critical thinking is demonstrated or communicated. The term 'standard' here would relate back to the discussion of standards in Chapter 4.

More than the relation of epistemological belief to reading comprehension, Ryan found that the individual's standard of epistemological belief also predicted course grades 'even after the effects of academic aptitude or the amount of college experience [had] been eliminated' (Ryan, 1984). It is interesting to relate this finding to a comment made by Chet Meyers (1986), that 'the real value of Perry's work is the insight it offers into the reasons why most students do not think critically' (p. 97) – they are just simply not yet able to conceive of knowledge in a manner that allows them to engage fully with the process of critical thinking. Kember (2001) reached a similar conclusion to Meyers. He makes a very significant statement that **'Critical and creative thinking is only possible if relativism is recognized'** – to which we will later return. He goes on further to conclude about his study that 'what comes through strongly from this study is the importance of [learners] making the transition from one broad orientation to the other'.

In an interview study of the learning of 'novice' and 'expert' part-time students in Hong Kong, Kember (2001) found it useful to conceive only of two sets of beliefs at either pole of the continuum. He described the least sophisticated pole as didactic and reproductive belief where knowledge is defined by authority, is absolute, where teaching is seen as transmission. In this state, the outcome of the learning is seen to be judged by the student's ability to reproduce material. This accords closely with the absolutist stage of Baxter Magolda. The other belief set is 'facilitative / transformative – where knowledge is seen as constructed and the student must judge alternative theories on the basis of evidence', where 'the student is responsible for learning independently with guidance from the teacher', where the student works towards understanding of relevant concepts and where the outcome of learning is transformation of knowledge for the student's own purpose. This description relates closely to the contextual knowing stage of Baxter Magolda (1992). Kember did not consider it necessary to class the intermediate progression between these two stages, or 'orientations' as he terms them. His view was that that there may or may not be intermediate stages. He observed that students would hold a range of beliefs that related to both stages at the same time. We would tend to agree with Kember's position that it is the continuum that is important. Learners in contact with appropriate stimuli progress along it, all be it, in a 'back and forth' manner. We return to Kember for some important conclusions at the end of this section.

Another question that has often been raised about the role of epistemological beliefs in the classroom is whether different disciplines foster different rates of epistemological development. There is conflicting evidence on this matter. Schommer and Walker (1995) studied this with around a hundred students. The students completed epistemological questionnaires and read a passage about either mathematics or social sciences, or did both as a control group. The results showed no significant differences in the epistemological beliefs in the groups. However, it seems significant that the students were actually all psychology students. It might be reasonable to consider that one's epistemological stage is related to one's core discipline rather than the material being processed at the time.

In a much more detailed study on the issue of discipline, Palmer and Marra (2004) disagreed with Schommer and Walker and demonstrated that the picture might be more complex. They also used a group of similar background students (engineering and science majors) who were studying a wide range of subjects, and spending different amounts of time in their other subjects. They compared the students' responses in their experiences of science, humanities and social science disciplines and proposed that students encountered two significant epistemological shifts in their development that were related to the disciplines studied. They identified the first shift as one between single and multiple perspectives – and suggested that this is facilitated in the humanities because essentially the notion of multiple perspectives is the basis of the humanities disciplines and is less often the case in the sciences. The second shift involves a development of the understanding that 'knowledge is not static', and that it must be appropriately evidenced and it is related to a particular context. This shift, Palmer and Marra saw as being facilitated in the sciences because science '. . . curricular experiences provide opportunities to develop these rich and deep understandings'. There are many queries that might be raised about the research of Palmer and Marra (as is acknowledged by the researchers) but their findings are very interesting and have substantial implications for the management of student experiences in relation to their epistemological development. The outcomes of the research are broadly upheld by Lonka and Lindblom-Ylanne (1996) who worked with medical and psychology students. Paulsen and Wells (1998), using Schommer's questionnaire (and thereby basing their work on her schema of components in epistemological development), related the components to disciplines that were grouped according to the simarity of the subject matter of the disciplines. In some respects they also agree with Palmer and Marra – for example, humanities students were less likely to have naïve views about knowledge as composed of 'definitive and absolute facts'. However, there are many variables in how a subject is taught, whether there is choice within it, whether it is modularized or integrated, the attitude towards knowledge of teachers, the stage of the learners – that make these generalizations about discipline and epistemological development difficult.

Like Kember's, a number of studies consider the manner in which students can be helped to make the transition from the unsophisticated absolutist view of knowledge to the sophisticated stage of constructed knowing. It is not surprising that one of the most significant factors is the nature of the teaching and the interactions with the teacher. For this reason it is relevant here to step aside from the consideration of student learning issues and consider the developing epistemological beliefs in relation to the teacher. Brownlee (2001) investigated the epistemological beliefs of (graduate) pre-service teacher education students. Like Kember, she conceived of epistemological beliefs as two poles of a continuum, though she created a category for those who held a mixture of beliefs in between the two. She interviewed 29 students (mean age 27). All of the students except one 'described some relativistic views about knowledge', but 17 'described mixed beliefs that individuals construct reasoned truths and receive absolute truths'. The other 11 students were 'aware that truths are predominantly constructed and reasoned'. This finding would be consistent with other observations (e.g. Baxter Magolda, 1992) that most Bachelor's degree graduates have not reached a 'pure' state of contextual knowing. These were trainee teacher students, but Brownlee cites research to suggest that teachers with more relativistic views of knowledge are likely to be more effective teachers. Brownlee's work should perhaps alert us to the need to ensure that higher education students are taught by those whose epistemological beliefs are reasonably sophisticated and relativistic, but, nevertheless, can recognize that many of their students are at earlier or less sophisticated stages of development. It is the experience of the writer that this may not always be the case.

Clearly there is much more work to do to clarify the role of the development of epistemological development per se and its role in learner development, in critical thinking and in everyday life as well. In 2004 a whole edition of *Educational Psychologist* was devoted to epistemological development and its role, and in a summarizing article Bendixen and Rule (2004) endeavoured to pull together the range of factors that are associated with epistemological development. The 'integrative model' addresses additional factors such as the stimulus and circumstances for epistemological shift and the roles of environment, motivation and emotion. They suggest that while there is a general developmental trend in the understanding of knowledge, there may be regression and 'regrowth' that is then 'stronger'.

There might be a drive to create an actual model of epistemological development with all the various factors and influences sewn firmly into it – or maybe, since there is usually no 'instruction' in how to progress (generally, as learners, we find our own way), there is no one model. Are we not showing absolutist tendencies if we seek 'THE model' as opposed to something that describes the kind of journey in learning, and not the exact route.

The development of the conception of epistemological beliefs – a conclusion for the purposes of pedagogy and critical thinking

Since higher education seems to be a phase during which there is potential for considerable development of epistemological beliefs, there is a need to work out a position for the relationship between student learning and specifically critical thinking and epistemological development. If we consider that we work solely as researchers, we can afford to wait for the detail of this continuum of epistemological beliefs to be elicited. However, if there is a concern for pedagogy – for example, for a means of understanding critical thinking – we need to conceive of a framework that can enable us to understand better the manner in which students see knowledge. From the review of the literature here, this writer tentatively puts forward a simple model rather like that of Kember or like the two extremes of the Baxter Magolda scheme. In this model students generally progress from absolutist to more sophisticated conceptions, but they do this by shifting forwards and sometimes backwards in different elements of this progression as they encounter different challenges to their learning. There seems to be some suggestion that when we encounter very complex ideas, we may regress and treat them in a more factual manner at first (Baxter Magolda, 1996). This may be what happens to some students on entry to higher education, when they are somewhat daunted by the ethos of higher education and the discipline 'experts' who now teach them. In particular it may happen for students from non-traditional (e.g. non-'A'-level) backgrounds (Moon 2005c).

Furthermore, without clear evidence of separate 'strands' to the epistemological continuum, it would seem useful to consider that there are central principles of epistemological progression with many related 'implications'. For example, if the epistemological beliefs mean that the learner sees knowledge as absolute and factual, then a likely implication of this is that the teacher is seen as an expert who holds those facts and transmits them to the learner in a didactic manner. It is not surprising therefore, that some students want to be 'spoon-fed' – because spoon-feeding as a process matches the conceptions of knowledge as an entity that these learners entertain. As the epistemological beliefs of the learner change, and she realizes that there is uncertainty and that it is possible for two experts to disagree, so the implication is that her views of teachers and teaching will need to accommodate to this change. The learner will also expect to take more responsibility for her learning.

We have tended to indicate above that epistemological progression seems unlikely to be as simple as a step-by-step pattern and we have tended to see it as a sequence of shifts back and forth but usually overall in a forward direction along the continuum. However, we should not ignore the occasions when learners reach epistemological crises (Carey and Smith (1999)). An epistemological crisis occurs when learners are suddenly confronted with a need to see knowledge in a different way. Most usually this will be represented in a shift between descriptive material presented as 'fact' and the introduction of a range of perspectives which can only be comprehended in a relativistic mode of understanding. Morgan (1995) provides a useful example of a personal experience of an environmental science course when students were asked what had been learnt from a series of lectures (p. 22). One response was, 'Well, it's all about these conflicting theories as I see it. I suppose we just have to guess which one is the best one.' Another was, 'But do we have to choose one?'. There were then questions about which one should be revised for the examination. Morgan comments that this session 'brought together' some of his reflections on how knowledge was not reproduction of fact but the construction of knowledge. The current writer similarly met an epistemological crisis in a zoology degree programme (see Chapter 1). In the first two years of the programme, subjects such as anatomy, chemistry and physiology and biochemistry were taught as facts to be learnt. In the third year, she studied ecology and ethology. In these (then newly introduced) subjects there was much uncertainty, much use of models as a means of understanding. The dramatic change in the epistemological basis of the programme caused an uncomfortable crisis and loss of progress on a course in which she had been doing well. It is interesting to reflect that with different specialist teaching staff involved in each area of teaching, there was no one teacher who had had to confront the change in approach – and it is questionable whether the writer as a learner then could have explained the difficulties that she was having at the time. More open discussion about personal epistemological crises among teaching staff would probably be helpful as a means of increasing their ability to help students.

We add a thought here. The writer has often pondered on how learners cope with material of teaching that is presented in a manner that presumes them to be at a more sophisticated stage of epistemological development than is the case. This might, for example, be a lecture in which several different theories are presented to account for an experimental observation – a modelling of critical thinking. Students who are absolutist should be disturbed by the issuing of several alternatives. One manner of coping is for learners to believe that the teacher is 'training them to think' by providing alternatives – but does the teacher really know which is the 'right' theory? Another method for them to adopt is to learn the material in an absolutist manner – in other words, memorize the details of the theories in order to issue them on demand in examinations or essays. Perhaps we encourage the latter approach by setting assessment tasks in which the reiteration of the theories is acceptable without any actual evaluation (or will we have presented them with evaluation data too?!). Perhaps understanding more about the ways in which learners view the world, we could enable them better to cope with such learning.

Teaching, learning and other experiences that enable epistemological development

Baxter Magolda subsequently explored the later development of some of the sample of students that she followed through college, and was able to indicate some of the factors that contribute to further development. She found that the nature of postgraduate education drew students towards contextual conceptions of knowledge (Baxter Magolda, 1996), as did situations in professional life that confronted these young adults. The particular kinds of situation were those that 'held participants responsible for making their own decisions, required direct experience in making decisions and involved interactions with peers or co-workers to explore and evaluate opinions' (Baxter Magolda, 1994). Baxter Magolda suggested that the involvement of college work with 'real-life' situations such as work in student affairs (student unions etc.) and placements could furnish these kinds of experience very helpfully (see below), thereby enabling students to progress in the development of their epistemological beliefs. We might take from this the implication that we ignore the potential for epistemological development of activities that are outside formal education at a cost.

Another aspect of the later work of Baxter Magolda, still of relevance to critical thinking, broadened the picture so that she looked at how epistemological development interacted with interpersonal and intrapersonal development (self in relation to others and the development of personal identity). She used the conception of development towards self-authorship (1999, 2001). We touched on related points in Chapter 6 in the development of academic assertiveness.

Adding the epistemological development dimension to critical thinking

We have now reviewed the ideas from the literature on epistemological beliefs. The studies draw on issues which are within the realm of critical thinking. There are, in addition, a number of studies of critical thinking that have been described earlier in this book that have findings that relate to the general shift from absolutist thinking to contextual knowledge thinking. Mingers (2000) and Phillips and Bond (2004) are examples. Similarly, Ford, Johnston, Brumfit, Mitchell and Myles (2005) use concepts that relate to epistemological development in the context of their work on the development of social work students as critical practitioners.

A few studies, however, directly link critical thinking and developmental epistemology. We have noted Kember's stance – that 'critical and creative thinking is only possible if relativism is recognized'. Kuhn's paper is theoretical (Kuhn, 1999). She notes that critical thinking has not traditionally been seen as subject to a process of development like other aspects of academic development (e.g. mathematics and reading). She argues that one reason for this is the lack of clarity as to the nature of critical thinking – she would say that its central activity is metacognitive. As well as the thinking about knowledge itself, metacognition includes the thinking about one's strategy for working with knowledge and the broader epistemological understanding. Like Kember (see above), Kuhn asserts that real critical thinking relies on a well-developed epistemological understanding. She says:

> Although often overlooked, the evolution of epistemological understanding is a fundamental part of metaknowing and of cognitive development more broadly. Indeed . . . epistemological development may have a pivotal role to play when we turn to the concerns of educators concerned with critical thinking.

A similar line was taken by Moon (1999, 2004) with reference to reflective learning – another aspect of meta-knowing.

Where Kuhn ends – saying that there are important messages here for instructors – Kloss (1994) starts. He relates his work primarily to that of William Perry's scheme and focuses on the pedagogical implications for teaching critical thinking for college students. He relates the development of the learners to the transitions from dualist to multiplist to relativist thinking, in other words, from absolute thinking – knowledge is right or wrong – to the notion that knowledge is a matter of opinion – to the recognition that there can be different views of knowledge because it is constructed. He argues that teachers should deliberately select material that displays ambiguity and the possibility of multiple perspectives in order to stimulate the thinking of students. He chooses fiction and poetry, and talks of the challenges for the learner and the teacher (see Chapter 11).

We can suggest that many new higher education students or other learners are in a position in which they treat knowledge as absolute (a dualist position). They progress, during their education, towards the consideration of knowledge as constructed and based on evidence that relates to the context (a relativist position or stage of contextual knowing), but it seems that few undergraduates would reach full development in this latter stage (Baxter Magolda, 1992). We note again the significant comments of Meyers (1986), Kember (2001) and Kuhn (1999) that critical thinking is not possible for those whose thinking is absolutist or dualist ('if something is right, it is just right and there is no justification needed'). Similarly, 'evidence is evidence and there is no need for evaluation of it'. Correspondingly, the descriptive statement about critical thinking that we have tentatively developed accords with relativistic or contextual knowing – a stage which, if it is attained at all, is attained usually after graduation from a first (Bachelor's) degree. If we are to take the view that students follow a strict sequence of epistemological development, it would be appropriate to say that 'true' critical thinking is a process in which few undergraduates can engage. However, we do not take that strict view, favouring the notion that the development is a general shift from absolutist knowing to contextual knowing, with jumps forward, and regressions. That means that most students in the early stages of their higher education are unlikely to be able to think critically in the full sense because of their inadequately developed epistemological beliefs – but that this gradually occurs over their undergraduate years, in fits and starts and varying over different subject matter changes.

Brief summary of this chapter (for those who do not wish to read it in detail)

The term 'epistemology' is used here to relate to the learner's view of the nature of knowledge. We use the terms 'epistemological development' and 'epistemological beliefs'. Epistemological development has been the subject of a number of studies over the last half-century that indicate that there is a developmental sequence in learners' epistemological beliefs and that this influences the manner in which learners function – significantly affecting their capacity for critical thinking. Four substantial studies broadly coincide in the nature of the continuum that they document on relevant experimental samples. The studies differ in the terminology that they used, in the populations that they studied, in their focus on gender, and in the number of stages in the continuum that they identified. The studies were those of Perry (1970), Belenky et al. (1986), King and Kitchener (1994) and Baxter Magolda (1992, 1994, 1996). With the exception of King and Kitchener, a research method of semi-structured interviewing was used. King and Kitchener asked subjects to work with ill-structured problems and then discussed with them their experience of the process.

Broadly the studies suggest that there is a qualitative change that occurs in learners' conceptions of knowledge and this is important for the processes of learning at the higher education stage. In this model students generally progress from absolutist understanding, in which they tend to see knowledge as 'right or wrong', black or white – as a series of facts that they will absorb from a teacher who has the facts. They shift towards conceptions in which they can recognize the constructed nature of knowledge, and therefore can take a relativist view of it, seeing that there may be a range of perspectives on any matter. They shift along the continuum, but they do this by shifting forwards and sometimes backwards in different elements of this progression as they encounter different challenges to their learning. There seems to be some suggestion that when we encounter complex ideas, we may regress and treat them in a more factual manner at first (Baxter Magolda, 1996). This may be what happens to some students on entry to higher education, when they are daunted by the ethos of higher education and the discipline 'experts' who teach them. In particular it may happen for students from non-traditional (e.g. non-A-level) backgrounds (Moon, 2005b).

Fully developed critical thinking involves the making of a judgement, and involves an inherent recognition that knowledge is contestable. It follows from this that fully developed critical thinking is logically not possible until the learner can function – at least some of the time – at the contextual knowing pole of the epistemological continuum.

Thinkpoint

It's summer. My head and hands are in the washing machine and I am hastily disentangling a pair of red socks from an otherwise white wash when the postman squashes a large brown DO NOT BEND envelope through the door. . . . Yes, it's the degree certificate. . . .

Barely a year ago now, overdue bags of books were returned to the library, final submissions stamped in acceptance . . . and I recall the heavy silence of the exam hall. In recollection, for this 'mature' undergraduate with young family, that student time was on the one hand an oasis of separateness, but also crucially a time of connection through argument.

(Jacobs, 2000: ix)

9   Depth in critical thinking

Introduction

Developmental theories of learning are important underpinnings for the thinking of any who work with learners. However, the viewpoint of most teachers in higher education is the subject matter to be taught and a class in front of them, and not a view of the learners changing over the period of their degree. The concept of depth in critical thinking allows us to bring developmental issues into the 'here and now' of the classroom, and as such this chapter creates a bridge between theory and classroom practice in critical thinking. As far as we know, the content of the chapter breaks new ground in the manner of exploring the idea of depth in critical thinking by way of particular types of examples. As with reflective learning, our day-to-day language seems to be inadequate as a means of communication of 'what you should do to think critically' in an effective manner. Other writers, such as Cottrell (2005) and Bell (1995), have also gone the way of including examples as a means of conveying their intended messages about critical thinking.

The first part of this chapter explores the need for a concept of depth in critical thinking and its relationship to epistemological development (the subject matter of the last chapter). We then use examples both to illustrate what is involved in increasing depth in critical thinking, and from which to generate a more general framework for depth (see a Framework for Critical Thinking and its Representations, p. 198). Since these examples are designed for use directly with learners, in the context of pedagogy, they are located in the Resources section in which they may be photocopied. The Framework is included in the Resources section.

Issues of depth – epistemological development in critical thinking

Suppose we set a critical thinking task for a year group of learners who are at the same level in higher education – perhaps the class in which Jez is a student. They are asked to critique or evaluate or review a particular theory in their discipline. They hand in their work. Their work is, of course, likely to vary greatly in the knowledge base that individuals have used for the critical thinking that is represented in the writing, but there are variations in the quality of the thinking. We can just accept that at face value in the sense that learners vary in their abilities, but alternatively we can assume that there is more to explore. The differences in quality of the represented thinking might be due to differences in:

- the quality of the writing (i.e. the representation of the thinking);
- factors in the environment of learning;
- personal factors in the learner;
- the knowledge base of learners;
- the quality of the thinking or other factors.

These factors are some of the more obvious sources of 'limiting factors'* to the quality of critical thinking (Moon, 2004).

Going back to the group of learners in the classroom and the qualities of their thinking: at a first glance, it is likely that some will appear to have taken what might be described as a 'deeper' approach to their critical thinking than others. The concept of depth is related to the ideas of deep (and surface) approaches to learning (Marton, Hounsell and Entwistle, 1997; Moon, 2004). Depth is used here to indicate that the learner evidences a seeking of meaning in the critical thinking process, is analytical and does not take ideas at face value – the details are expanded later. Those who take a 'less deep' approach tend to write more descriptively, mentioning superficial or face-value ideas and characteristics of the material. In this classroom of learners, these differences in depth may be seen as due to:

- longer-term differences in the learners' general study abilities;
- differences in the learners' skills of critical thinking;
- developmental factors – such as differences in epistemological stage or understanding.

In other words, with two more years of higher education experience, those who have written more superficially may be able to write at greater depth because they may have advanced in the epistemological progression. It is not likely to be as simple as that. Advancing epistemological development (even if we can conceptualize that clearly) is unlikely to operate independently of other factors such as the knowledge base on which the learner draws, or the structuring of the writing – there will be an interaction of factors. However, it may be useful to suggest that the epistemological development itself seems likely to act as an important limiting factor* in critical thinking (Moon, 1999, 2004). In effect, we reiterate the message

---

* 'Limiting factor' is a term used in ecology (Odum, 1968) and adapted to the description of learning where it can be described as follows:

> The success of learning depends on a complex of factors, so that any factor that approaches or succeeds a particular tolerance so as to limit the quality of learning is the limiting factor in that situation.

(Adapted from Moon, 1999)

(In this context, we substitute 'critical thinking' for the word 'learning'.)

of the last chapter, but now in relation to practical tasks – the stage of epistemological development might set the most (or one of the most) significant limits on the quality of a learner's critical thinking.

In talking of epistemological development, however, we are talking about progression and long-term change through time. When we are working in the one time dimension of learners sitting in a classroom, the 'here and now' is all we have and while in an overall view of the learners it might be helpful to recognize that they are likely to be progressing in epistemological terms (with implications for appropriate support), our current 'material' is a diversity of performance in a group of learners. How do we work with that? We cannot expect to be able to explain how they will reach more sophisticated thinking stages when they are not at those stages – can we?

Depth in critical thinking – the development of the concept of depth

We take on this term 'depth' because it is useful for describing these differences in the quality of critical thinking in the present, while also relating to the epistemological development of the learner. It provides us with language with which to describe aspects of the quality of critical thinking. We need this language for pedagogical purposes – as teachers, for guiding learners and for giving good feedback on their work, and for learners, as an indication of how they can improve their work. The discussion (below) of the development of a language of depth also provides background information for the development of assessment criteria.

There is not much reference in the literature to a conception of depth in critical thinking so it is necessary to indicate from where the ideas have been derived. (There is not an obvious reference to 'depth' in the vast set of resources in the website of The Foundation for Critical Thinking – *www.criticalthinking.org*). First there is the conceptualization of a developmental sequence in critical thinking in Chapter 3, with Kuhn's work the most significant (Kuhn, 1999), and this thinking was amplified in Chapter 8 with reference to epistemological development. There is also a series of papers, all previously mentioned, in which the qualities of critical thinking have been analysed or scaled in some way. In particular we refer to Mingers (2000) and Phillips and Bond (2004). The latter's analysis of the dimensions in variation of 'critical reflection' is particularly relevant (see Chapter 2).

Another issue relevant to consideration of depth in critical thinking in this book is raised in the various references to the learning of critical thinking rules and methods – such as logic. We made reference the lively comparison of rule-bound ('mental ping-pong' and 'political') approaches to critical thinking by Sweet and Swanson (2000: 49). We would argue that most of the approaches to critical thinking that involve rule-following are unlikely to achieve real depth of thinking, because the achievement of depth is more holistic and organic – and, in particular, it is related to an individual's state of epistemological understanding.

An important source of thinking on depth in critical thinking, and the method used here to illustrate it, has also been the writer's work on the issue of depth in reflective learning (Moon, 2004). We have seen that reflective learning and critical thinking appear to have much in common, especially in their deeper aspects of functioning. We summarize the work on depth in reflective learning and look at its relevance to critical thinking in the next paragraph.

From comments in running workshops on reflective learning, it seemed that there were two difficulties that are commonly experienced in endeavouring to encourage learners to reflect. The first is the difficulty in trying to encourage learners to reflect at all. They do not know what reflection is or how to 'do it'. As with critical thinking, the thinking of their tutors is often unclear. It is a common experience with reflective learning also that even when learners manage some reflection, it is usually descriptive and superficial – and teaching staff find it difficult to help learners to write at greater depth. In tackling this, initially the writer drew on work done on this issue by Hatton and Smith (1995), changing the wording of their hierarchy of depth in reflective learning to make it more comprehensible for learners. Then, drawing on the work of others who talked about 'levels' of reflective learning, she drew up a more comprehensive framework to describe levels in reflective learning (Moon, 2004: 214, 2006: 161).

This Generic Framework for Reflective Writing is abstract – and learners need examples. There are similar problems for learners wanting to learn to think critically – they need examples as well. Sets of scenarios like 'The Park' were written (Moon, 2004: 196). 'The Park' is a brief description of an event, rewritten three more times, each repeat being written at a deeper level of reflection (freely photocopiable). The Generic Framework for Reflective Writing informed the writing of the accounts, and was informed by the writing – and was modified. It has been further modified as a result of feedback and observations in many subsequent workshops. It seemed that workshop participants (tutors or students) could talk about reflective learning volubly in relation to examples, but had difficulty if they were working only with abstract concepts. The provision of examples of reflective writing at different 'depths' seemed to be a key to helping both learners and their tutors to understand reflective writing and how to deepen it. The framework also informed the writing of assessment criteria for reflective work.

Many of the issues above apply to critical thinking, not only in respect of the difficulties and means of solving them, but also in the actual criteria developed for deep reflective learning. For example, the following is a summary of the main ways in which the four levels of reflective learning in the framework change from the first descriptive level to the deepest level.

In deepening reflection, there are shifts:

- from description to a reflective account;
- from no questions (and narrative) to the asking of questions, to responding to questions, to a stage where the response to questions is implicit in the text;
- from the recognition of emotional influences to increasing effectiveness in handling emotional factors;
- There is progressively a 'standing-back from the event';
- There is an increase in self-questioning and a challenging of own ideas;

- There is an increasing recognition of relevance of prior experience;
- Increasingly others' views are recognized to have value, are reviewed and taken into account;
- There is increasingly a reviewing of one's own reflective processes – i.e. meta-cognition.

There are many features in common with depth in critical thinking, as is demonstrated below.

The development of three examples of depth in critical thinking

A set of scenarios to illustrate increasing depth in critical thinking was developed. The first example was deliberately chosen to be close to a reflective task. It is a self-appraisal process written by a person who is learning to sing – 'A first attempt at singing'. In terms of critical thinking activities, it is therefore 'Critical thinking about the self' (Chapter 2) – which is, of course, only one of a number of different kinds of activities in which critical thinking is enacted.

The subject matter of 'A first attempt at singing' was selected because it was relatively simple. Other texts that provide examples of critical thinking tend to work with more complex examples, and hence make it difficult for the reader to extract the principles from the example, especially where the subject matter is related to a discipline. 'A first attempt at singing' is presented as an illustration of the concept of depth in critical thinking in this chapter, but is described as a pedagogical exercise in Chapter 11 and Resources 1 and 2). The piece itself is presented in Resource 3, from which it may be freely photocopied. There are also two more illustrations of depth in critical thinking: 'The discussion about learning' (Resource 4), which is an example of the critical thinking activity of making a constructive response to the arguments of others, and 'An incident on a walk', which is an example of the activity of reviewing an incident (Resource 5).

Issues that arise from the development of the three scenarios/examples of the representation of depth in critical thinking

As the first piece ('A first attempt at singing') was developed it became evident that time was an issue. In account 4, Jay notes that the emotional sensations of the experience of singing were still felt when she started to write this critique of self and that she had to – in her words – wade through it to get to the subject matter on which she wanted to focus for this task. The notion of 'standing back' from a personal event is common in the literature of reflective learning (Moon, 2004). The question that Jay asks, about delaying the consideration of the event, is a valid one for this book on critical thinking. It might make sense in this way: that the emotional experience of an event seems to 'drive' the thinking for a while. We are caught up in the subjectivity of the event and have to work hard to get through it to view more clearly the processes of the event that, in this case, needs to be the focus of the critique – i.e. the improvement of the singing. Leaving the writing until a few days later, Jay might have been more able to 'objectify' the thinking and see it more clearly for the purposes of critical thinking.

Understanding the effects of time on the personal view of an issue is an important factor in personal critical and reflective thinking. This issue does not seem relevant in the second example ('The discussion about learning'), where personal issues are not so central, though emotional issues are still mentioned and taken into account. In several of the accounts, in particular, account 4, there is observation of the persuasive 'mood' of the statement – which could lead the reader to tackle the critical thinking task in a biased manner.

There is another factor that comes into the second, third and fourth of the accounts of 'The discussion of learning', but not so much in the other two examples of depth in critical writing – and that is the potential knowledge base. In a task of critical appraisal of the self, we might assume that any learner has the opportunity to gain the same range of knowledge about herself – and hence the skill in critical thinking need not be limited by knowledge base. In the second example of critical thinking about 'good' learning, it is possible that some learners simply might 'know' more and be able then to draw on broader ideas. The knowledge base is not the same as 'depth', but it needs to be recognized as potentially having an effect on the quality of critical thinking. The issue of creativity might be another factor that comes in here. The accumulation of evidence can be deemed to be a creative act, with the more able creative mind more wide-ranging, more able to recognize unusual linkages of conception.

The development of a framework for critical thinking

Using all the literary resources mentioned in the earlier part of this chapter, as well as the work on the Generic Framework for Reflective Learning, and, in particular, using feedback from development and use of the three examples of depth in critical thinking to which reference is made above, we have developed a 'Framework for Critical Thinking and its Representations' (Resource 7, p. 198). Like the similar framework for reflective learning, it is designed as a continuum with markers on the way which are not seen to be 'stages'. It is only coincidental that there are four parts to both of the scenarios and to the framework. No exact matching is intended – except in the general trend of development. Critical thinking differs from reflective learning in being represented in different activities (Chapter 2). As a result of this some of the vocabulary in the framework may need to be modified to relate to the vocabulary of different activities (e.g. evaluation of an object). Clearly not all the elements mentioned in the framework are relevant to each and every critical thinking activity or task. In addition the framework is described in terms that mainly relate to writing. We have acknowledged that not all critical thinking is written – so again, some translation may be needed in order to apply it to non-written formats.

We start by listing the qualities that tend to shift as a piece of critical thinking becomes deeper. As in the framework itself, we use the word 'issue' as a shorthand for the topic that is under consideration. This material and the framework itself are also reproduced in the Resources section of the book (Resource 6 – which may be photocopied and replicated).

The text shifts:

- from description of the surface matters of the issue (possibly a narrative) to text that is shaped by the critical thinking process towards the required outcome;
- from the absence of argument and comparison to the presence of argument;
- from dealing with surface characterisics of the words and ideas in the task to a deeper consideration (for example, assumptions about word meanings will be dealt with in deeper accounts, but not in descriptive accounts);
- from a descriptive text to one in which questions are raised, to one in which there is a response to questions raised;
- from the giving of opinion to the presentation of considered and justified evidence;
- from a structure in which there is little focus to a structure that is focused and purposive;
- from not noticing or not dealing with emotional aspects of the issue – to noticing, dealing with and reasoning about emotions in relation to the issue;
- from the giving of unjustified opinion as conclusion to the presentation of a considered conclusion based on evidence provided with a note of limitations of the thinking;
- from a one-dimensional account (with no recognition of there being further points of view) to a recognition of other points of view;
- from non-recognition of the role of prior experience to the taking into account of prior experience and the effects it might have on judgement;
- from a text in which there is a drift from idea to idea to a deliberate persistence in dealing with selected and relevant topics;
- from no metacognition or reflexivity to reflexivity and metacognition.

These shifts are represented in greater detail in the four levels of the 'Framework for Critical Thinking and its Representations' which is in the Resources section, from which it may be copied (Resource 7).

The uses of the framework

The framework is a tool under development. It needs to be used and can be modified in use to enable it to work better. It also needs to be tested against what others consider to be the main features of critical thinking. In addition, it is important to recognize that there are other issues relevant to the quality of critical thinking other than deepening it. Some of these features have been mentioned earlier in this chapter (e.g. breadth of knowledge) and the general ability of the learner to represent her thought clearly and in a manner that enables effective communication. Another factor is the academic assertiveness of the learner. These, together with depth or epistemological development, could be said to be further potential limiting factors to the quality of reflection that is possible.

We return to the beginning of the chapter and the reasons given for the consideration of the depth of critical thinking. There was discussion of how some of the variations between learners at one stage in their ability to think critically are likely to relate to differences in stage of epistemological development. We saw that while this may be a useful partial explanation, it does not help the teacher to aid the learner in the classroom. The concept of depth, as described in the framework, provides for this.

The framework can be used on its own or as a back-up to use of the scenarios for pedagogical activities. In Chapter 11, we describe the use of these scenarios, drawn up in three or four 'depths' of critical thinking, to act as a tool for working in staff and learner development on critical thinking. In these cases, it is likely that the role of the scenarios will be to enable the groups to discuss what critical thinking is, and to learn how to guide their own or their students, using the exercise. As with reflective learning, the framework can be used both to introduce critical thinking and to deepen it or improve its quality in student work. An issue that may need to be discussed in some circumstances is 'how deep' the critical thinking should be – sometimes a relatively superficial mapping of issues is appropriate to a task while on other occasions, a deeper treatment is necessary.

Of course, the scenarios that have been given are only samples. Another use of the framework is to guide the writing of more scenario materials on critical thinking for learning. This is a very useful activity for those who need to work at deeper levels of critical thinking (e.g. at Master's level). In addition, the framework can be used for assessment purposes. It provides information that could be turned into a set of assessment criteria for a designated level of critical thinking, if the depth and quality of critical thinking is a quality to be assessed.

Concluding comments

In this chapter we have begun to create a bridge between the theoretical approaches to critical thinking and pedagogy, particularly in the development of the scenarios and in the development of the framework.

Thinkpoint

From a novel, Iris Murdoch's *Under the Net*, a character in the novel speaks:

> at that time I used to read Hegel . . . though I confess I never understood [the ideas] very much, and I hoped to be able to discuss them with Dave.

But somehow we never seemed to get anywhere and most of our conversations consisted of me saying something and Dave saying he didn't
understand what I meant and I saying it again and Dave getting very
impatient. It took me some time to realise that when Dave said he didn't
understand, what he meant was that what I said was nonsense. Hegel
says that Truth is a great word and the thing is greater still. With Dave
we never seemed to get past the word; so finally I gave up.

(Murdoch, 1954: 22)

Part 6

Critical thinking and pedagogy

10 A defining statement on critical thinking and an introduction to the pedagogy

Introduction

This chapter represents the opening of the pedagogical task of the book and to fulfil this task, the chapter deals with many 'loose ends'. It starts by reviewing the issue of the terminology of critical thinking. The second section returns to the statement on critical thinking in Chapter 7, tightens it and, most significantly, integrates the ideas from the two chapters on developmental epistemology and the issue of depth in critical thinking. This version of the defining statement then stands as the working model on which are based the chapters on the pedagogy of critical thinking. We move on to looking at the relationship between critical thinking and a number of issues that have general relevance to the pedagogy of critical thinking: its relationship to reflection and argumentation, the link with progression through a higher education programme, and issues of importance to work with non-traditional students.

The third section of the chapter provides an overview of pedagogical issues in critical thinking by identifying some principles on which it is based. The last section of the chapter returns to the activities of critical thinking and what it is that a learner needs to be able to do in order to think critically in the context of the various activities. While we have studied in Chapter 9 the various capacities of deep critical thinking, the manner in which they are deployed in relation to the activities of critical thinking may differ. This last section can usefully inform the writing of modular learning outcomes.

Terminological issues around 'critical thinking' – and a reluctant resolution

With the clear recognition that true critical thinking resides in the brain, and that it is the represented form that we see, it would be preferable to use the generic term 'critical activity' for most of the content of this book. However, as soon as we use the term 'critical activity' we draw in other meanings, such as the literary and sociological term 'critical theory', which do not concern this book. We can avoid the overlap into critical theory by stressing that the critical activities with which we are concerned are generic in terms of discipline – and thus we arrive at 'generic critical ability'. 'Generic critical ability' is jargon of the first order and will not necessarily be related to the notion of critical thinking that has been discussed in this book so far. Reluctantly we return to use of the term 'critical thinking', taking care to recognize that thinking and the representation of thinking are different activities. It is simply a term too much in common usage to alter.

Towards a defining statement about critical thinking – final statement for this book

There is no one definition of something like critical thinking – but this is the final version for this book. It is a 'tighter' and more comprehensive version of the definitional statement in Chapter 7 and includes reference to the work on depth in critical thinking and epistemological beliefs. The definitional statement is as follows:

> Critical thinking is treated here as a general term that tends to be used to cover both the mental activities of thinking and the various representations of the thinking that include action, speech, writing and so on. We should see the various terms such as 'critical appraisal', 'evaluation', 'reflection' and 'understanding' as elements of critical thinking where there is an emphasis on specific kinds of mental activity.
>
> Critical thinking is a capacity to work with complex ideas whereby a person can make effective provision of evidence to justify a reasonable judgement. The evidence, and therefore the judgement, will pay appropriate attention to the context of the judgement. Critical thinking can be seen as a form of learning, in that new knowledge, in the form of the judgement, is formed in the process.
>
> The meaning of a 'judgement' may relate to a judgement of one thing against another or others (like a decision) or the judgement of the merit of one thing (sometimes in relation to a purpose or set of criteria that have been agreed). The idea of effective judgement implies effectiveness in the thinking, reasoning or argumentation and in the quality of the representation of the thinking in writing, speech etc. It is an important characteristic of deep critical thinking that the thinker takes a critical (metacognitive) stance towards her actual process of critical thinking and its representation.
>
> The fully developed capacity to think critically relies on an understanding of knowledge as constructed and related to its context (relativistic) and this is not possible if knowledge is viewed only in a dualistic or absolute manner (i.e. knowledge as a series of facts).
>
> The notion of depth in critical thinking is closely associated with the level of epistemological development of the thinker. Generally speaking, deep critical thinking can be equated with 'good-quality thinking' which involves analytical thinking rather than surface description of issues. The variation in depth and its association with epistemological development indicate that critical thinking develops as a capacity and that this development may need to be taken into account in pedagogical thinking.

There is a sense of precision, good organization, effective reasoning, and the ability to work reflectively among other skills in critical thinking, but it is much more than the deployment of a set of skills. There is also a concern with 'standards'. 'Standards' can be interpreted in relation to the standard or quality of the thinking, or the sufficiency of the quality of the outcome or conclusion to the thinking.

Critical thinking and its representations are affected by the personal characteristics of the thinker. For example, emotion is recognized to play a part in critical thinking as it does in all cognitive processing. There appear to be different ways in which emotion interacts with cognitive activity but the thinker should monitor its various influences, articulating this where appropriate and where possible. Similarly a person's ability to use language skilfully is relevant to the language-based representations of critical thinking and the thinker needs to be sensitive to different usages, connotations and understandings of words and ideas. Intellectual curiosity and interest are relevant to the willingness to pursue a line of critical thinking and in addition the effective critical thinker will be reasonably effective in the capacities that have been grouped under the term 'academic assertiveness' – having due courage and effectiveness in the assertion of ideas and a willingness to 'change her mind' if necessary.

There are different representational activities within which critical thinking is applied. They may include: the review of someone else's argument; the evaluation of an object; the development of an argument; critical thinking about the self; critical thinking about an incident; a constructive response to the arguments of others; and the disposition of critical thinking as a habit of engagement with the world.

There are different approaches to the teaching or presentation of critical thinking and its representations. While as a whole the presence of various approaches enriches the general conception of critical thinking, it also contributes to confusion about its nature and identity. There are approaches, for example, that focus on logic, on skills, on pedagogy, on personal dispositions, and so on.

The notions of objectivity and subjectivity are not clear cut in critical thinking. The naïve view would say that critical thinking yields objectivity – but a more sophisticated thinker can comprehend that to be objective, she needs to take into account the essential subjectivity of the process of knowing. In a sense, objectivity is sought through the understanding of, and ability to work with, subjectivity.

There should be a recognition that critical thinking and its representation is a culturally influenced process. There is evidence to suggest that it is essentially a Western way of processing ideas, and that learners from other cultures may confront difficulties in understanding it because they work in different ways.

Widening the view of critical thinking

Having worked towards this concise statement about critical thinking, it is time to open it up again. At this point the language and nature of analysis of critical thinking and its representation might make it seem to be a grand and expert process – but opportunities for critical thinking occur all of the time. We go back to Barnett's notion that higher education should be about the development of the critical being (1997) – the person who thinks critically as part of her way of life, and who is willing to act on her understandings. We all make judgements all of the time. In their educational context, students make judgements all of the time – in the process of revision of a piece of writing; in a decision on how to tackle an experiment; in the organization of time in relation to tasks to be done; in decisions as to what to revise; in the judgement as to what are the important points in a text and so on. They take evidence into account in making those judgements often without ever recognizing the process as critical thinking. This is not a process only to be engaged when the essay title asks for it – but effective critical thinking needs to become a habit of mind alongside the development of students' conceptions of knowledge. It is relevant to all learners despite the fact that the term is used much more in the arts and humanities, and less in the sciences. However, in what might be seen as a subject that bridges humanities, science and psychology, the literature would suggest that critical thinking is seen as particularly important.

Perhaps it is not just critical thinking with which we are concerned. We might suggest that the frequent allusion to critical thinking in higher education is actually a reference to the underlying epistemological development and not just to the thinking process, and thus another way of saying that educational processes should support the shift of learners from absolute conceptions of knowledge towards contextual knowing.

Linking critical thinking and other academic activities – 'reflection', 'argument'

'Reflection' and 'argument' are terms that we have used in previous chapters. In this section, we make a closer consideration of the relationships of these two terms to critical thinking. 'Reflection' and 'argument' as terms are, of course, no more absolute and definite than 'critical thinking' – they are human constructions in just the same way.

Reflection

What we say in this section follows on from the references to reflection in Chapter 9 and from previous writings on reflective learning elsewhere (Moon, 1999, 2004, 2006). We start by saying that critical thinking involves reflection – and that reflection may involve some activities that could be termed critical thinking. Reflective learning is seen as a form of cognitive processing of complex issues when the material under consideration is largely already known (Moon, 2004).

This could also be said of critical thinking and in both it is possible to conceive of superficial and descriptive aspects in a continuum to deep reflection or deep critical thinking. At the deepest level of both, there is a conscious taking of multiple perspectives, engagement with relevant prior experience, metacognition and the taking into account of the broader context of the issues. There is also an awareness of relevant emotional issues and the manner in which they can relate to and influence thinking. We cannot therefore say that critical thinking and reflective learning are completely separate activities. They overlap. However, there are shades of difference in connotation between critical thinking and reflection. There is a sense that critical thinking is more purpose-driven towards the reaching of a judgement. It is more focused on the identification and evaluation of evidence. There is a connotation of precision and the matching of standards in critical thinking that is not generally associated with reflection, even in the academic situation. While identification and evaluation of evidence may be involved in reflective learning, the latter may be more concerned with the exploration of ideas, which can be about seeking the potential for evidence rather than established evidence. Also reflection is often (but does not need to be) associated with the functioning of the self, whereas we have seen that only one activity of critical thinking is concerned with self as subject matter. Metacognition is common to both reflection and critical thinking and, in particular, it seems that the development of effective reflection and effective critical thinking are both contingent on the progression of the learner away from an absolutist position and towards contextual knowing.

Generally speaking, there seem to be more similarities between deep reflective learning and deep critical thinking than the surface forms of both, which are descriptive. Superficial reflection might therefore be seen as exploratory, whereas critical thinking is still a process that focuses on the making of a judgement, albeit with only surface issues described and under consideration.

Argumentation

As with reflection, there is a broad literature on argument in the higher education context. Like critical thinking, the nature of argument has local meanings in different contexts (see chapters in Mitchell and Andrews, 2000). It can exactly fit the statements about critical thinking on occasion. It is dependent on a reasonably sophisticated set of epistemological beliefs for the appropriate management of evidence and the qualities of representation (Jackson, 1997; Andrews, 1997; Sweet and Swanson, 2000). Sometimes, as with critical thinking, there are more formal aspects of argument (e.g. use of the language of logic – Mitchell (1997)). There can also be some differences in connotation between argument and critical thinking. There is a sense that one argues for a specific purpose, perhaps to 'win a point', while the statement about critical thinking above emphasizes the 'good' processing of evidence rather than the final making of a judgement or conclusion.

Whereas we would not be happy to say that 'argument' is an alternative term for critical thinking, because the latter has many more and broader elements, we would see the processes of argument as being a part of the process of critical thinking.

Critical thinking and the progression of student learning

We have suggested above that the development of critical thinking may usefully be considered as paralleling epistemological development – and that it is likely that treating these two features of cognitive growth together may be a productive approach to pedagogy. We explore this a little further in connection with the progression of learning over the period of higher education.

If it is reasonable to suggest this parallel development (and we follow the research of those like Baxter Magolda (1992)) learners' capacity to think critically will grow in relation to their epistemological development. A consequence of this is that we cannot expect new students in higher education properly to understand what to do if we ask for critical thinking, though there are activities that can help them to shift towards this ability. As they progress, so the fostering activities can progress, always just moving beyond what is 'easy' for the majority, and recognizing that some will need more support than others. The nature of the supportive activity for critical thinking will differ as the student progresses. One reason for this is that the nature of the relationship between learner and teacher tends to change as the learner's view of the nature of knowledge develops.

Based on the work that has gone into this book and many years of work on level descriptors for higher education, we can make some suggestions as to what we might expect from students at different stages of their undergraduate studies in terms of critical thinking, and the pedagogical implications. The writer invites comment and suggestions for amendment. A chart is placed in the Resources section (Resource 13, p. 219) as it is suggested as a stimulus for a staff development activity (Chapter 11) on critical thinking and would need to be copied.

Critical thinking and pedagogy – the aims and some principles

It is time to relate all these ideas to pedagogy. The aims of a pedagogy of critical thinking are to enable learners to:

- shift from an absolutist conception of knowledge towards contextual knowing (in Baxter Magolda's terminology (1992);
- shift from superficial or descriptive responses to critical issues, towards depth in response (largely a restatement of the above);
- understand the context in which critical thinking is required, and to respond at the appropriate depth;
- display flexibility in thinking;
- display metacognition;
- use creativity in critical thinking in an appropriate manner;
- (in more sophisticated thinkers) discuss issues of objectivity and subjectivity with respect to their thinking processes.

There are some general principles that overlay the pedagogy of critical thinking. In this section the principles are presented in a discursive manner with the main points picked out in bold text. We start with a general statement that applies to any learning – but it is a point that is often lost in the manner of writing about pedagogy. The nature of thinking of an individual is under the control of that individual and **one person cannot make another think critically**. A teacher cannot make learning happen. The most likely occurrence that may arise in this connection is that tutors assume more advanced conceptions of the nature of knowledge than students possess (Chapter 9). As Meyers (1986) indicates, we facilitate or foster critical thinking through the tasks set, the habits formed by learners, the careful provision of feedback and explanation and the understanding of the teacher and the classroom atmosphere. Similar ideas are presented by Belenky, Clinchy, Goldberger and Tarule (1986), who use the analogy of the teacher as a midwife who focuses not on her knowledge but on the encouragement of the student's knowledge in the process of 'connected teaching'.

There are a number of major strategies for encouraging critical thinking – but no one strategy is the 'right' or the only option. The different approaches to critical thinking (Chapter 3) tend to yield different teaching strategies. We look at three examples. Lipman (1991) suggests that critical thinking is facilitated through the teaching of philosophy to all students. This view is exemplified in the pattern of the International Baccalaureate (IB) in which there is study of 'Theory of Knowledge' alongside several other disciplines (International Baccalaureate, 2005). Theory of knowledge seems to be an important support to the learning of IB students, and appears to be very helpful to subsequent higher education learning – and probably also professional learning. It is no coincidence that the British government has announced that the provision of opportunities for learners to opt for the IB system is to be expanded.

As an example of a second strategy, Brookfield (1987) advocates the introduction of critical thinking as a topic apart from the disciplines studied. Along the lines of Brookfield's ideas, non-discipline-related work with critical thinking is probably justified in another way. Carey and Smith (1999), talking about younger (school) students, suggest that there may often be a discrepancy between the stage of 'common-sense' learning and the stage that drives thinking on scientific work at school or college. If this is the case, then it may be possible to work at more sophisticated levels of thinking when the topic is related to everyday life, and then to draw the ideas from the everyday examples into application to the disciplinary studies. A third approach is taken by Meyers (1986), who suggests that discipline staff need to work with overt and well-understood concepts of critical thinking in their subject classes.

The line taken here is that none of these, or many other approaches, is wrong and there is much in common between them in the way in which they work (though we would not favour very rule-bound approaches). An important principle is that the support of critical thinking development in a student needs to be the responsibility of all staff who work with students (we return to this later). These are many means to the same end and the best strategy is likely to incorporate aspects of all of them. All teaching should challenge the learner to shift her thinking along the epistemological development continuum as well as developing critical thinking.

A general principle that emerges from the epistemological literature is that **the functioning of learners is drawn towards contextual knowing by just challenging them beyond their 'comfort zone of knowing'.** King and Kitchener (1994) advocate this principle and it accords with Vygotsky's conception of teaching in the zone of proximal development (1978) and much of the literature on critical thinking. Meyers, for example, talks of the presentation of paradoxes to 'set students' minds to pondering . . . [so that] . . . disequilibrium . . . will challenge their old ways of thinking and prepare . . . them for change' (Meyers, 1986: 44). The draft chart of progression (Resource 13, p. 219) has this principle at the centre of its construction and aims to guide the application of the idea.

Another general principle about the fostering of critical thinking is the need to recognize **the significance of the atmosphere of a class.** This is inferred by the use of the terms 'nurture' and 'foster'. The reasoning that underpins this principle is covered generally in Chapter 6 in discussion of academic assertiveness. Learning to think and express oneself critically involves the taking of risk. Learners can feel daunted by academia and the cult of the expert, and challenged by the notion that their familiar absolutist conceptions are no longer appropriate. It seems that this may be a particular difficulty for some non-traditional students entering higher education (Moon, 2005). Recognition of the challenges in formal education can be a key to the success of facilitating critical thinking. Meyers (1986) says: 'Students must be led gently into the active roles of discussing, dialoguing and problem solving. They will watch carefully to see how respectfully teachers field comments and will quickly pick up non-verbal cues that show how open teachers really are to student questions and contributions' (p. 67). **The classroom should feel as if it is a place that will tolerate risk-taking.** It is a place for the exploration of ideas, rather than the simple transmission of knowledge; it is a place in which there is time in which to tease out problems rather than jump to a solution in an absolutist manner. There are often difficulties in implementing this philosophy in current UK higher education with large student numbers, the pressures of research and administrative tasks, and the sometimes naïve introduction of technologies. These can work against the provision of an atmosphere in education in which good critical thinking is fostered.

Another aspect of educational work that can help the development of critical thinking is **the deliberately encouraged interaction between students.** We have seen that critical thinking is a social activity because the agreement that knowledge is acceptable is a social process. An 'agreement' 'holds' within that social and cultural context or community of practice at that time. A more practical reason for interaction relates to the need to understand that there can be different views of the same idea. The exposure to the multiple perspectives that can occur within a group of students can facilitate the shift from absolutist thinking.

A further principle is that **we should overtly encourage students to engage in thinking.** The increasing use and acceptance of reflective learning, of learning journals and self-appraisal in the form of personal development planning (PDP) could seem to be leading in this direction. However, sometimes in these tasks we may be valuing a box that has been filled, a task that has been done, without paying attention to any real depth of the thinking. This sort of mechanical approach is also encouraged by the increasing numbers of students.

While we say that we should encourage learners in their thinking, the reality is that it is within the process of writing that the quality of thinking is most evident. **In order to facilitate critical thinking, we need to take writing more seriously – it seems reasonable to say that writing is central to the development of critical thinking in current higher education**. In most programmes, the numbers of learners are too great to support development of effective oral language in discussion. There are many more ways than essays to encourage the processes of critical thinking in writing. We explore this in Chapter 11 – and an excellent website is Thinkingwriting (n.d.).

Learners need to be shown examples of critical thinking. This is put forward as a principle that goes beyond critical thinking. Many students, in particular those from non-traditional backgrounds, do not know what is expected of them in their studies (Moon, 2005). They often ask for examples but it is common for higher education teachers to decry the use of examples because 'students might copy them' or 'think that there is only one way of doing a task'. Providing students with examples of the quality or standard of work expected and that for the next level provides them with a view of what they should be doing and what they should aspire to achieve. The process of using examples is aided more if students are also shown poor work in which critical thinking has failed to occur. The examples need to be accompanied by a commentary or annotated with respect, in this case, to the critical thinking (and not the content). The work described in Chapter 9 (on depth), and Resources 3, 4 and 5 (pp. 181–96) can aid the fulfilment of this principle.

Although critical thinking is very much in the language of education, it remains a term that has multiple and unclear meanings. **Learners need definitions of critical thinking and other such terms – but these may be overtly 'local' definitions** – for example, those developed for a programme, and agreed between the staff who work on that programme. Learners need to know that they are 'local' and it is possible that others will use different definitions. Once definitions have been agreed they need to be used and discussed regularly and deliberately.

Assessment is a strategy for the encouragement of the kinds of learning that we require from learners – and can be used in the process of fostering critical thinking. Assessment is not just about giving marks. Learners should be shown the importance of critical thinking overtly in the manner in which their work is assessed – because what we assess is seen as a pointer to what it is that is important for them to achieve. We can show the role of critical thinking in assessment by talking about it and by making it very evident in the criteria for assessment. Assessment serves many purposes in education (Moon, 2002). The opportunity for feedback can also occur through assessment.

Part of the generation of a nurturing atmosphere in a classroom is a matter of ensuring that **teachers model critical thinking** in the manner in which they teach (Meyers, 1986; Topping, Crowell and Kobayashi, 1989). We reiterate a point made earlier. There is interactive teaching and there is presentation. Traditional lectures are 'presentation'. Even the vocabulary gives it away – the material is 'delivered' to the students – which is an absolutist conception of teaching, though more advanced learners can use such material to evaluate or advance their own thinking. The tendency to use pre-prepared material, as in PowerPoint, encourages the presentation of ideas and takes us further from the methods in which teaching was seen clearly as a thinking process instead of the 'thought-out product' with no room for deliberation (Moon, 2001).

Staff knowledge and development have a key crucial role in fostering critical thinking. If critical thinking is closely associated with the student's progression along the continuum of epistemological development, then it might be a reasonable suggestion that staff, who facilitate the learning of students, should be aware of the continuum and use it to guide their teaching of and interactions with students, including assessment (Chapter 9). Meyers demonstrates in his book (1986) that **a fruitful manner in which to enhance critical thinking is to work with teachers, helping them to clarify the idea in their own disciplines and contexts**. Through a dialogue method in a series of seminars, Meyers suggests how such developments can be initiated. In one of the sessions, teachers are asked to visualize their disciplinary framework for critical thinking (1986: 19). Working with staff within their disciplines can be one of the most effective strategies for the development of critical thinking among students. In particular, it is important to **ensure that teachers have sufficiently developed epistemological beliefs before they are in contact with students**. We have noted already Brownlee's findings (Brownlee, 2001) which suggest that the epistemological beliefs of teachers may not be fully developed. We have to recognize that it is common for students to be taught by postgraduate students whose development may not be complete – or whose lack of confidence in the classroom may lead them back into more 'fact-giving' strategies. They may, themselves, have only completed an undergraduate programme in the previous year.

The fostering of the epistemological development of a group of students requires careful overall management. If we are to take the epistemological development of students into greater account, there are implications for the management of student learning and their autonomy. It has been suggested that in the same classroom learners may well be at different stages of epistemological development. Learners need to be challenged and not 'spoon-fed' (Furedi, 2005), but some will require greater support in order to shift from their absolute position (Moon, 2005b). Both good support and challenge may be correct strategies for the same group of learners – and methods of managing this situation need to be found, preferably without sending the non-progressing absolutists to a remedial service.

As a final remark, it is always worth remembering that **presenting critical thinking in any way that requires the following of rules is anathema to the very nature of sophisticated critical thinking. These points made here are principles and not rules!**

What do learners need to be able to do to think critically?

This last section of this chapter returns to the listing of the activities of critical thinking (Chapter 2). While the material on depth in critical thinking indicates what is required for good-quality critical thinking, the capacities of the learner may need to be deployed in different measures in the various activities, alongside the demands of the self – in particular, academic assertiveness (Chapter 6). This section may be useful as language to underpin the writing of learning outcomes with regard to critical thinking processes in the curriculum.

For an effective review of someone else's argument, learners need to have:

- an appropriate conception of the nature of knowledge;
- a capacity to think at least at the depth of the argument;
- a will to pursue the task within reason;
- sufficient ability to focus appropriately;
- self-authorship – willingness to declare and stand by their own judgement;
- willingness to query and examine their own biases;
- an ability to sort out the structure of the argument (elementary logic);
- (sometimes) a capacity to use formal logic in order to question the process of argument.

For the effective evaluation of an object, learners need to have:

- an appropriate conception of the nature of knowledge;
- self-authorship – a willingness to express their own voice and views;
- an ability to work at an appropriate depth – in relation to the object and to others' conceptualization of it;
- the ability to express clearly the representation of their thinking in an appropriate form;
- an ability to recognize the difference between their personal view and a community view;
- knowledge of the general area of culture (appropriate theory);
- the ability to use the conventions for evaluation of the discipline and – perhaps – to go beyond this.

For the effective development of an argument, learners need to have:

- an appropriate conception of the nature of knowledge;
- clarity about the direction and aim of their argument;
- ability to represent their thinking clearly (good signposting);
- creativity in assembling the evidence;
- ability to work at sufficient depth in assembling evidence;
- self-authorship – willingness to stand by the point(s) that they make – to 'take a stand';
- openness to – and to taking into account – their own biases;

- willingness to be critical of their own process of argument;
- the ability to draw a clear conclusion.

To engage effectively in critical thinking about the self, a learner should have:

- a willingness to reflect on their own functioning (mental and physical);
- ability to represent this form of thinking in an effective format;
- self-authorship – the confidence to recognize and be open to personal error or ineffectiveness;
- a willingness to work with the views of others about their own functioning or work;
- a constructive and creative attitude to critical thinking about the self;
- the ability to be persistent and to focus appropriately in self-criticism;
- (possibly) a sense of humour about the self;
- (probably) an openness to the possibility for change.

To review an incident, a learner should have:

- an ability to recognize the impact of one's own position in relation to the incident;
- a recognition of the role of emotion on interpretation of the incident;
- an understanding of the need to see the broader context of the incident (i.e. stand back);
- a willingness to recognize and work with others' perspectives on it, listening to others' views;
- the ability to seek a broad review of evidence required for the judgement.

To engage in the provision of a constructive response to the argument of others, learners should have:

- academic assertiveness – a willingness to state their own views – have a 'voice';
- willingness to stand one's ground, challenge but also change one's mind;
- a pursuit of clarity in thought and expression;
- appropriate framing of the issue and focus;
- appropriate management of one's emotional state;
- flexibility and creativity in thinking in new areas.

To display a critical habit of engagement with the world, learners should have:

- an appropriate conception of the nature of knowledge;
- an ability to represent their thinking in a clear and appropriate manner;
- good organization in the representation of their thinking;

- flexibility in their thinking – not to be rigid;
- a willingness to question and challenge ideas;
- an ability to reflect in a deep manner;
- a generally constructive outlook – seeking improvements in the status quo;
- a willingness to accept that others can have different views of the world and to work with this.

Thinkpoint

The marble not yet carved can hold the form of every thought the greatest artist has.

Michelangelo

This quotation is from the *Pietà Rondanini* in Milan Cathedral.

11 The pedagogy of critical thinking

Introduction

This chapter is closely linked to the Resources section of the book. Chapters 11 and 12 are the most practical chapters of this book. They contain the description of a range of activities and exercises that can be used to stimulate critical thinking and its various representations. This first chapter is generalized, while the second refers to academic assertiveness (see Chapter 6). Where there are materials associated with the exercises, they are contained in the Resources section from which they may be freely photocopied.

In this chapter, headings used for sections are largely a matter of organization and there are overlaps between them. To make it easier to find exercises, the sections and exercises or points made are numbered. There are references sometimes to the stage of learners, mostly in higher education, for which most of the exercises will be most suitable – but their use is a matter for the judgement of the tutor. We must reiterate that we would see critical thinking as developing in parallel with epistemological beliefs, but for convenience, largely refer to critical thinking. None of these developments begins or ceases in formal education.

The exercises are both derived from and should pay due attention to the principles for the pedagogy of critical thinking (Chapter 10) and also the range of activities of critical thinking (Chapters 2 and 10). With regard to the activities of critical thinking, we have not dealt with the activities separately in this pedagogy – but it is sometimes worthwhile checking that learners are engaging in an appropriate range of them for their full development.

In some of the sections below, a listing of references to other work is provided. Apart from the obvious introductory activities, the content of the rest of this chapter is designed for 'picking and mixing' according to the judgements of the tutors involved.

The main headings are as follows:

1. Direct methods of introducing critical thinking and deepening it (p. 139)
2. Teaching of philosophy or theory of knowledge (p. 140).
3. Working directly with epistemological beliefs (p. 141).
4. Drawing from the everyday – critical thinking and 'real-life' issues (p. 143).

5. Encouraging the development of critical thinking through placements and out-of-class activities (p. 144).
6. The use of reflection to enhance critical thinking (p. 145).
7. The deliberate provision of thinking time (p. 147)
8. Encouragement of critical thinking through the processes of assessment (p. 148).
9. Critical thinking developed through oral work (p. 149).
10. Writing and critical thinking (p. 151).
11. Reading and critical thinking (p. 155).
12. Critical analysis of another's work (p. 156).
13. The development of critical practice (in brief) (p. 158).
14. The techniques of argument (in brief) (p. 158).
15. Focuses on reasoning and logic (in brief) (p. 159).
16. Educational development and critical thinking (p. 159).

1. Direct methods of introducing critical thinking and deepening it

1.1 The use of scenarios and the framework for critical thinking

Resources 1–7, pp. 177–201

In Chapter 9 three illustrations of the qualities of critical thinking are described, using the continuum from descriptive and superficial critical thinking to the qualities of depth ('A first attempt at singing', Resource 3 (p. 181)); 'The discussion about learning', Resource 4 (p. 186); 'An incident on a walk', Resource 5 (p. 191)). The illustrations are in the form of four accounts of the same scenario written as a result of increasingly deep (and better quality) critical thinking. The accounts are supported by a list of the characteristics of critical thinking that change as the scenarios become deeper (Resource 6 (p. 197)) and 'The framework for critical thinking and its representations' (Resource 7 (p. 198)). The background theoretical thinking is described in Chapter 9 and other earlier chapters of this book. The scenarios were presented in Chapter 9 as a means of illustrating the concept of depth in critical thinking. We return to them now in order to use them as exercises with the following aims:

- to introduce critical thinking by way of an example (explained through the Framework);
- to demonstrate that the critical thinking can vary in depth and that deeper thinking is more rigorous and desirable than superficial and descriptive thinking. This is illustrated in the Framework.

The exercise is developed in response to the observation that learners who are asked to think critically tend initially to lack understanding of what to do and then tend to work at rather superficial levels of thinking. It is suggested that learners have two experiences of the exercises – first as an introduction to critical thinking and then later as a means of helping them to deepen the quality of their critical thinking. The instructions for the uses of the exercises are in Resources 1 (face-to-face situations) (p. 177) and 2 (online version) (p. 179).

From the writer's experience of wide use of this kind of exercise in enabling the comprehension of reflective learning, the disciplinary nature of the topic or event does not matter. It can actually be disadvantageous to use an exercise with subject matter that relates to the discipline of the group because the group will then tend to put on their disciplinary 'hats' and examine the content, rather than consider the quality of the thinking and writing. However, as we have indicated, there are different activities of critical thinking (Chapter 2). It can be useful to think about which kind of activity is involved in the exercise and to choose an exercise that represents the closest actual activity to the current work or the learners.

1.2 Demonstrating the deepening of critical thinking by development of scenarios

This is an exercise for more advanced learners (e.g. Master's level) who have worked on the scenarios above and used the Framework. Learners are asked to develop their own scenario and write it descriptively as in the first of the accounts in Resources 3, 4 and 5 and then, using the list of shifts (Resource 6, p. 197), and the Framework (Resource 7, p. 198) for reference, writing further accounts at one or two deeper levels.

2. Teaching of philosophy or the theory of knowledge

2.1 Introduction

Philosophy used to be a usual first-year subject in higher education. It has been edged out, but it is surprising how many higher education teachers still wish it to be in place. Philosophy, of course, has a number of 'movements', one of which is logic (in its various forms). Lipman is one of the main proponents of the view that critical thinking can be facilitated if learners are introduced to a basic course in philosophy (Lipman, 1991). It may be that the way in which philosophical study can enhance critical thinking is by its demand on the learner to think, rather than to pack away a series of 'facts'.

2.2 Philosopical underpinnings to critical thinking in practice situations

In a number of practice-based disciplines, what may be called 'critical practice' is covered. It includes material such as reasoning and the fallacies of reasoning, ethics, dealing with moral dilemmas and the management of the thinking processes that guide practice (Mumm and Kersting, 1997; Gibbs and Gambrill, 1999; Brown and Rutter, 2006).

2.3 International Baccalaureate (equivalent stage to UK 'A' level) 'theory of knowledge'

In order to help learners to understand the structure of disciplines, and the differences between them we use the 'theory of knowledge' (TOK) (International Baccalaureate, 2005). Although they may find it hard to start with, they are better equipped for any further study and appreciate that. It seems reasonable to assume that well-taught TOK helps them along the continuum from absolutist conceptions of knowledge towards contextual conceptions. Such study would seem particularly to support students who are covering several disciplines, where no one teacher has the experience to help them across their range of study. It also provides an excellent basis for the development of the lifelong learner. TOK may be used twice in the course of an undergraduate programme – once early on and then later in a more reflective and metacognitive mode, as a review of the nature of learning over the whole of the programme. The various websites associated with TOK contain much material.

3. Working directly with epistemological beliefs

3.1 Introduction

We have discussed at length the manner in which critical thinking is closely related to epistemological development. It would be useful to show learners at entry to university how their conceptions of knowledge are likely to change in the period of their education; however, there could be a logical contradiction in this in the sense that if they can understand the kind of thinking that they will be doing, it could be argued they are able to do it now. We have said that there is evidence that learners are not fixed at a particular stage, but for different areas of knowledge, they may be working with knowledge at different stages. On this basis, it is worth doing some work with them on the conceptions of knowledge. Whether the stages are named or not is a matter for the judgement of the tutor. Some of the exercises below explicitly mention the stages of epistemological development and are probably most suitable for more advanced learners.

3.2 An exercise for advanced learners to introduce the ideas of and behind epistemological development

Resource 8, p. 202

A form of this exercise has been used extensively with teaching staff in workshops on reflective learning, critical thinking and student learning, and here it has been adapted for use with learners. The original process for the exercise involved the preparation of twenty quotations from subjects (students) who were interviewed in Baxter Magolda's (1992) study. Five quotations were taken from each of the four stages (see Chapter 9) and printed on cards – so there were twenty cards.

Participants in the exercise are given a description of the stages that were identified by Baxter Magolda, and asked to group the quotations appropriately. They were asked to think about what their own students might say to them. The version printed in the Resources section is similar but uses fictitious 'quotations' that are more overtly related to the four stages (Moon, 2005b). This exercise is a way of opening a discussion about critical thinking in learners' education. Although presented here for students, it is important that their teachers have the same understanding – maybe also having done the exercise.

The exercise could either be related to 'epistemological development' or 'epistemological beliefs', or may be introduced as 'ways in which we think about knowledge'. The important message for Master's level students is that they should be contextual knowers.

3.3 Helping learners to understand what it is to think in a more sophisticated manner

Resources 9, p. 207 and 10, p. 210

This is another form of exercise either overtly presented to learners as representing epistemological development (e.g. using the terminology of Baxter Magolda (1992) – use Material A in Resource 8, p. 203), or presented in the context of critical thinking. In either case the aim of the exercise is to demonstrate the progression from descriptive and non-critical work to deeper and more effectively critical work. In the exercise, learners are asked to look at paragraphs made by three students about a given topic and to sequence the paragraphs in terms of their depth and criticality. They then have to justify their sequence. Two different examples of this exercise are given.

3.4 Exercise on the relevance of epistemological development for the relationships between learning and teaching

Resource 11, p. 212

Epistemological development does not just relate to the learning process. Absolutist learners, seeing facts as facts that they need to 'collect', require teachers who simply just provide clear facts, organized in a manner that best suits the learners. Sophisticated teachers understand that their role is to stimulate learners to construct their own knowledge. This exercise is based on cards, and invites participants to match teacher and student quotations to the stages identified by Baxter Magolda (Resource 8, p. 203, part A). It is useful for advanced learners or new teachers.

3.5 Using poetry and fiction

Kloss (1994) describes how he 'nudges' learners through 'the Perry scheme of intellectual development'. He uses fiction and poetry 'because it provides more possibilities for ambiguity, varied interpretations and multiple perspectives, three of the challenges that constrain adoption of multiplicity and relativism'. Kloss's paper contains a number of more detailed suggestions as to the use of this material and other methods for 'nudging' the development of learners. Capossela (1993a) also advocates the use of story as a means of supporting epistemological development for similar reasons.

3.6 Creating deliberate dissonance (or disequilibrium)

Various writers have associated the deliberate creation of dissonance in the learning environment as a means of promoting shifts in epistemological beliefs (e.g. Meyers, 1986). Bendixen and Rule (2004) say, 'The first condition for conceptual change is that individuals must feel that current beliefs are no longer working satisfactorily (i.e. dissatisfaction with current conceptions).' Learners should be exposed to ambiguities and confusing issues in their disciplines.

3.7 Creating environments in which epistemological beliefs are both valued and questioned

Bendixen and Rule (2004) suggest that the development of environments in which epistemological beliefs are both valued and questioned aids the increase in sophistication of beliefs (see also Meyers, 1986). They suggest that learners need to practise 'making and defending claims'. They say that learners need the valuing of epistemological reasoning in the environment in which they grow up as well as in formal education. Perhaps the main factor in the stimulating environment in this respect is other people, so, in effect, this is a comment on the interactions. Those who work on questioning skills work towards this (Brookfield, 1987; Morgan and Saxon, 1991; Paul and Elder, n.d.).

3.8 Other literature that addresses the pedagogy of epistemological development

This includes Belenky, Clinchy, Goldberger and Tarule (1986) – connected teaching; Hines (1988) – useful material; Baxter Magolda (1992, 1999, 2001); Baxter Magolda and King, 2004); Kitchener, Lynch, Fischer and Wood (1993); King and Kitchener (1994); Kuhn (1999); Kuhn and Udell (2001) – 'the path to wisdom'; Meyer and Land (2003) – relevant concepts though epistemological development not explicit.

4. Drawing from the everyday – critical thinking and 'real-life' issues

4.1 Introduction

There are many justifications for talking about critical thinking in terms of real-life experiences. First, it is important for students to realize that critical thinking is an everyday activity and not confined to the academy – even if the term is not commonly used. Second, students' epistemological beliefs may be more advanced in relation to everyday issues than in academic material. These experiences of critical thinking may enable them to feel more familiar with it and to think more effectively in their academic subjects. Kegan (1994) and Baxter Magolda (1999, 2001 and Baxter Magolda and King, 2004) have described the kinds of experiences that have enabled learners to shift towards sophisticated epistemological beliefs. 'Real-life' issues arise out of the everyday situations of students' lives – personal experiences in which judgement has been made or has to be made. We have noted earlier that there is some evidence that learners who grow up in situations in which there is discussion or even argument, may advance more easily in epistemological development continua (Bendixen and Rule, 2004).

4.2 Working with the experiences of making judgements

Learners can be asked to discuss some of the more complex judgements that they have had to make in their everyday lives and the process by which they have reached a decision.

4.3 Newspapers

A session or two of working on the critical thinking represented in a variety of qualities of newspaper can provide good examples and poor examples of critical thinking for learners who have done some basic work on critical thinking. More advanced learners might be interested to identify the epistemological beliefs represented in a range of newspapers.

4.4 Other literature that addresses critical thinking and everyday experiences

Though de Bono does sees 'critical thinking' as criticizing (1983), much of the material in his many books is relevant to critical thinking in terms of how the term is used in this book. See also Nelson-Jones (1994) – in relation to self; Brookfield (1987); and Young (1980b) and other papers in Young (1980a).

5. Encouraging the development of critical thinking through placements and out-of-class activities

5.1 Introduction

Baxter Magolda identified the qualities of experience that supported development towards self-authorship (see above), and identified situations in which these might occur for students at college or in their early post-college years. Placements seem to be a promising source of such experiences during the formal education years. These ideas have been linked with the observation that students who go out on work placements within a higher education programme, tend to achieve higher classes of degree (Lucas, pers. comm., 2005). Clearly this cannot be generalized for all work placements – some are dreary and routine and the student has little responsibility. However, it is possible in a placement to enable the student to have more opportunities to make real judgements and decisions, to meet conflicting views, and to lead others, and these situations seem to enhance these aspects of development (Service learning, n.d.).

5.2 Work experience

It would seem useful to employ some of the ideas in the section above as criteria for the design of good-quality work placements. However, many programmes do not involve placements. Work experience may provide a similar experience and it is possible in a number of programmes for learners to gain credit for work experience – sometimes basing this on the work that students are doing to support themselves financially (Watton, Collings and Moon, 2002). There are other examples in which, for example, local employers provide students with real projects that are incorporated in their programmes of study – and which demand the making of professional judgements. This is probably an activity more suitable for more advanced students. The value of work placements and of the experiences that we have mentioned above, is enhanced when students are asked to engage in reflection, sometimes in a learning journal for example (see 6.2).

5.3 Other literature that addresses critical thinking developed through placements and similar experience

Such literature includes Astin, Vogelgesang, Ikeda and Yee (2000); Ford, Johnston, Brumfit, Mitchell and Myles (2005) – social work; Adams, Dominelli and Payne (2002) – social work; Knight and Yorke (2002); Hannay (2006); Lucas and Tan (2006). Gibbs and Gambrill (1999) contains many exercises to develop critical thinking, particularly in the practical aspects of social work. Some of the exercises could be adapted for use in similar placement situations.

6. The use of reflection to enhance critical thinking

6.1 Introduction

We have seen that deep reflection is similar to critical thinking but tends to be more often associated with exploratory thinking about, and more often is devoted to, the self and personal activities, whereas critical thinking tends to be more associated with the need to arrive at a conclusion or judgement. More superficial reflection is probably less closely related to critical thinking (Chapter 10). Reflection, in essence, is a process of dealing with uncertain and ill-structured ideas, and contact with this kind of material is likely to support the development of critical thinking so long as the reflection is sufficiently deep. There are many activities in reflective learning that could also be used to develop critical thinking (see Moon, 2004 and 2006).

6.2 Learning journals and critical thinking

Learning journals are containers for reflective work (Moon, 2006). They take many different forms and may be designed directly to underpin critical thinking activities. They may, for example, be the 'thinking place' for research projects, or the place in which there is critical thinking about (appraisal of) of the quality of personal (perhaps professional) activities. There is an issue of risk for the student working on a learning journal where the journal is to be seen by another or marked by a tutor. A strategy to avoid this situation can be to ask students who have kept a journal, to write an account of the learning done in the journal, with quotations from the journal – a form of secondary reflection. It is this that is marked.

6.3 Secondary reflection

Secondary reflection is reflection on earlier reflection. In many ways a first reflective account is like raw lecture notes and it is the second look at them which can draw together the material into themes or can provide a more organized account from which to learn. One means of managing secondary reflection is in a 'double-entry journal' – wherein one page of the double-page spread of a journal is for the initial reflections and the other page is for the later secondary reflection (Moon, 2006). This may well match a description of 'critical thinking about the initial reflection'.

6.4 Critical thinking about the self

Personal development planning (PDP) is a reflective process in which most UK students are now engaged. PDP mainly involves self-appraisal – a critical thinking process about personal experiences, progress, decisions etc. within a higher education programme. There can be a danger of the appraisal being a strategic tutor-pleasing account, or a box-filling exercise – neither of these has much to do with real critical thinking. If there are questions, they should be challenging to the student either in the range or novelty of information to be taken into account, or in the depth of consideration required. It is worth explaining to students, the link between critical thinking and PDP, recognizing that critical thinking is a broad concept with many links into higher education activities.

6.5 The development of metacognitive modes through reflective learning strategies

Metacognition (or reflexivity) – the critical reviewing of one's own processes – is central both to deep reflective learning and critical thinking. The focus is not on the content of the work, but on the cognitive or emotional processes that have operated on the content – and it is encouraged when students are asked to discuss the manner in which they have tackled a task. They might be asked to discuss their research strategies for writing or for conducting a project, for example. While the term does not automatically imply evaluation or a notion of 'what I would have done better or differently', it is useful to incorporate this idea. It is probably an area of activity that should be brought further to the fore in later undergraduate education.

6.6 Critical thinking on critical incidents, scenarios and story material

A critical incident (scenario, case study or 'story') is written, elicited, developed, or told to a group of learners who then use various techniques to reflect on the material in a manner that is relevant to the purpose of the exercise and also is critical. It might be retold from another's point of view or looked at in a different way. The group reflects together and may then write up the exercise separately. Brookfield (1998) is a useful source of such material. See also McDade (1995) and McDrury and Alterio (2003). Gold, Holman and Thorpe (2002) talk of the use of story in management studies and George and Cowan (1999) use critical incidents technique in formative evaluation.

7. The deliberate provision of thinking time

7.1 Introduction

It often seems that while higher education is meant to be about the promotion of thinking, the manner in which pedagogy is conducted provides little time for thought. Lecturers start speaking and continue to speak until they end the lecture and learners need to move on to the next class. If we believe in the encouragement of critical thinking, we should build time for it into academic work. (The use of reflective activities can be construed as one means of providing thinking time.)

7.2 Develop a vocabulary for thinking

A helpful means of acknowledging thinking time is to develop a terminology for it, such as 'stop and think' and 'thinktime'. These terms might imply the stopping of a seminar or lecture in order that students can think about a particular point, or write notes down on it, or make critical comments (see 'quickthink' below).

7.3 Thinking and teaching

The idea of providing thinking time relates back to the teacher also. She should give students time for reflective listening. This means that she does not just give a direct answer to a student's question (as an expert) but, where appropriate, engages with the thinking process with the learner. It is worth considering the styles in which people teach. There are forms of teaching that are little more than 'presentation', where the thinking process has gone on before the session and where it is simply given to the learners. The typical PowerPoint presentation is of this kind – though it does not need to follow this pattern. 'Chalk and talk' (or 'whiteboard and talk') might epitomize the other end of the continuum – where the thinking is done aloud and at the time of the teaching (Moon, 2001).

7.4 Wait time

'Wait time' is a concept developed by Tobin (1987). Tobin found that where lecturers used a speech style that involves brief pauses (e.g. asking rhetorical questions, building in reflective pauses, making pauses between topics) students learned better. It seemed that their brains had time to process information and to think. This seems to be one of the most meaningful findings in educational research – and yet we so rarely deliberately take note of it.

8. Encouragement of critical thinking through the processes of assessment

8.1 Introduction

Critical thinking is involved in assessment in a number of ways. First, the act of developing an assessment method and of assessing the work of another is a matter of making a judgement. It is critical thinking and we would do well to involve learners more in this process for that reason among others (as we do in peer and self-assessment). It is worth noting that attitudes towards assessment often reflect somewhat absolutist values – it is seen as a mysterious judgement that is made by an expert who somehow 'knows' (as in knowing a fact) the mark to attribute. Learners need to understand that the selection of assessment criteria is a matter of (contestable) judgement – and better still, they should be engaged in the selection of the criteria. Angelo (1995) describes the use of classroom assessment techniques for the development of critical thinking.

   In addition, we may well be interested in judging the quality of work using criteria that represent the quality of the critical thinking in the work. Critical thinking, as we have said, is implied in most sets of level descriptors for higher education. Learners need to understand what critical thinking is in order to meet criteria that are constructed. It is widely said that assessment drives learning – if that is the case, and we consider critical thinking to be important, then we have to think carefully about how we do it.

8.2 Involving learners in the development of assessment criteria

If students are to be engaged in the development of assessment criteria, a decision needs to be made as which kind of criteria are to be developed – threshold criteria, or those associated with marking, grading criteria (Moon, 2002). Students are asked to produce a sample of the material that will be assessed, or are given sample to read (if it is written). In groups, they generate some assessment criteria that they consider to be appropriate. One method is to take one criterion from each group in turn until all of the criteria are 'used up'. The list of criteria is then reconsidered, and a suitable number are selected for use (Moon, 2002, after Brown and Dove, 1991). In this case, the element of critical thinking is the selection of appropriate evidence for making the judgement. In the literature there are a number of suggestions of criteria for critical thinking (see Fisher, 2003; Kaasboll, 1998; Cottrell, 2005).

8.3 Peer assessment

Peer assessment – which may or may not involve the learner-generated assessment criteria – is related to critical thinking because it provides practice in making the judgement on the basis of evidence (see Moon, 2002). It involves students in marking the work of their peers on the basis of the given criteria. Students learn much about standards of work expected and ways of writing (and otherwise representing their work) through this process. A general principle if we are to get learners involved in looking at each other's work, is that we need to ensure that they understand the difference between being critical in a negative manner and being constructive.

8.4 Self-assessment

In the process of self-assessment, students assess their own work against a set of criteria. They thereby learn metacognitive skills (see above), they learn to make judgements, and usually they learn how to do their work better the next time.

8.5 Testing as a means of fostering critical thinking

There are a number of 'tests' of critical thinking available (for example, see *www. criticalthinking.org*). One means of encouraging learners to develop their critical thinking skills is the use of tests (Young, 1980c). This will enable them to learn where they are working appropriately and where inappropriately – so long as the test matches the conception of critical thinking that is used by the teachers with whom those learners are working. Most pre-designed tests would not relate to the conceptions of critical thinking in this book. See also Cottrell (2005).

9. Critical thinking developed through oral work

9.1 Introduction

We have said that critical thinking has social dimensions. It is valuable to encourage the oral expression of ideas for several reasons. First, self-expression is an important self-development skill – Baxter Magolda (2001) associates it with self-authoring (see earlier) and in this book we have developed the term 'academic assertiveness' (see Chapter 12) which is very relevant to this section. Secondly, the exposure to the views of others helps learners to recognize the need to take multiple perspectives into account in the process of critical thinking. Any form of group discussion can be helpful, but there can easily be 'drift' in the discussion of a group. Good 'chairing' skills from a tutor help – but learners need those skills as well.

9.2 Group critical thinking tasks under time pressure

Time pressure can create focus in a group where there is a decision, a judgement or a conclusion to be reached in a limited period. The identification of someone as a 'chair' can maintain criticality and keep the process moving. Several groups set up in competition to reach a well-evidenced judgement in a certain time can raise the tempo and maintain engagement effectively as well.

9.3 Debate

Debate is designed to enact critical thinking – with evidence given, evaluated and judged. Tutorial groups can be good situations for debate. One problem is that in traditional debate situations, not everyone is involved. One way of ensuring some involvement from everyone is to give learners the subject matter of the debate and ask everyone to prepare a case either for or against. The choice of who are to be the actual proposers and seconders is only made at the beginning of the session itself. In that way, everyone is prepared, and can therefore contribute. See also Brookfield (1987).

9.4 'Quickthink'

The writer uses the term 'quickthink' for short exercises wherein learners are asked to think about a particular issue in groups of three for three or four minutes. The subject matter is likely to be the definition of a contentious term or a difficult idea. One of the learners in each group writes notes. Responses from some or all of the groups may be requested, though the outcome may be less important than the process of discussion and sharing of perspectives. It is a useful technique for the introduction of a topic.

9.5 Controversial questions

Meyers (1986) suggests that a pattern be adopted in which each class is introduced by the posing of a controversial or difficult question. At the end of the class, there could be a five-minute discussion of the issue.

9.6 Critical friends

A system that involves the pairing of 'critical friends' can generate critical thinking and associated metacognition. A critical friend is a person who considers and is constructively critical of the work of another. The roles would usually be reciprocal. A critical friend system can be associated with a single task or the work of a whole year or module. There may be some learning associated with the role so that the critique follows specific lines. It might be linked, for example, to work described in other sections of this chapter.

9.7 Other literature relating to the oral aspect of critical thinking

Many of the publications on written critical thinking can also apply to oral critical thinking. This means that the samples of their material may be useful. Bell (1995), Cottrell (2005) and various papers in Capossella (1993a) are useful – there are many more. Also, Meyers (1986), Brookfield (1987) and Brookfield (1998) provide many further ways of exploiting critical thinking orally. For more advanced learners, Poulson and Wallace (2004) provide excellent examples on pedagogical and educational topics.

10. Writing and critical thinking

10.1 Introduction

The most obvious link between critical thinking and writing is in the use of writing to represent the process of thinking. Some people can better express what is in their minds than others because, for example, they have a better capacity with language in the form of writing. The capacity to write clearly and precisely is particularly associated with critical thinking, both in the sequencing and layout of evidence, but also in the broader summing up of the case.

The links between critical thinking and writing go beyond the process of getting the content of the critical mind onto paper or screen. The production of a written version of thoughts provides a chance for review. It is a chance to engage in metacognition about our own critical thinking as we judge whether the material on paper or screen says what we need it to say – and we duly revise it, or not. Once thinking is represented in writing, it can also be seen by others, who can also comment and make judgements about it – as in the process of peer review of academic papers or the assessment of student work, or cooperative working in groups.

Exercises in writing skills (below) may concern the skills of writing that are associated with critical thinking or critical thinking as represented in writing. The exercises are roughly grouped according to where they might be used in a higher education curriculum, though this is only for guidance. A sophisticated critical task with simple text might be of the same difficulty as a simple critical task with a text dealing with complex material.

10.2 Writing tasks that aim to improve the representation and process of critical thinking in the early stages

The subject matter for writing exercises of the types described below could either be within or outside the discipline studied. It could be drawn from politics or current affairs; it could be a common philosophical debate or an everyday application of the discipline studied. Most of the subject matter for these exercises will involve issues that might be called 'ill-structured' – where there is no obvious right or wrong response. The first five exercises are particularly useful for students in the early stages of critical thinking.

Summarizing and the ability to write a conclusion: a learner is presented with a piece of writing that represents critical thinking about a particular (given) topic. The purpose and/or audience may also be specified. The learner is asked briefly to evaluate the evidence and write a conclusion. This exercise is for the purpose of enhancing the understanding of critical thinking, the ability to conclude a piece of writing.

Summarizing the evidence: a learner is presented with a piece of writing that represents critical thinking, as above. Here the emphasis is put on the production of a good summary of the evidence.

Taking different disciplinary perspectives: a topic is given and learners have to make notes on the different views of the topic from different perspectives. The topic may or may not be fictitious. For example, it is proposed that a new road should be built to bypass a village, and some details about the situation are given. Notes are made on the way in which different disciplinary perspectives might be presented – whether they are in support of or in opposition to the argument itself.

Making a judgement: learners are asked to make a judgement about something unfamiliar – for example, a piece of artwork, a piece of aesthetic writing, a sculpture, a film. When they have made the judgement, they are asked to identify the criteria on which they made the judgement, and to compare them with those used by other students. The focus is not on the content of what they have written, but on the criteria used and how they contribute to the arrival at a judgement.

Making a judgement, starting from another perspective: perhaps as a follow-on from the previous exercise, learners are asked to make a judgement about something (work of art, poem etc.) for a given purpose, and the judgement is made a second time from the viewpoint of another or others – e.g. much older, much younger in age, or with a different cultural or educational background. The focus of this exercise is on the ways in which different perspectives might cause us to evaluate evidence in different ways.

10.3 Writing tasks to further the capacity in critical thinking

The next set of exercises can be useful for students in the middle or towards the end of their undergraduate studies.

The use of concept maps

Learners share thought processes on a particular (contentious) issue or matter for judgement in the form of concept maps, and note, discuss and write about the different views indicated, trying to resolve them.

A fictitious debate

A group of students construct notes towards an oral debate or write a piece that has the structure of an oral debate on a given topic. They will need to consider the nature of the characters who propose and oppose the motion and note the points that they make with evidence that they give. This exercise could be done by an e-mail group.

Practice of peer review skills

A simplified or fictitious version of a research paper is given to students to read in a 'mock' peer review situation. Learners are asked to make a judgement of the paper (e.g. as suitable for publication). They are asked to consider assumptions made, to consider the quality of the evidence for the findings, to identify gaps in the research evidence etc., and to provide justifications for their decisions.

Mark an essay in which critical thinking is represented

Learners are given prepared essays (made up, or by agreement with the writers) that have required critical thinking. They are asked to mark them for the quality of the critical thinking. They compare their marks and identify the criteria on which they did the marking. It is useful to use good and poor essays so that there can be direct learning from the good ones and the recognition of problems in reasoning in poor essays.

Recognition of the roles of referencing in the written form of critical thinking

In the earlier stages of higher education, learners tend to be led to view referencing as an acknowledgement of sources and 'avoidance' of plagiarism, but it has also much to do with the breadth of consideration and the quality of the evidence consulted – in other words, the critical thinking processes. It supplies information that helps a reader to evaluate sources of evidence. In the assessment tasks that are set in order to evaluate student knowledge and ability to think critically, the listing of references demonstrates to the assessor the breadth and quality of sources of evidence to which the student has referred in making judgements. The discipline of writing references is a form of training for the student in the proper communication of academic knowledge.

Recognition and development of the 'playing with ideas' form of writing
Critical thinking in its written form also relates to writing in a further way that is not often overtly considered – when writing most clearly interacts with thinking and learning. It is the use of writing when ideas are explored, 'toyed with', tried out in the notes in the notebook. It is the scribble of the idea on the back of the envelope, the concept maps and other graphic depictions, the layouts of lists, models and plans that all come into this group. It is an under-exploited form of writing that has much to do with critical thinking in the processes of higher education. We could ask learners to discuss their methods and demonstrate ways in which they plan. Simply giving a name to this process might help, asking them as a task to sketch out notes towards something.

10.4 Some more general writing exercises to support the written form of critical thinking

The next set of exercises can be helpful at any stage in higher education, though the complexity of the subject matter will and should vary.

Short-answer tasks
Learners are asked to respond to critical thinking tasks (e.g. to respond to short statements) in 300–400 words. This will force them to be precise and succinct in their writing and reasoning.

A demonstration that people understand things differently
A lecture or talk is given on a topic that is reasonably complex and probably on a topic within the discipline. Learners take notes at the time and afterwards are asked to compare their notes.

The identification of main points and important evidence
As above, learners are asked to listen to a lecture or talk in which evidence is given for a particular stand. Learners are asked to summarize the subject matter of the talk or lecture, focusing on the main points made, the judgement, and the nature of the supporting evidence.

Looking critically at one's own work – drafting and redrafting
This is an exercise in clear writing. It is also a means of showing learners that their perspectives change over time and as they learn more. A set of learner's writing (e.g. essays) is kept, or copies are made. After the passing of a period of time (e.g. 3 months or longer) the material is given back and learners are asked to edit the material, clarifying the points made and identifying what they would change now.

Practice in metacognition
Learners are asked to go back over a piece of work that has involved judgement and to write a reflective commentary on their process of going about the task – the research and the writing. They are asked to consider areas of the process that they would change another time.

'Compare and contrast' tasks

Learners are asked to compare and contrast two views, interpretations, theories etc. This could be done in columns, notes or text depending on the exact emphasis of the exercise. There could be a restriction on the number of words.

Learners write a discussion between two theorists (could be fictitious or real) about a topic in their discipline

They are asked to think about the position that each would take, and the kind of evidence that they would bring to the discussion. The aim of this exercise might be to demonstrate how two experts can apparently disagree about the same subject matter.

10.5 Groupwork activities in writing and critical thinking

In any situation, including many of those above, where learners work together in a group towards a common end, they will be recognizing that they have different perspectives on the same issue, and thereby will be learning about critical thinking. Underwood and Wald (1995) and Cooper (1995) are useful references.

10.6 Other literature on the pedagogy of critical thinking and writing

Since most critical thinking is actually represented in writing, there are many other relevant materials – in particular, Meyers (1986), Brookfield (1987), Kiniry and Rose (1993), Caposella (1993b), Kloss (1994), Bell (1995), Cottrell (2005) and, for advanced learners, Wallace and Wray (2006). There are also many relevant books on student writing issues, e.g. Lillis (2001).

10.7 Another source

Another source of excellent material is the Thinkingwriting initiative at Queen Mary University of London (*www.thinkingwriting.qmul.ac.uk*).

11. Reading and critical thinking

11.1 Introduction – the role of purpose

This section is concerned with more general aspects of reading for critical thinking. The academic process of critical review, which is an amalgamation of reading and writing skills, is covered in the next section (12.). Reading with a critical view may be a very general activity or it may be focused. Many of the activities listed in the section on writing and critical thinking (10.) would be relevant to the development of reading skills since there is a mutual reinforcement in the processes. The role of purpose in reading critically is very important. A sense of purpose should direct the criticality. Is the reader seeking to know the approach of the writer? to judge the quality of the writing? to judge the argument or the outcomes? Or is she reading in order to select and extract evidence for her own use in critical thinking about her own topic? These purposes may, of course, overlap. If one is selecting evidence, one wants a sense of its quality.

As in writing, there are generic skills involved in reading, in addition to those directly associated with critical processes. As in many activities, however, there are two activities involved in reading – the mental reading process and the representation of that reading, the notes made. However adequate is the initial reading, it is often the adequacy of the notes, read later, that determines the real outcome of the reading.

11.2 Reading and note-making

Learners are asked to read a piece of reasonably complex text for a particular purpose, and to make notes on it. Afterwards they compare their notes on the text and discuss different systems of note-taking, perhaps trying out different systems. Some might try using concept maps rather than linear text. They could be encouraged to try a new method on another text.

11.3 Recognizing the structure of text

The discussion of notes in the section above might be directed towards the learners' capacities to recognize the flow of meaning though the paragraphs of the text and the main points made in it. Some work on 'reading for learning' that the writer very much values is that of Augstein and Thomas (1973) and Harri-Augstein and Thomas (1991). Good readers are able to discern easily the main points made by paragraphs and use the signposts in the text to build up the meaning in relation to their purpose for reading (Moon, 1975).

12. Critical analysis of another's work

12.1 Introduction

We said that critical review overlaps with the processes of reading and writing since, in order to review something appropriately, it is important to be able to read it appropriately. It is a process that some would say epitomizes critical thinking in academia – but as we have indicated in Chapter 2, the reviewing of the argument of another is only one activity of critical thinking and there are a number of others (some of which would also utilize some critical review). While critical review is likely to be involved to some extent at undergraduate levels in higher education, it is likely to be required in its sophisticated forms at postgraduate level.

Generally in critical review there is an intention to make a judgement of value – in other words to evaluate. The evaluation of work might be as an academic exercise in review or critical thinking (evaluation) for a student. Alternatively it may be a means of assessing the value of the argument or new knowledge for the purpose of furthering one's own knowledge. In terms of the latter, the new knowledge might be for the academic needs of research, or for interest. We could also, however, be talking about assessing the value of ideas in a newspaper article, or it might be a book review that we look at, or publicity for a new restaurant. In this context, however, we will focus on the kind of literature that would be more typical of higher education.

While epistemological development is relevant to all areas of critical thinking, it is particularly relevant to remember that learners will have different views of how to go about the writing of a critical review according to their epistemological beliefs. Proper critical review requires relatively sophisticated understanding of the nature of knowledge and may also require detailed knowledge of research methodologies. There are many approaches to critical review that are fairly mechanistic (for example, the approaches that provide ordered recipes for the stages of a review). An absolutist learner, given a recipe, is likely to 'go through the motions of review'. That may or may not be sufficient for the context.

12.2 *A general guide to critical review*

Resource 12, p. 215

This resource is designed for direct use by students. It is not meant to be a set of rules, but a series of prompts that should enable them to be more able to review material in an appropriate manner. If the students have worked on critical thinking through the exercises in Resources 3, 4 and/or 5 and the Framework for Critical Thinking and its Representations (Resource 7), their attention should be drawn to the fact that critical review is a form of deep critical thinking, in other words, including similar criteria to the Critical Thinking 2 in the Framework (or the fourth account in the examples).

12.3 *Other literature on critical review*

There are many study guides that provide guidance as to how to review academic material – some more mechanistic than others. Some examples to which we have referred are Bell (1995), psychology but adaptable to other disciplines; and Cottrell (2005). Both give examples and would be more suitable for undergraduate education where there is unlikely to be deep analysis of the research methodology and data.

At postgraduate level critical review becomes more significant because the learners are likely to be using it either in professional education and/or development, or in research. They are no longer 'just practising' but are engaged in the proper building of knowledge for others. Books providing guidance in postgraduate research are plentiful on library shelves. Two books, however, are designed to provide support specifically in the activities of critical review for postgraduate-level research. Poulson and Wallace (2004) is an edited collection that begins with both a guide to critical review and examples of good practice in the writing up of research as material on which students can practise their reviewing skills. The subject matter is education (teaching and learning), but the theoretical material has more general application, in the social sciences at least. Wallace and Wray (2006) has more general application in the social sciences and is a detailed guide to the theory and practice of critical review.

13. The development of critical practice (in brief)

13.1 Introduction and suggestions for further reading

This is one of the more specialized topics in pedagogy that we are not covering in more than an introductory manner. 'Critical practice' is a term used in some areas of professional work, such as social work, where there is a concern for the appropriate application of knowledge in practical situations as well as the constant reflection on personal actions. This reflective element is often called 'reflective practice' (Moon, 2004). Critical practice seems to imply the taking of a more proactive stance. It has been linked with the notions of 'critical being' (Barnett, 1997; Brown and Rutter, 2006) to which we referred in earlier areas of this book (Chapters 2, 3). Literature that deals with critical practice in professional situations is Plath, English, Connors and Beveridge (1999), Gibbs and Gambrill (1999) – with many practical exercises; McDrury and Alterio (2003); Ford, Johnston, Brumfit, Mitchell and Myles (2005); and Brown and Rutter (2006).

14. The techniques of argument (in brief)

14.1 Introduction and suggestions for further reading

Argument may be written or oral and tends to differ in interpretation according to discipline. There is not a unified approach to it in the literature. We have taken a relatively broad approach in this book, seeing it as an element of critical thinking, but not the whole. We use this section to direct interested readers to more detailed accounts of the more focused approaches to the pedagogy of argument. A number of these accounts emanated from a project on argument based at the University of Middlesex a few years ago, which focused on the improvement of argument skills in the disciplines. This material was broadly based on the work of Toulmin (1988). Some of the relevant publications are Riddle (1997), Mitchell and Riddle (2000) and Mitchell and Andrews (2000). This last is an edited book of papers written by subject specialists with reference to their disciplines. Other relevant material is Bensley and Haynes (1995); Phelan and Reynolds (1996) – an academic approach based in social sciences; Bonnett (2001) – also a social sciences approach, but at undergraduate level; Cottrell (2005) – a study skills approach. Other study skills books may cover argument, though they can vary in their interpretations.

15. Focuses on reasoning and logic (in brief)

15.1 Introduction and suggestions for further reading

We attempted to locate the place of logic in critical thinking and interpreted it as a specialized system of thinking that may have a place in critical thinking, but is not critical thinking as such. There is no good evidence that good critical thinkers have acquired their capacity through a background in logic. Some books that explore the elements of logic that are appropriate for higher education learners are: Baron and Sternberg (1987) – some papers; Phelan and Reynolds (1996) – for advanced learners in social sciences; Bowell and Kemp (2002); Van Den Brink-Budgen (2000); Fisher (2001).

16. Educational development and critical thinking

16.1 Introduction

Staff development, as Meyers (1986) has said, is of central importance to the development of critical thinking in learners. The present book started with a list of conceptions of critical thinking from staff. The conceptions differ, as do the activities to which they referred. If tutors know what they are aiming to facilitate in learners, and can be clear and explicit about it, there is a greater chance that learners will be enabled to achieve this. Brownlee's work has explored the epistemological development of trainee teachers and has indicated that it is likely that there are teachers who may not be sufficiently developed in their own epistemological beliefs to guide learners (Brownlee, 2001; Bendixen and Rule, 2004).

16.2 Workshops on critical thinking

The writer has been running workshops on this topic for a while. As has been shown a few times in this text, the workshops have informed the writing of the book. The aim of the workshops has never been to propound one view of critical thinking but to indicate the complexities, the range of approaches and some of the theoretical underpinnings (in particular epistemological development), and promote thinking about critical thinking. As we have seen earlier, what is important is that tutors work with a clear definition for themselves, colleagues working with a group of students, and that group of students. Students need to know that there are different definitions in operation. This approach is similar to that recommended by Meyers (1986).

16.3 Exercises on introducing and improving the quality of critical thinking

Resources 1–7, pp. 177–201

The exercises on depth and quality work well in staff development sessions. They can help in the formulation of a common approach to critical thinking in staff groups and in the development of assessment criteria for critical thinking itself. Resources 1 and 2 are the instructions for the exercises; Resources 3, 4 and 5 are exercises themselves. Resources 6 and 7 support work done in the exercises (see 1.00 above).

16.4 Development of own scenarios

Based on Resources 1–7, pp. 177–201)

Better than 'doing' the given exercises on introducing and improving the quality of critical thinking is the development of own exercises, based on the framework and the indication of shifts towards deeper critical reflection (Resources 7 and 8). The aim might be to develop materials for students to use.

16.5 Exercises on epistemological development

Resources 8–11, pp. 202–14

An exercise such as Resource 8 is used in nearly all of the workshops run by the writer since the principles of epistemological development seem to underpin so much in higher education. The other exercises reinforce Resource 8.

16.6 A particularly useful source – Meyers (1986)

We have said that Meyers puts much emphasis on the teacher's understanding of critical thinking and her ability to make it a part both of what she teaches and of the manner in which she teaches. In Meyers's book there is a format for a seminar for teachers on critical thinking to enable them to develop their own conceptions of critical thinking (see also Resnick, 1987).

Thinkpoint

A story about human knowledge.

The Blind Ones and the Matter of the Elephant
(an ancient story from Afghanistan)

There was a city in which all the inhabitants were blind. A great king came and set up camp in the nearby desert. He possessed a very large elephant, both for protection and because it was a mark of his importance. He entered the city with the elephant. The people of the city had never encountered an elephant before and were very keen to know what it was. A group of them rushed forward. They touched and groped, but there were so many of them that each only felt a part of the elephant. One felt the ear, one the legs and another the trunk. When the guards pushed them back into the crowds, people flocked around those who had touched the elephant, asking what it was like. The man who had felt the ear said that it was a large and flat thing – rough, like a rug. The man who had felt the leg said that it was a mighty, firm pillar. He who had felt the trunk described it as a swinging hollow pipe that could sweep people away. Those who heard the stories told others, and they told others. Each knew something but none had the whole picture. Soon everyone in the country knew something, but none had the whole picture.

Another ending to this story, according to the original, is that those who are created cannot use science to have the vision of the divinity.

(This story is retold from Shah, 1979: 84)

12 The pedagogy of academic assertiveness

Introduction

We have argued in Chapter 6 that there are some capacities of academic assertiveness that could be developed in learners that can help them to manage better their academic experiences, and specifically the critical thinking demands of their programmes. This was illustrated with a number of examples. We have argued additionally that academic assertiveness could be valuable for learners in much wider spheres of their academic, professional, social and career lives. This chapter tentatively explores some pedagogical ideas for academic assertiveness. In terms of the examples we have used, the chapter is primarily designed to support the academic and critical thinking activities of learners – but it could very easily be generalized to use in other spheres of student or life experience. Indeed, it is likely that the scenarios that learners provide within a course would address broader issues. It is a sketch of the topic only – partly because of the constraints of space, but also because this is early days in this topic and it will be developed in a further publication.

The ideas around academic assertiveness have emerged alongside the processes of thinking about critical thinking and the writing of this book though they have been well supported by colleagues as they have been described. There is more thinking and development still to do. Because it is largely new material, we do not stint space in this chapter.

In Chapter 6 we defined academic assertiveness as:

> A set of psychological and emotional orientations and behaviours that enables a learner to manage the challenges to the self in progressing in learning and critical thinking as well as in general social situations in the experience of being a student.

We identified areas of academic work in which academic assertiveness is involved as:

- the finding of an appropriate 'voice' or form of expression through which to engage in critical thinking or debate;

- the willingness to challenge or disagree and to seek or accept a challenge;
- the ability to cope with the reality or the likelihood of not being 'right' sometimes; of making an error or failing; the effective recovery from these situations; the willingness to change one's mind if necessary; the openness to feedback on one's performance (academic or otherwise);
- the willingness to listen and take account of the viewpoint of others; awareness that others can make mistakes and then have a reasonable tolerance toward their failings;
- autonomy – a willingness to be proactive; to make and justify independent judgements and to act on them;
- an appropriate level of academic self-esteem.

General issues in a pedagogy of academic assertiveness

The suggestions in this section on academic assertiveness are based on the writer's reading, research and practical experience of assertiveness training, other forms of personal development, and student learning. There are many books on assertiveness training. Some are developed for named situations, but generally most follow cover similar issues. Examples are: Smith (1975); Alberti and Emmons (1970); Back and Back (1982) – workplace situations; Lindenfield (1986); Dickson (1992) – for women; Gillen (1992) – for managers; and Moon (1993) – for older adults. General assertiveness courses or advice are occasionally offered to students within the context of a student union (e.g. Hinton, 2006). In the books, there is material on skills and capacities, psychological aspects, practical advice and techniques for handling situations.

The context: It is convenient to describe the sessions on academic assertiveness as if they are sessions within a short course – we discuss the potential arrangements later. Basic to the course are the eliciting of examples of situations in which more assertiveness would be helpful to the learner, and the presentation of a series of principles and practical ideas and their illustration in non-personal (given) scenarios and then in relation to past and anticipated or imagined personal situations. The sessions are best if they are interactive at all stages. It is crucial that the learners are able to relate the learning material to their own lives, their academic tasks, including critical thinking, and to behaviours in the present and the future. However, there are other less interactive formats for presentation that can still be helpful because they invite the learner to think out personal situations. It would be possible to construct an online version of this material, recognizing that there would be limitations to its effectiveness.

It is useful to think of the issues that are covered in academic assertiveness sessions as remaining similar but the illustrative scenarios would be different at different stages – e.g. as a learner, in a professional situation etc. It is subject matter best addressed, therefore, at several times in a programme, or it could be seen as a 'language' taken on and used in an ongoing and adaptive manner.

The contexts for work with learners on academic assertiveness will vary according to what is possible within the broader programmes. Since it is important that learners relate their own experiences to what they are learning, ideally work would be done in a small group with a high staff-to-student ratio. This ideal will rarely be reached in the context of most higher education situations. However, there may be ways around this (see next topic).

Location of the sessions: In higher education, it is well known that learners do not like 'skills' inputs that are not directly related to their programmes. An alternative to the separate 'skills' module (taking a broad view of 'skills' here) is to embed material in other modules. However, this material on academic assertiveness may not be best served by embedding it. The principles need to brought to mind in relevant situations as a set of principles to guide action – as a kind of 'language'. Embedding them will not necessarily achieve this.

An alternative to embedding the material is to present it within the (UK) personal development planning (PDP) agenda of the programme or institution, there dealing with broader issues of student experience than just the academic. It is, for example, very much a set of employability capacities. A final suggestion is that the sessions be located in the student union. Sometimes material that is not well accepted as part of a programme is suddenly acceptable to students when it is presented through the union as part, for example, of a student development programme.

Format for presentation: In discussing 'location' above, we ignore the possibility that the course could be presented in other than face-to-face formats. The latter may be ideal, but not possible. There are many books on general assertiveness, and there are also CDs and DVDs or videos from the business sector from which ideas can be gained. However, more interactivity is possible when the material is presented in a virtual environment.

Length of course: There is not a great deal of 'input' material, but there is much to learn from discussion and the other activities that might be involved in sessions. Since the material can be presented in many different ways, format could be mixed in order to make best use of staff time and facilities. In any case, working with real-life and familiar issues is engaging and can be entertaining.

Content and the role of the tutor: The material proposed here is based on that which is common to many forms of assertiveness training, but it is adapted to the academic work side of student life, and in particular to situations in which critical thinking is involved. Clearly students live real lives, so it is easy to find examples that relate to other than academic situations. The content of this chapter could easily be adapted to other situations (e.g. professional situations), simply by using different examples.

Generally in assertiveness courses, the principles put over are explored through stories and scenarios, ideally in role play by participants (though actors could be used), or in discussions held about written or presented scenarios, or failing those, the scenarios can be read with an invitation to react (e.g. 'What would you have done?', 'Think of a similar situation in which you were involved.').

The scenarios may be imaginary, provided by the tutor, or they may be provided by the learners from their own or vicarious experiences, or they may be scenarios developed from imagination. More general scenarios may be derived from media productions such as 'soaps' or other works of fiction.

The tutor's role: The tutor for academic assertiveness is a facilitator. Many tutors will be able to gain personally from the material and a demonstration of their experiences and needs in learning to handle situations better can be very helpful to the students who themselves need to learn that tutors are their partners in the construction of knowledge. Everything that we would say here about the appropriate facilitation of academic assertiveness will be said in the context of the facilitation of critical thinking, and therefore we do not expand on this here.

Working with international students for whom assertiveness is not a culturally 'natural' stance: We have talked about the cultural issues that may confront some international students in Western higher education (Chapter 4). Clearly there is vast diversity of behaviour in the population of international students, but there are some who could gain more from Western styles of education if they were more assertive. The culture of some students may favour non-assertive or sometimes even what to Westerners might seem to be aggressive styles of behaviour. Learning something of academic assertiveness should never be presented as an attempt to change cultures but to help learners to help themselves within the context of Western styles and practices in education, including the 'critical style' (Chapter 4).

Some sample learning outcomes

If academic assertiveness is included within the structure of a programme, then it is likely to need to be described as learning outcomes which can be assessed. We have suggested that it may be revisited as the issues change in the course of a programme. These learning outcomes might be useful for students in the early stages of a programme.

When the sessions on academic assertiveness are completed, it is anticipated that the learner will be able to:

- in a brief form, relate the major principles of assertiveness (could be listed) to academic situations that she has met;
- describe three situations in which she can illustrate the use of the principles she has learned to a positive effect (could be imaginary);
- discuss given case studies with respect to principles of assertiveness;
- put forward her point of view in a seminar situation with reasonable clarity and confidence;
- make valid observations about more and less effective behaviours or 'voice' in seminar or discussion sessions where the object is for participants to learn from each other. The observations may apply to herself and/or to others. (The discussion session may be real or recorded – or virtual.)

These are sample learning outcomes. There are many possibilities that work with either imagined or real scenarios or with descriptions of actual behaviours.

Some suggested subject matter for a course in academic assertiveness

We provide subject matter that is related as much as possible to processes of critical thinking and academic situations. However, depending on the rationale for the course, the participants, and the implications of any learning outcomes, broader areas of experience can be drawn in. The use of more everyday examples can help in the comprehension and practice of the principles.

We stress that this is a sketch of a course – the outline of possible sessions and a demonstratration of the relevance of the material to critical thinking and academic life in particular. General texts on assertiveness provide more detail. There are whole courses detailed on the web (e.g. Team technology, 2006), though we should be critical of them.

Introduction: what is academic assertiveness?

(The word 'behaviour' is used as a general term to denote the observable ways in which a person reacts to a situation.) In a course in an academic context it is usually helpful to give a definition and summarize the forms of academic assertiveness mentioned and identified in Chapter 6 and as above.

Alteratively, learners might be asked to describe situations in academic life (or any educational experiences) that they find difficult. As a graphic illustration of academic assertiveness, difficult situations could be illustrated in film, video, role play, text or the oral description of scenarios.

The characteristics of assertive behaviour

Typically assertive behaviour is expressed in a range of behaviours such as voice, posture, use of personal space, eye contact, content of words or gestures.

It is a good idea to define it in relationship to non-assertive behaviour and aggressive behaviour, with some references to manipulative behaviour (which may be defined as a form of aggression).

It is easiest to demonstrate assertive behaviour by the use of scenarios in which learners are non-assertive and then become more assertive. Scenarios role-played or discussed will demonstrate the kinds of behaviours that change. Examples might be drawn from situations in which learners receive (negative) criticism, get low marks, feel intimidated, need to seek help but are not sure of how to ask – and so on.

We can relate being academically assertive to the list of characteristics given above, or, in more general terms, being assertive means that a person is direct and can state clearly what she needs. In an academic situation, she has 'voice'. She knows her rights and responsibilities and can ask clearly for what she needs. She is not afraid of meeting challenges, can express feelings comfortably, gives and receives compliments easily, and can give and receive constructive criticism easily. She is also aware if she is in a 'no-win' situation and can back off.

Aggression in assertiveness training is described as 'going for what one wants without taking account of the needs of others' – a fairly broad definition. It might be illustrated in situations of critical thinking, by the person who pursues her point with a loud voice or an aggressive stance, or one who does not listen to other points of view, or 'takes over' a situation regardless of the rights or feelings of others.

The manipulator works to achieve what she wants regardless of others too. She, however, uses techniques that others may not notice, by working round others, by leading them into making mistakes or displaying weaknesses that she can put down. The manipulator 'sucks up' to the tutor, lies in order to ensure that a late assignment is marked, manoeuvres others into situations where they give a wrong response or answer, tricks others into giving the answers to her – perhaps by charm and so on.

Examples of these behaviours are common and we all engage in all of them at times. There is much to learn of the management of aggressive and manipulative behaviour in, for example, learning to live away from home and learning to live in shared accommodation.

In this section, a useful form of exercise is to ask learners to imagine four named students who display predominantly assertive, non-assertive, aggressive and manipulative behaviour (as in Dickson, 1992). Some situations are then provided and learners are asked to describe how these stereotyped students might behave in the situations. Some sample stereotypes that could be expanded are:

Assertive – Shanti. Shanti is of British Asian origin. Her family put much pressure on her to achieve a professional career. They keep a shop. Shanti has had to think hard about how she manages her own needs and those of her parents and has learned much in how to be effective.

Non-assertive – Simon. Simon is tall and good looking but as soon as you talk with him, you find his voice is weak and 'whiney'. He tends to sit in the back in classes, not speaking unless he is spoken to. Posture-wise, he hangs his head.

Aggressive – Angela. Angela needs to dominate every social situation that she is in, speaking loudly and giving her opinion and expecting others to agree with her. She is abusive to those who challenge her. In her written work she declares her opinion clearly but may not be good at supporting it with evidence.

Manipulative – Gemma. Gemma is quiet, but she is used to getting her way. She is good at winding people up or putting them down in order to take advantage. She often goes to chat with tutors, smiling and trying to find out from them what she needs to know for her assignment.

Gender stereotypes might be introduced here and returned to later.

Exercises

These stereotypes can be explored in situations such as the following:

- The academic situation generally. How do these learners cope with being at the bottom of the pecking order with titled and esteemed figures (Doctors, Professors) entering their lives, tutors with little time, being one of a hundred others in a module and so on?;
- Student behaviour in a seminar or in a tutorial where there are several present. It can be interesting to consider with learners the ways in which a tutor might manage different and difficult behaviours;
- Student group or project work;
- Laboratory situations;
- Issues around the setting, writing and handing in of the first assignment.

Assertive behaviour and the self

In this section the discussion of assertive behaviour is expanded and applied to the self. Assertiveness is displayed in voice, posture, breathing patterns, use of silence in speech, content of speech, etc. These features are explored, and ideally they are demonstrated and experienced in role play in which various aspects are exaggerated (e.g. dealing with a difficult situation in an unassertive way, with no eye contact, etc.; dealing with it aggressively, etc.). Learners describe how they feel when they see themselves as strong and assertive or less strong and unassertive.

Exercises

- It is probably easiest to deal with the initial illustration of this section in relation to simple and common situations such as complaining about cold coffee or poor food in a restaurant or the bar. The situation can be re-run in role play with different behaviours on the side of the complainer and the waitress, manager, etc. It can then be applied to academic situations.
- Learners might be asked to work in pairs and to explore real experiences in the academic context, and the manner in which they behaved. They might be asked to talk through how they could have handled situations more effectively.
- The characteristics of personal assertive behaviour can be the subject of reflective exploration in writing – e.g. 'Exploring my own assertive and non-assertive behaviour'.

The effect of the context: the origins of behaviour styles

This leads on directly from the last topic. It is a closer exploraton of situations which encourage or discourage assertive behaviour. It is an opportunity for learners to explore more closely the influences of people, environments and situations.

It can be useful to introduce this topic through some sort of a questionnaire (e.g. assertiveness inventory – Alberti and Emmons, 1970) in which different situations are listed and learners are asked to think of those in which they can feel effective and assertive and those in which they behave in less effective ways. It will be as well to generalize this section beyond the directly academic.

Exercises

- Learners might work in groups to grade academic situations which inspire non-assertion (understanding that individuals may think differently), recognizing that different people will grade the situations differently. They should be persuaded to retain their list of situations.
- It is worth extending the discussions in this section to consider the ways in which we come to behave in particular ways – genetic origins, family, peers, education, etc. Who have been the key figures as models for them in behavioural terms, and what behaviours have they learnt from those people?
- Academic scenarios that can elicit discussion are:

  - classes in which the tutor directs questions at individuals;
  - aspects of seminar or tutorial situations;
  - seeking help from a tutor who is known to be intolerant of undergraduate students;
  - the student is called in to talk over an assignment that has been handed in late;
  - being overwhelmed by too much to do.

- The question might be asked: in what circumstances in academic life, do you feel at your strongest and most assertive? What are the conditions under which that takes place?

Your rights as a person

It is usual in assertiveness courses to provide a list of 'your rights'. Alberti and Emmons point out that this list is very similar to the Universal Declaration of Human Rights in 1948. It includes the following, though this should be regarded as a flexible list. It is derived particularly from Dickson (1992), but there are many versions (see also Smith, 1975).

As a human being, you have the right to:

- be treated with respect as intelligent, capable and equal;
- state your own needs and priorities independently of your different roles;
- express your feelings;
- express opinions and values;
- say 'yes' or 'no' for yourself;
- make mistakes;
- make your own decisions and deal with the consequences;
- change your mind;

- say that you do not understand something;
- decline responsibility for other people's needs;
- deal with others without being dependent on them.

To allow others their rights, we need also to accept corresponding responsibilities which will match the rights (e.g. treat others with respect as intelligent, capable and equal; allow others to state their own needs, etc.).

The listing of these rights and responsibilities provides subject matter for development of scenarios and discussion of them and, in particular, personal reflection on times when the rights have been abused by others and times when the learner has abused the rights of others. Many aspects of academic assertiveness are addressed quite specifically in these rights, such as making mistakes and the expression of opinion and values. Cultural issues are particularly relevant here because the interpretation of these rights can vary in some religious or national settings – but perhaps that is also the case within an institution too. Would we say that higher education really provides the 'right' to make a mistake or to fail? An interesting issue is whether we should enable learners to feel better able to fail or to do less well in order to encourage them to experiment and to be more creative (Ireland, pers. comm., 2006). There are gender issues to be discussed here too.

Exercises

The exercises in this section will be a matter of discussion of situations in which learners need to stand up for their rights. They can provide their own scenarios or imagine scenarios on which to work.

Some samples are:

- Anthony has written a poor essay. He knew that he did not give it enough time – he had broken up with his long-term girlfriend and was so devastated that he went home for two weeks. His tutor has called him in.
- Adam has argued that a set project should be conducted in a particular manner. The others disagree. He now begins to realize that they are right but does not want to lose face. He quietly asks the tutor if he can join another group.
- James finds the writing up of laboratory reports easy. His friends often ask him for help with theirs and this is beginning to take a lot of time and he feels that they are beginning to copy parts of his work.
- Sally has tutorials with a young postgraduate research student. Sally is conscious that the tutorials are poor and that she and her colleagues are not getting the support from them that they need at this stage in their programme.
- Sue feels that her fellow students are ignoring her and possibly belittling her behind her back. She is dyslexic and feels that her brain seems, at time, to work in different ways. She gets special help.
- Tutor Simon has brought the wrong set of notes to a lecture. He does not like to admit his error and waffles on the subject matter in such a way that the

students know that something is wrong. There is an issue for him and for the students too in dealing with the situation.

- In a debate on an ethical issue in social work, Janette begins to feel that she is changing her mind and favouring the other side of the argument. However, she has already said a lot in support of her starting view, and would feel awkward to admit her different line of thinking.
- Jerry is a new lecturer. He tried to describe something to a group of students and was not clear. He ploughs on. In a class test the students do badly. Jerry comments that they obviously did not have the standard of basic knowledge to understand what he has been saying – then he decides to deal with the situation more honestly.
- There is a Chinese student in your tutorial group. She speaks very quietly and is not proficient in English. She seems very intimidated by the situation and others talk over her.

The ability to change

This is a topic that is not necessarily addressed directly in assertiveness courses, but Dweck's work on self theories is relevant here. Dweck (1999) suggested that learners who believe that they are as they are because they have a fixed potential (e.g. by having a particular intelligence quotient, or a fixed set of abilities) are much less able to change than those who believe that these qualities are not fixed. Other work (e.g. Perry, 1997, cited in Knight and Yorke, 2002) has shown that learners can be enabled to change their view of their abilities in order that they can improve.

Exercises

- It would be worth talking about the beliefs about learning to which Dweck refers in her research and then ask learners to reflect in discussion or in writing how they see their own qualities and level of intelligence – as changeable or as fixed.
- It would be worth looking at some particular scenarios. For example, Andy has received his essay back. He was asked to critically review two alternative theories about social behaviour. The comment was that he has not been suffi-ciently critical. He goes home feeling very negative and fed up and shoves the essay and the comments into the bin, saying and feeling that he just has not got the ability to suceed.
- Another kind of exercise with scenarios could be used. For example, the following is given. Lee is in a first-year laboratory class. The tutor tells the class that if they think hard, they will work out how to do the experiment that is required. Lee's friends seem to understand, but he does not. This has happened before and this time Lee is very depressed. He is persuaded by his flatmate to go and see a student counsellor. The participants are asked what advice they would think of giving to Lee about his problem. He does get reasonable marks for most of his work.

Managing better

This topic is a return to a deeper consideration of what influences the development of assertive, non-assertive or aggressive behaviour. Ideas can be developed through scenarios, discussion and individual reflection, and possibly through references to examples of characters in stories, in the media and so on. Excellent support material is provided in Davies (2003), which could be useful as a course text.

Managing our thoughts: Learners encounter many situations in which they are stressed, fear failure, feel out of their depth and so on. There are several techniques that can be taught that may help. They are simple and are described in books on assertiveness – stress innoculation, thought stopping, relaxation techniques, the use of positive self-statements, the rethinking of one's self-image and so on (e.g. Dickson, 1992; Team technology, 2006). Learners might be encouraged to try out the ideas in the situations that they identified as difficult (see above).

Managing self-esteem: Topics to be discussed under this heading are: the belief in personal change (see above), the willingness to identify and enjoy challenges; endeavouring to be oneself, learning to be more comfortable with others, being more generous in praise to others, listening better and so on.

Watching how others manage better and not so well: Increasingly, at this stage in a course, it is important to encourage learners to try out ideas, observe what is happening in the world around them – so that they notice assertive, non-assertive and aggressive behaviour and learn from the situations (how to and how not to). Students can be encouraged to notice and bring in for discussion, events that they have observed between sessions where assertive behaviour either has or has not been displayed.

Managing specific situations

Learning what it is to be assertive does not make difficult situations go away. This is an important point to make. Others will still behave with anger, in a manipulative manner, through the use of put-downs and so on. Knowing how to be assertive gives people more choices in how they manage situations and more understanding when they go wrong. There are a number of useful techniques that are taught on courses that help learners in dealing with:

- situations of aggression or anger;
- 'put-downs';
- the giving or receiving of compliments;
- the giving of constructive criticism;
- the receiving of constructive criticism or feedback;
- saying 'no';
- issues around disapproval and prejudice;
- competitiveness.

There are plenty of academic situations from which to draw illustrative material in these sections, and again references on assertiveness training will provide suggestions of techniques that can be useful. As above, practice, discussion and reflective writing are useful methods to enhance learning in these areas. It is always useful to ask learners to identify a difficult situation that they are likely to confront in the near future and to work on how to manage it more effectively.

Looking at some personal goals

At this stage in a course, it is useful to ask learners to identify some situations that they would like to manage better in their lives as students or in academic situations. They could either write reflectively on these situations or identify them and discuss them with a selected other. The chosen situations (three would be a good number) can then be the subject for further consideration for the rest of the course – perhaps in reflective writing. If there is opportunity for role play, some of the situations can be examined through this medium, and some better forms of management discussed.

Some further scenarios as material for sessions on academic assertiveness

We provide some scenarios that are particularly relevant to the use and development of critical thinking. Participants will produce many other examples, though early in their academic programmes they may not be aware of some academic situations that they will need to manage. This might argue for working with groups of learners at different stages in their programmes. In terms of designing and using scenarios, Alberti and Emmons (1970) suggest that in the early stages of working on this material it is better to keep the examples generalized, shifting to the scenarios suggested by learners later. It is easy, early on, to get 'bogged down' in specific examples and feel obliged, as a tutor, to pursue them.

- Ellie does not understand the instructions for the dissertation project that she has to do. Her tutor is a professor with a difficult manner and she feels very intimidated. What can she do?
- Juan has to choose an essay to write. He is deeply interested in his subject of philosophy. One of the essays is set by a tutor who is known to give good marks if the thinking in the essay is explained simply and Juan knows that he could get good marks for this essay. However, he is much more interested in exploring the ideas posed in another essay title that would be more challenging to him and he knows that it would be much harder to get good marks. What is his thinking on this?
- Magrit has been asked for a seminar task, to prepare a critique of a paper of a well-known theorist in her discipline, who happens to work at the same university. She feels deeply intimidated by the man himself and is horrified that she could be asked to criticize his paper. What are her thinking processes? What should she do?

- Joanne is told to be more independent in her studies but has insufficient understanding of what is required. What should she do?
- Kate has been asked to write an essay but is not clear what in it will be valued in terms of allocation of marks. She knows that those who seem to be able to write well get good marks. When Anne, the tutor, is asked about the marking scheme, she is not clear what is required, and how many marks will be attributed for style and how much for content. What should happen here and how could the situation be resolved?
- Read, Francis and Robson (2001) mention Denise who was asked to criticize 'leading historians'. Denise says 'you can't turn round to someone like that and say, "sorry, I think you're rubblish!"'. But what should she do?
- Angio has always done well at school. He is used to being top of the class, the best at sport, the student with the voice that is listened to. He struggles when he gets into his first-year law class and tries to dominate his seminar with his loud voice. His tutor calls him in for a one-to-one.

Thinkpoint

When we encourage students to articulate and process experience through storytelling we provide them with opportunities to clarify and question their assumptions . . .

(McDrury and Alterio, 2003: 175)

Part 7

Resources

The resources in this section are freely photocopiable. This is in order that they may be used as classroom exercises or examples. The exercises largely relate to the content of Chapter 11.

The resources in this section are:

RESOURCE 1

Instructions for face-to-face group exercises on depth and quality of critical thinking

(see *Chapters 9 and 11*)

Introduction

The aim of these exercises is to enable participants to see what critical thinking looks like, to recognize that critical thinking can vary in depth and that there is more potential for learning from deeper rather than superficial critical thinking. The exercise is developed in response to the observation that learners who are asked to think critically tend to work at rather superficial levels of thinking. In the exercises there are four accounts of the same event or topic. In each case a person (writing at different levels) is – or different people are – thinking critically on the topic. The accounts are written at increasingly deeper levels of critical thinking.

From the writer's experience of wide use of these exercises, the disciplinary nature of the topic or event does not matter. It can actually be disadvantageous to use an exercise with subject matter that relates to the discipline of the group because the group will then tend to put on their disciplinary hats and examine the issues from that point of view, rather than consider the quality of the thinking and writing. However, as we have indicated, there are different activities of critical thinking (Chapter 2). It can be useful to think about which kind of activity is involved in the exercise and to choose an exercise that represents the closest actual activity to the current work of the learners. The text of the book associated with these exercises is Chapter 9.

Procedure

The procedure for the exercise is described as a group process, though it can be used individually. The process works best when it has a facilitator who is not engaged in the exercise. The exercises take around an hour in all and work best when the facilitator is well in control of the situation. It is important, for example, that the pages of the exercise are not leafed through in advance other than as instructed and when participants follow the instructions – in particular, not beginning the discussions until everyone has read the relevant account.

- The exercise is introduced as a means of helping the group to see what critical thinking looks like and to demonstrate that there are different

continued

depths in it and that deeper critical thinking probably accords with better learning.

- The groups are told that there are four accounts of the topic/event, and that they will be reading them one after the other, with time after each reading for discussion about the content of the account.
- Small groups are formed (ideally with no more than six in each).
- The groups are told to turn to the first account and read it quietly to themselves, considering what features that they think represent critical thinking – if any!
- When it is evident that most people have read the first account, the groups are invited to discuss the account and identify how it involves critical thinking. They are given about five to seven minutes for each discussion session (or until the conversation dries up, as it might after this first account).
- After the discussion session, the participants are asked to read the next account in the sequence (and they are reminded not to turn pages beyond the account in hand). Then they discuss it as before.
- After the last account has been read and discussed, groups are asked to go back through all of the accounts and to identify features that represent critical thinking that progressively change through the accounts. For example, the accounts change from being description or story to focusing on issues in the topic. In the later accounts there is more recognition that there are multiple perspectives, etc. The groups are asked to list (e.g. on flipchart paper) the ways in which the accounts 'deepen' – but not just to describe the qualities of each account. They may be encouraged to create some sort of graphical representation if there is time.
- In a plenary session the groups share their lists (as above) and discuss the whole exercise. One way to do this is to ask each group in turn for one feature that has changed. It is at this stage that the participants can be referred to the list of features that change (Resource 6, p. 197 and Chapter 9) and to the Framework for Critical Thinking (Resource 7, p. 198 and Chapter 9), which provides a general guide to features in the deepening qualities of the thinking. The accounts are not intended to accord directly with the stages described, but both are like continua running in parallel.

Later it might be suggested that as an exercise to consolidate their thoughts about critical thinking, they might be asked to develop their own topic and write about it at four depths of critical thinking, using the framework as a guide.

RESOURCE 2

Instructions for online exercises on depth and quality of critical thinking

(see Chapters 9 and 11)

General introduction for participants

The aim of these exercises is to enable participants to see what critical thinking looks like and to recognize that critical thinking can vary in depth and that there is more potential for learning from deeper rather than superficial critical thinking. The exercise is developed in response to the observation that learners who are asked to think critically tend to work at rather superficial levels of thinking. In the exercises there are four accounts of the same event or topic. The accounts are written at increasingly deeper levels of critical thinking. In each account a person working on the account several times, or different people are thinking critically on the topic, but at different 'depths'. The subject matter does not matter – in fact, subject matter that is related to the person's discipline can 'get in the way' because the concern comes to be with the content issues and not the kind of critical thinking that is occurring. It is the quality of the thinking that matters.

Procedures

General instruction
In whatever manner it is run, the exercise works better when people follow the instructions. There is no need for the facilitator to comment on the discussions of participants during the presentation of the four accounts – it is better that she simply manages the presentation of the accounts, in this way showing her online presence.

Aim of the exercise
The exercise is a means of helping participants to see what critical thinking looks like and to demonstrate that there are different depths in it and that deeper critical thinking probably accords with better learning.

The first account is provided. The instruction is:
Read the account in order to consider what features you think represent critical thinking. When you have read it, comment on how it involves critical thinking and engage in online discussion with others on this.

 continued

The next account is provided after an appropriate period of time. The instruction is:
Read the next account in the sequence and discuss what represents critical thinking and how deep it is, engaging in discussions as before.

Account 3 is given (same instructions).

Account 4 is given (same instructions).

After the four accounts have been received and read by participants, the following instruction is given:
Now look through all four accounts and decide what it is that represents the features of critical thinking that progressively change through the accounts. For example, the accounts change from being 'story' to focusing on issues in the topic that need to be considered critically. In the later accounts there is more recognition that there are multiple perspectives, etc. Discuss this with your colleagues online and list the ways in which the accounts 'deepen' – but do not just describe the qualities of each account. The idea is that, as a group, you end up with a list of features that change through the accounts and that characterize progressively better-quality critical thinking. The fourth account, being the last presented, is not presented as 'perfect' – there could be other end points beyond it.

The list of ways in which the accounts change is then given and participants are asked to compare it with their own list. Then the Framework for Critical Thinking and its Representations (Resource 7) is given.
Participants are told that the accounts are not intended to accord directly with the stages described, but both are like continua running in parallel.

Later it might be suggested that as an exercise to consolidate their thoughts about critical thinking, they might be asked to develop their own topic and write about it at four depths of critical thinking, using the Framework as a guide. This would mostly be useful for those at Master's level.

RESOURCE 3

An exercise for introducing and improving the depth and quality of critical thinking about the self

Linked to Resources 1, 2, 6, 7 (For discussion, see Chapters 9 and 11)

The critical thinking activity here is critical thinking about the self (Chapter 2).

Background

Jay is on a professional education programme and is learning how to think critically about her actions or the actions of others. She is expected to demonstrate that she can consider critically her experience or evidence about her performance so that she can learn usefully from it. This is a series of attempts to engage in critical thinking done in the course of an exercise. The main concern of the tutor is that Jay can demonstrate sufficient depth in her thinking to make appropriate judgements about how to learn from her performance, and thereby work out how to improve. She takes the example of learning to sing.

A first attempt at singing

Account 1

This is about my relationship with singing. I cannot sing. I always thought that it is because of what my mother always said about singing (an indulgent waste of time) – but I have now sung two songs in public at the Golden Lion folk night. I used only to be a storyteller there. I practised the songs, thinking that I might get around to singing but I kept making excuses. Friends said I could sing but I did not know if I could believe them. I had gone for a long drive on the day that I sang and I worked at learning the words – and the idea of actually doing the song grew. I took the song-sheets as I set out for the pub. Sam came up as usual, arranging the list of performers for the evening. He asked if I had a story – and I said that I might surprise him . . . and left it at that.

Others sang and played. The people before me were superb – unfortunately. Then it was my turn. I walked up, sweating. I had rehearsed how I would introduce myself. I did that and then I could not find the first note. I tried again and it was there and my voice came – 'As I walked out one evening fair . . .' – 'The Dark-Eyed Sailor'. The words were on the sheet in front of me and I held onto the music stand but then I wanted to move and let go and then I was swaying in an ungainly manner. My hands were

continued

everywhere, holding each other, flaying about, trying to express something, but the words did flow and people seemed to be listening. I thought: 'they are surprised to hear me sing. Good!' People joined in too. I liked that and the way in which my voice emerged from the mass of voices when I was into the verse again. I had to keep referring to the words though because I did not know them well enough. This tied me to the spot.

One song went and then there was the other. I fluffed the start again – but then I was off and the flow was on. There were wobbles when the nerves got the better of the voice. There was a misreading of the lines – whoops. Then there was a stage when thoughts got in the way ('What am I doing here? Stick to what I can do next time') but I got to the end and slid back to my seat amidst clapping. I wondered if the clapping was just polite or if it was sympathetic or for me making the effort. But I had done it.

Account 2

I have now sung in public – at a folk night – on my own for the first time. I had it in mind for a while that I would sing sometime despite the various messages from my mother that we are non-musical and was there something about music being an indulgent waste of time? I had questioned this but had not countered it until now. If I am so non-musical, how could it be that I actually liked music so much? A couple of friends, hearing my nervously delivered bars, said that they thought that I could sing but I needed confidence. Were they right or just patronizing me? What does it mean 'to be able to sing' – is it more than to keep in tune? I even found it difficult to ask these friends about these things because they might laugh if I said that I might actually want to sing in public. I do know that I like to perform because I tell stories in public.

I practised the songs, but was not sure that I would really do it. However, I have a sense of adventure – you only live once so I do take risks. When, at the session, Sam asked me if I was going to do my usual story, I heard myself saying that I might surprise him – I was then on the slope. I do like to surprise people – so that was a further drive.

My turn came and I was there. I put the song-sheets on the stand. Having words to follow is an odd experience for a storyteller. Stories are in my head and storytelling is describing a series of visual images. I am free to move. Being tied to a sheet of someone else's words was strange.

I sung the two songs. I fluffed the first notes of both because I could not find notes on which to start. How do I manage this another time – and will there be another time? There are lots of things to think about – that I felt I got wrong this time – what should I do with my hands? How should I move when singing? How do I express the ideas in the song? There is some mental directive too, about looking as if I am enjoying the song. I was asking

Resource 3, *Critical Thinking*, © Jennifer Moon, Routledge 2008.

myself if people were just being tolerant when they clapped – or was there something to clap about? I realize that I have now played the card of 'This is my first time of singing'. I no longer have that excuse.

Account 3

I have now sung two songs in public in a folk club. This was a challenge and an achievement for me. I already performed as a storyteller because I liked performing. I assumed that I could not sing. I want to reflect on what this experience means to me. There are several things: the taking of the risk; the motivation to sing; the fact that I actually sang and broke a long established directive. What did I learn from it all and where do I go from here?

So I look at taking the risk. I do take risks. I want to go on learning and getting the most out of life. I also value creativity – doing new things. It was good and satisfying doing this new thing. Nerves and the anxiety of 'am I making a fool of myself?' were better than the frustration of sitting back with excuses as before – so emotion was both stick and carrot. My emotional state was also related to old directives from my mother that 'we are not musical; singing is indulgent' – I seem to have interpreted that as 'do not waste time with music' because 'we' cannot do it. How deep-rooted are these directives! Breaking it was good.

I think about the way in which I sang. Storytelling is free from sets of words and for me physical movement seems to enable the flow of the story. Singing is different. I tried to learn the words to the songs, but for security I needed the words in front of me and I sang from them rather than from memory. And – to read I need glasses – and somehow they get in the way of the flow. I need to focus on letting the song flow and remove as many of the constraints as possible – nerves, eventually being one of them.

Nerves – what are they about? Getting as far as doing this song involved difficult processes that only started with mother and 'we don't sing'. I always sang to myself and liked the feel of singing in my mouth and to my ears – was there a contradiction? Eventually I worked up to saying to an opera-singer friend 'I would like to be able to sing'. He sang something and I followed. 'Yes', he said, 'you can sing.' Then he wandered off, singing his own songs. Obviously I could not sing enough to engage his interest. That about sums up several experiences of mine – very tentatively seeking help, then not getting what I needed in terms of support or positive comment and then feeling disenchanted again.

I realize in thinking back, I introduced myself that day with: 'This could be "try anything once" or "you've got to start somewhere"'. I think I got to the root of something in those flippant words. There are two issues – that performance and whether I do it again. Flippant words can carry truths. Is the issue the doing of it once or the idea of having started something to continue? I have focused so far on 'having done it once'. If I decide to continue, I need to question how I can improve my voice now. There were a few positive comments after I sang and they clapped – as they do – but that is not enough. I have to overcome this diffidence about talking with others about my singing. I need gentle honesty in comments from others. I have to face up to my fragility and nerves and get over that. I have to deal with the idea of being a beginner too – and as I write, it opens up. It is as if I have opened a door in my thinking, though I need to keep going back and checking that I am opening 'helpful' doors.

Account 4

I think back on my first singing spot in front of people in a folk club. It was low-key stuff, but I want to learn both from it and how to learn from it. My first thoughts on it were about 'surface' things – emotions, my confidence, the fact that I was contradicting a long-held belief-system. Those things were what I thought about at the time – but I realize that I just have to deal with that stuff. I will deal with it in time – but only if the singing itself is right. Sandy pointed out that that is the very point that I largely have ignored in talking around the experience. Improving the nerves is pointless if the singing is rough (and vice versa) – I do need to learn to manage nerves and so on – but alongside the development of the singing.

I asked Janice for some tips. She is an experienced singer and heard me that night. It is hard for me to ask for help. I am used to being able to do things and I hear inside me a voice saying 'I can get it right on my own'. But I am a novice and one with an 'inexperienced' ear as well as a novice voice. Janice was gentle. She gave me three things to consider and from those, a few more came to mind. On the technical side, she said that clearly I need to open my mouth more and that will let more sound happen. I tried this and it works. I imagine tension tightens up the mouth. I need also to pay attention to my breathing – it was all over the place that night. Janice suggested an exercise which I seem keen to do – good!

Janice is one of those who says that one must learn words in order to concentrate on expression of a song. I fought that one – words are a prop; and when I am nervous I can forget anything. Other people use words too . . . but she insisted. I guess I can learn words if I keep on practising in the car – a good place! It was singing in the car that enabled me to realize how my voice warms up after a few songs – it gets louder. I need to warm up before I sing to anyone.

So I need to take on board that I am a novice and that practice is what leads to improvement – and because practice will enable me to sing better, I will be less nervous and remember the words better and not need to read them – so I can express myself better and feel more confident and less nervous, so it goes on. It is all linked – how could I have doubted the worth of practice? It is like skiing, drawing, craft work – everything.

I think about how initially my thinking about singing was all caught up with what seemed to be the immediate and emotionally dominated parts of the experience. It was only after wading through this stuff that I could begin to unearth the quality of my singing as an issue and make proper judgements about what needs to be done there. That is a basis from which to move forward. I look at what I have just written and wonder if I could have seen more clearly the emotional and performance issues as well as the learning issues in one 'go'. Perhaps if I had not written about this so soon after the event – when I was still caught up with the feelings – I could have avoided that stuff, though it is relevant, and the emotions made the experience feel very close up and real. In future critical thinking about myself, I should try writing about some things straight away, accepting that there is further to go with it – then leaving it for a week or so and see if the perspectives change. I think they might and I might be able to get straight to the point.

Resource 3, *Critical Thinking*, © Jennifer Moon, Routledge 2008.

RESOURCE 4

An exercise for introducing and improving the depth and quality of critical thinking on a given statement

Linked to Resources 1, 2, 6, 7 (For discussion, see Chapters 9 and 11)

The critical thinking is about a statement that has been made. The activity of critical thinking here is the 'Constructive response to the arguments of others' (Chapter 2). It is the kind of activity that many learners will confront in essays where a title is given as a statement.

Background

In a seminar on the subject of learning in higher education for postgraduate certificate in education students, Sallyanne flippantly says: 'Good learning in higher education is simply all about getting good marks in the modules of the programme'. Martin, the tutor, intervenes and asks the learners to go away and think critically on the statement for half an hour. He indicates that he is less interested in the issues in the statement than the quality of the critical thinking that is involved.

A discussion about learning

Account 1

I have been asked to think about what I mean by 'good learning'. A programme in higher education is made up of a number of modules. In the average undergraduate programme of three years, the marks for the modules at level 2(i) and 3(h) are usually counted towards the degree grade and there is a formula used to determine which students get firsts, upper seconds and so on and which are the failures. Firsts and upper seconds are usually taken to be good degrees, although an upper second is also the average degree. It used to be that lower seconds were average.

Good learners usually get good degrees, though this is not always the case. A good learner might be ill or just have a bad time for a while and get lower marks and therefore not do so well on some modules. There are mechanisms of compensation and condonement that allow their better marks to make up for their less good marks.

Sometimes learners seem to be really good in the first year of higher education and then something happens to them and they do not do so well. Perhaps it is that they have really chosen the wrong subject or they get lazy and go out too much or they drink too much. Some students are not good at learning because they are out so much that they do not meet the deadlines that are set for their work. Some have jobs that take up – possibly

– too many hours of time and they just do not come to all of the lectures.

I can illustrate that last point by reference to an engineering student I know. He did really well in his first year, getting good marks for practically all of the modules that he studied. He found that he was getting short of cash and decided to get a job at the local pub. The landlord would only take him on if he would work five evenings a week, so he agreed. He started to get bad marks because he missed the first lectures in the morning quite often and did not have time to catch up by writing up notes. He would have been a good student though – and by that I mean a good learner.

Thinking critically about the statement, then, I would agree that good learning in higher education is about getting good marks in the modules of the programme because students who get good marks usually get good degrees.

Account 2

I have been asked to think critically about the following statement: 'Good learning in higher education is simply all about getting good marks in the modules of the programme'. What is the statement asserting? It asserts that students who are good at learning get good marks in modules. In general I would agree with that statement, though I need to look at it further because there are some ideas in it that need to be explored more. For example, what is meant by 'good' here?

I explore the notion of 'good learning'. A good learner is not necessarily a student who is passionately interested in his course and who asks questions about the work; in other words, one who takes a deep approach to his learning [reference given here], but usually it is a student who is also fairly strategic – in other words, can manage time reasonably well, can organize ideas, prepares well for examinations and so on [the learner gives references here]. It is such students who tend to do well in their modules and get good degrees so long as they put the time in. It is always possible that a good student can slip up or be ill for some modules.

It is also right to question the time scale of 'good at learning'. Does it assume that they were always good and will always be good, or just that they are good at the time of the degree? Since the word 'student' has not been used, we might be talking about a longer time scale than the time for the study of a degree. I also would question the use of the word 'simply' and what it is meant to imply. In addition another issue that needs to be discussed here is the assessment of the learning – to what extent is good learning defined as good marks in the assessment of a module?

It is also necessary to look at how module grades accumulate to a degree class and whether good learning in all the modules is reflected in good learning at degree level (or programme level).

Resource 4, *Critical Thinking*, © Jennifer Moon, Routledge 2008.   continued

In general, and after consideration of the facts, I think that I agree with the statement that good learning in HE (higher education) is all about getting good marks in the modules, because good learning is good learning. There are, though, some things to think about here, such as the meaning of 'good' and whether this statement would be true in other areas of education.

Account 3

I have been asked to think critically about the following statement: 'Good learning in higher education is simply all about getting good marks in the modules of the programme'. What is the statement asserting? It is saying that a student who gets good marks will be a good learner and that is all there is to it. There are some assumptions in the statement.

First I look at the words – what is meant by 'good learning'? There is an ambiguity here. The statement either implies that students who are good at learning get good marks in modules or that it requires the quality of 'good learning' – whatever that is – for a student to get good marks in modules. There are assumptions in the statement that 'good' is a similar quality in relation to learning in both uses of the word. 'Good' in relation to marks means that there are high marks. That is a different meaning from 'good' in relation to learning – which might mean that the learning is effective, or quick or thorough, or it can be applied and so on.

The use of 'good' in relation to good marks depends on the process of assessment. Some learners are good at assessment and others are less good. A student could be a good learner in one sense, but he is poor at the assessment, and in the sense of the statement we cannot say that he is a good learner – but equally it does not work around the other way. He is not a poor learner because he got poor marks.

In my experience, it is very possible for there to be students who I would say were 'good learners', who do not get very good degrees. The fact that they do not get good degrees is related to the fact that they have not got good marks for their modules. Some of these students make excellent professionals – sometimes they have more of the skills that are actually required for the profession – but they certainly could not be defined as good learners at the time of their graduation or on the basis of their actual marks.

So, in conclusion, I would say that the statement could be said to hold in a narrow sense – it is not untrue. However, there are many assumptions and distortions in it and I could not agree with it as it stands. In particular there is the issue of the use of the word 'good' in relation to assessment and its use in relation to the word 'learning'. They are different uses and confuse the statement.

Account 4

I am considering the statement: 'Good learning in higher education is simply all about getting good marks in the modules of the programme'.

In order to think critically on this statement, I first need to consider the meaning of the statement itself. It was given as a bit of a 'throw-away' line with slight cynicism. The words 'simply all about' feel persuasive without much room for disagreement, though I may ultimately disagree. I note the 'mood' of the statement. There is a message in it beyond the words.

The statement equates 'good' marks with 'good learning'. While there may be some disagreement about the term 'good' in relation to the marks, 'good learning' could mean many different things. Much of this question hinges on the meanings of the uses of the words 'good'. A set of 'good marks' is likely to imply that the learner has achieved well in the context of the modules of the programme and it may mean thereby that the learner does well in the overall degree. This may be true, but there is another issue hidden here. Good marks are defined as 'good' in relation to the assessment process which involves an assessment method and assessment criteria. Some students have great difficulties with some assessment methods (e.g. dyslexics may have difficulties with written work). The assessment criteria may reward particular kinds of learning – perhaps they reward those who just learn facts easily and not those who can reason, but are not so efficient in factual recall. In other words, being successful in the degree does not define a person as good at all learning because 'good' in the sense of the degree is relative to assessment methods and criteria.

I need also to question what is meant by 'good learning'. First, is there one thing called good learning? Different people might construe 'good learning' in different ways. In research by XYZ, in which the meaning of 'good' learning was examined in different contexts (school, further, adult, professional and higher education), different concepts of 'good' learning were evident in different contexts (XYZ, date – *i.e. the student gives a reference*) – so the interpretation of the word may differ. In the literature of learning, there are even different theoretical bases associated with the different sectors of education. Secondly, from my own and colleagues' experience of working in professional education, it is not necessarily those students with good marks who are most successful in the profession. Those who get high marks often lack the personal skills to start with. Indeed, we can take it further. Some who turn out to be the wisest or most clever in society had poor results in their higher education programme or were not in higher education. In this respect, there is a timescale that needs to be taken into account for this judgement. Are we talking about 'good learners' now or over their lifetimes?

Resource 4, *Critical Thinking*, © Jennifer Moon, Routledge 2008. continued

190

Within the time available for this critique, I have started to examine the statement that 'Good learning in higher education is simply all about getting good marks in the modules of the programme'. While the wording of the statement tries to persuade me of the case, I cannot agree with it, though in restricted senses it could be meaningful. As I have indicated above, the word 'good' can be interpreted differently in different contexts and by different people, and additionally, the notion of 'good marks' is relative to local assessment issues that define what 'good' means in that context of assessment.

RESOURCE 5

An exercise for introducing and improving the depth and quality of critical thinking about an incident

Linked to Resources 1, 2, 6, 7 (For discussion, see Chapters 9 and 11)

This is an activity of critical thinking about an incident (Chapter 2) and will be a common form of critical thinking in professional practice. In the last two accounts of this exercise, where the writing is deeper, there are more issues with which to deal and the text would be much longer. In these accounts, therefore, we deal mainly with the first of the points raised about the briefing. It is important to remember that it is the quality of the represented critical thinking that matters – and not the content.

Background

Sam and Gill are qualified walk leaders. They are leading a set of four one-day walks around the Shallon hills, on behalf of the Nature Authority. It is a fairly remote and rough area. An incident has occurred and they need to consider it for its implications for their practice as guides. They have a report to write on it. The four accounts are written at different depths of critical thinking.

An incident on a walk

Account 1

Saturday 6th July: We began the circular walk of the Shallon hills at 9.00. There were ten walkers. The briefing was done. Sam and I (Gill) had talked about what we would do if some of the walkers were not equipped for a walk in the hills in weather like that. It was very wet and the forecast was for it to continue over the whole weekend. Several of the walkers had lightweight jackets, one was without a hood and one had sandals on instead of walking boots. We were not really happy with the situation, but did not say anything – it was summer after all. Being warm, it was difficult to know what to say to them, especially when they had received the information pack and paid money to come.

We had walked for two hours in very wet conditions and stopped for coffee. Everyone seemed to be happy and they were all talking, including the two who subsequently had problems. We walked on and not far on I noticed that Sam was having difficulty keeping the back-markers up to the

continued

pace. We had a long way to go that day and needed to push on. Then I looked back and he had stopped with them; eventually I walked back. It seemed that one of them had got very cold and was wet through. We talked about the situation. She was getting a bit vague – a sign of hypothermia. She had to be got off the hills. According to the plans that we had made, Sam took her (with her friend) back. Meanwhile I went on with the rest of the group.

That evening, Sam said that the girls were very cold as he walked them off and one was well on the way to hypothermia – she kept wanting to lie down – a sure sign. It seemed that the incident affected the rest of the group quite a bit and we talked about that too.

There is some thinking to be done about walkers and their equipment. For example, what do we say to them if they are not properly equipped?

Account 2

Incident of hypothermia on the Shallon hill walk, July 6th 2006

We met the group of ten walkers for a briefing and as a means of checking their equipment. It was very wet and from the forecast was likely to stay that way all weekend. Several had inadequate gear for the conditions. What could we do? I realized that we had not discussed how to deal with this situation. Should we have told them to go away when they had paid? How could we have sent them away at this stage? I felt caught between my instincts as a qualified leader, and the contract we have with the Nature Authority. I was a bit disturbed by this dilemma and because of this and the fact that it was actually quite a warm day we said nothing. Maybe we made a mistake.

We started the walk and they seemed happy enough. We were watching those who were likely to be getting wet. It was after a coffee stop that Sam noticed that the two we were most concerned about were dropping back. On talking with them, he found that one was shivering a lot, and seemed vague. She was clearly too cold to proceed. We put her into dry clothes and, as agreed, Sam took her and her friend off the hills. He had difficulty with this; the woman kept wanting to lie down – hypothermia had set in.

I was surprised at the effect that the event seemed to have on us all. I was, of course, very conscious about looking out for signs of cold in the rest of the walkers and we were more careful after this incident. We did not stop for long at a time, for example, and kept moving.

So there were several things in this incident that we need to think about – what should we have done about the poor equipment at the stage of the briefing? Did we manage the situation right when we discovered that the girl was cold? Looking back on the event I recognize that there was the potential for a much more serious situation. We should use the incident to plan what we would do on other occasions which are wet or for other situations like this.

Account 3

Case of hypothermia on Shallon hills walk series, July 6th 2006

The walk was led by Gill D and Sam K and this is a jointly prepared report. The first issues on this walk arose at the briefing. There were ten walkers, eight were well equipped for the wet conditions and two inadequately dressed – in showerproof jackets, one with no hood. The forecast was for heavy rain all weekend, though it was warm. We were both concerned about the inadequate clothing, frustrated that they had ignored the instructions and worried about the reaction of the Authority if we sent them away. We should have been prepared to talk about it but it was difficult to deal with in this context. We needed to talk in private and make a decision about turning them away – even though they had paid. We did not create an opportunity for the private talk and, partly because it was so warm, we let them come. In retrospect, this was an incorrect decision.

We walked on for two hours, then stopped for 25 minutes. Prior experience should have indicated to us that you can get very cold if wet, even in warm conditions because then there is the issue of condensation. Stopping too long for coffee was probably a mistake. We walked on and at this stage Sam noticed that one of the two with inadequate clothing was a bit odd. He spoke with her and observed early signs of hypothermia. I went back and we confirmed that she needed to be taken off the hills. We got warm clothes onto her with difficulty and Sam took her and her companion back. During the walk off the hills, he observed that she was showing quite serious signs of hypothermia – wanting to stop and lie down, etc. It was only afterwards that we realized how dangerous a situation this could have been.

I (Gill) walked with the other walkers. Because I realized how easy it was to get cold even on that warm day, I took a lot more care to watch for signs of cold and we did not stop anywhere for long.

There are several issues here. (1) the adequacy of clothing and how we handle that at the briefing; *(2) the management of the walk, given that we had two ill-equipped walkers with us; (3) the management of the situation when we realized that we had a case of hypothermia and (4) the management of the rest of the walk (only the first of these is discussed below).*

1. With regard to the clothing issue, we were disturbed by that. The girls had had the instructions but maybe they thought that they had adequate clothing – it is hard to tell what people understand by 'adequate clothing'. Perhaps the instructions need to be better and they need to be clearer that

 continued

people could be turned away. In that respect, we were worried that the Nature Authority might not support us if we turned them away. The walkers had, after all, paid for the walk, but safety is an issue that cannot be ignored. There was a difficulty too in how we could manage the situation at the briefing – we need to ensure that we do talk in private and share opinions after the briefing and before we walk. There may be things in that decision-making process that we also need to discuss.

(To keep accounts equal, we have dealt only with the non-italicized item.)

Account 4 (Shallon walk, July 6th 2006)

A case of hypothermia on a one-day walk

This is a jointly written incident report (walk leaders, Gill D and Sam K). We have discussed some of these issues with colleagues before writing it and this version of the report includes issues raised by our colleagues. We note how easily this situation that we describe could have become a dangerous one.

The incident

The ten walkers were sent usual instructions about the importance of appropriate equipment in advance. At the briefing, we noted that two were ill equipped – having shower jackets, one without a hood and one with sandals, not boots. It was very wet, with rain forecast to continue but it was warm and we let them proceed. When we talked about this later, neither of us was happy about the decision that we made at the time, but we tended to hold back that expression of doubt – perhaps because it was the easier option to let them walk. We have realized that we need to be able to get away from the group to have a conversation after the briefing, sharing any concerns – and we need to be honest – only then should we make a decision.

We walked for two hours, stopped for 25 minutes, then walked on and it became evident that one of those in inadequate clothing was becoming hypothermic. Having put warm clothes on her, Sam took her and her companion off the hills. During the walk off the hill, it became evident that the hypothermia was quite advanced. The event had a considerable impact on the day and we wish to consider our management of the situation within this report, as well as the incident itself.

Considerations

There are several issues here for more general consideration.

1   The broad issues of equipment; the instructions about it in the joining information – and the management of ill-equipped walkers at the briefing.
2   *Our management of the walk under those weather conditions, given that we had let ill-equipped people come.*
3   *Our handling of the case of hypothermia.*
4   *The overall management of the walk once the incident had happened.*

And other issues may emerge.

To keep accounts equal, only the first of these points is discussed below.

1. We deal first with issues around equipment, reference to equipment in the joining instructions and the management of the briefing. In going over the situation in several discussions and in writing this report, we feel that we made an error in allowing the ill-equipped walkers to come with us on that walk.

We noted that the walkers had received instructions to wear suitable clothing and they had a warning that they may not be able to proceed if they did not wear enough. However, it is very difficult to turn them away at the briefing situation. They have paid for the walk, travelled here, and are expecting to go walking. However, there is the safety issue, obviously theirs, and, one could argue, that of the other walkers who were left with one leader for a long day in difficult conditions.

Clearly we have to be able to turn people away on occasions. It may be that the joining instructions could be strengthened. For example, they could stress the distinction between waterproof gear and showerproof jackets. It is possible that the girls thought what they were wearing was adequate. Just because we know the nature of proper equipment does not mean that more casual walkers understand. They probably had no understanding of just how wet these hills can be. It would be useful to get the opinions of the occasional walkers about the issues of clothing and what they think they need for particular conditions.

There is also the relationship between us and the Nature Authority. Both of us, as leaders, were disturbed by the kind of relationship we have with the Authority and it influenced our decisions on the day of the walk. We know of an incident four weeks ago when a walker in sandals was turned away. He complained to the Authority and the guide was 'ticked off'. We, as leaders, need to feel confident enough to turn people away if necessary and we should not be concerned about the Authority when we make such a decision. We have talked to other colleagues and we feel that we would have better confidence to make decisions if we knew that we had the full backing of the Nature Authority.

A problem arose at the briefing when we did not feel at ease to have a private talk away from the group in order to discuss our concerns and make a decision about action. There seemed to be an assumption that the briefing was about the walk itself and not about preparedness for the walk. We need to be clearer about the briefing, and to build in a brief meeting between the two leaders in order to go over any concerns (there could be other issues) and – as would have happened in this case – to decide on whether we should turn away the ill-equipped walkers.

Actions on point 1: (*Gill and Sam drew out issues for action or for further consideration at a meeting with colleagues after consideration of each of the points made.*)

RESOURCE 6

Shifts in the texts of the scenarios (Resources 3, 4, 5) as the critical thinking deepens

Linked to Resources 1, 2, 3, 4, 5 and 7 (see Chapters 9 and 11)

In the shift from superficial critical thinking to deep critical thinking, text changes in the following ways:

- from description about the surface matters (possibly a narrative) to text that is shaped by the critical thinking process towards the required outcome(s). There is a shift from a structure in which there is little focus to a structure that is focused and purposive;
- from the absence of argument and comparison to the presence of argument/comparison;
- from dealing with surface characteristics of the words and ideas in the task to a deeper consideration (e.g. assumptions about word meanings will be dealt with in deeper accounts, but not in descriptive accounts);
- from a descriptive text to one in which questions are raised, to one in which there is a response to questions raised;
- from not noticing or not dealing with emotional aspects of the issue to noticing, dealing with and reasoning about emotions in relation to the issue;
- from the giving of an unjustified opinion as conclusion to the presentation of a considered conclusion based on evidence provided with a note of limitations of the thinking;
- from a one-dimensional account (with no recognition of there being further points of view, perhaps of others) to a recognition of other points of view;
- from non-recognition of the role of prior experience to the taking into account of prior experience and the effects it might have on judgement;
- from a text in which there is a drift from idea to idea rather than a deliberated persistence in dealing with selected and relevant topics
- from no metacognition/reflexivity, to reflexivity and metacognition.

RESOURCE 7

Framework for critical thinking and its representations

Linked to Resources 1 – 6 (see Chapters 9 and 11)

In these descriptions of critical thinking, the word 'issue' is used as a shorthand for the topic or task that is under consideration. Different activities of critical thinking and different forms of representation may necessitate some modification of the language.

Descriptive writing with little evidence of critical thinking

The text is descriptive and it contains little questioning or deepening of any issue. It may provide a narrative account which is from one point of view, in which generally one point at a time is made. Ideas tend to be linked by the sequence of the account rather than by meaning and there may be no overall structure and focus.

There is no real argument and not much comparison.

Any introduction to the issue to be examined may tend to miss the point of the issue and pick up the surface characteristics of it – such as words used, rather than the meaning of them. It is taken at face value.

Assumptions are likely to be left unexamined and probably unnoticed.

The text may refer to past experiences or opinions, but just as direct comment with no analysis and all in the context of this single viewpoint.

There may be references to emotional reactions but they are not explored and not related to any conclusions that may be drawn.

There may be ideas or external information, but these are not considered in depth, questioned or integrated.

There is little attempt to persist in focusing on particular issues. Most points are made with similar weight.

A conclusion may either not be properly drawn, or it is drawn but it is not justified by the text. It may be opinion and unrelated to any reasoning in the text.

Descriptive text that moves towards critical thinking

This is similar to the above, but there is some attempt to recognize the task and broadly, but still descriptively, structure the material towards the reaching of some sort of conclusion. It is not the kind of structure that will enable proper critical thinking.

There may be some comparisons made between ideas but probably no more than two ideas at a time.

There a form of introduction of the issue to be discussed, in which something of the critical thinking task is recognized.

Assumptions or points for analysis may be noted or questioned but they are not explored in depth – or they not are fully related to the task or not drawn into any conclusion.

There may be some drawing in of additional ideas, reference to alternative viewpoints or attitudes to others' comments, but these are not explored in depth or focused on in working through the issue towards a conclusion.

There is recognition of the worth of further exploring but it does not go very far.

Any conclusion tends to be partly opinion or not fully or justified by the text.

Critical thinking (1)

The structure of the text begins to change towards being a vehicle for critical thinking. It is no longer a straightforward account of an event, but it is definitely reflective and analytical and the writing seems more intentionally designed and focused. The issue is introduced and probably the wording is explored in order that any deeper meaning or assumptions can be elicited.

There is a more appropriate conclusion that does relate to the text, drawing from it and relating back to the issue raised in the introduction.

There is evidence of external ideas or opinions and, where this occurs, the material is subjected to reflection and consideration in relation to the task.

There is appropriate questioning of the ideas and assumptions; some obvious mulling over. Assumptions are examined and sub-conclusions are drawn into the text.

Where relevant, there is willingness to be critical of the action of self or others. There may be evident willingness to challenge one's prior ideas or those of others.

There is evident 'standing back' from the event, consideration and reconsideration of it.

There is recognition of emotional content, a questioning of its role and influence and an attempt to consider its significance in shaping the views presented.

There may be recognition that things might look different from other perspectives; that views can change with time or the emotional state. The existence of several alternative points of view may be acknowledged, though not necessarily fully analysed (depending on the task).

The text may recognize in a limited way that personal and others' frames of reference affect the manner of thinking, but analysis of this is not fully demonstrated in the making of the judgement or conclusion.

The conclusion is based on evidence in the text.

Critical thinking (2)

There is an introduction of the issue, an examination of the wording (e.g. meanings and assumptions) or context of it, as appropriate. It may be reinterpreted so that it can be more clearly analysed.

The context, purpose for or limitations of the current thinking may be mentioned.

The selection of the evidence for examination is appropriate and sufficiently wide-ranging.

The evidence is examined in a systematic manner that is well structured in relation to the task or issue. There is an appropriate balance between discussion of evidence and deliberation towards the response. There is good 'signposting' within the writing.

The account shows deep reflection, and it incorporates the recognition that the frame of reference or context within which the issue is viewed, could change and affect the conclusion.

A metacognitive stance is taken (i.e. there is critical awareness of the processes of critical thinking in themselves).

The account may recognize that the issue exists in a historical or social context that may be influential on the response to the task. In other words, multiple perspectives are recognized and taken account of.

There may be evidence of creativity in the processes of thinking and reasoning or in the range or nature of evidence used in the critical thinking.

Self-questioning and possibly self-challenge is evident.

There is a recognition of any influences on thinking and judgement such as the timing of the response, emotion, contextual matters, prior experience, personal interest in the outcome, etc.

The conclusion effectively draws together the ideas developed in the text as evidence and makes a judgement in response to the topic introduced or given, recognizing any particular limitations of the judgement.

RESOURCE 8

An exercise in the recognition and understanding of epistemological beliefs for staff or more advanced students

(See Chapters 8 and 11, section 3)

This exercise is based on M. Baxter Magolda (1992) *Knowing and Reasoning in College Students*, San Francisco, Jossey-Bass. It uses fictitious statements from learners but is based on Baxter Magolda's scheme for epistemological development. Most undergraduate students will not have fully reached the stage of contextual thinking at graduation, but it may still be useful to give them the exercise and then to describe the stages of thinking. It is a valuable exercise for staff development. It is best if participants work in groups of around six. The materials required for the exercise are as follows (A, B and C are below).

A – for each participant, a description of the stages of epistemological development (perhaps adapted to the level of the student group).

B/C – materials B and C use the same material, but processed differently. To make 'B' material, photocopy the material below, enlarging it – and cut up the quotations so that each quotation is on a single strip of paper (or better – on card). Discard the headings and introduction. One set of cards or slips of paper is needed for each group.

C – the handout for C is as the text is printed below (B/C) – and one is required for each participant. This is, in effect, the 'solution' to be given after the exercise.

The process for the exercise is as follows. A brief explanation of epistemogical development is given (Chapter 8). It is useful to introduce the exercise as a means of stimulating participants' thinking about how they or their students think about the nature of knowledge. It is worth telling them that when they do the exercise, they are not likely to get all of the quotations in the 'right' places, and that it is a constructed exercise with the aim of helping them to understand an important concept that relates to their learning.

Each participant is given A, and asked to read it for a few minutes.

Each group is then given the sets of cards (B) and the group is asked to classify them under the four stages as identified on A. They will need at least

15 minutes for this process. It is useful if they start by writing the headings for the stages on scraps or yellow sticky notes.

When they have finished (or time is up), the handout C is given, which shows the 'correct' solutions. They will need around 10 minutes to compare their work with the 'solution', then to relate the actual quotations to the stages in handout A.

There should then be time for discussion and thought about the relationship of this material to their observations of the exercise, the theory that it illustrates and their personal experiences of learning.

Material A: The stages of thinking described by Baxter Magolda (1992)

Absolute knowing stage

In this stage knowledge is seen as certain or absolute. It is the least developed stage in Baxter Magolda's scheme. Learners believe that absolute answers exist in all areas of knowledge. When there is uncertainty it is because there is not access to the 'right' answers. Such learners may recognize that opinions can differ between experts but this is differences of detail, opinion or misinformation. Formal learning is seen as a matter of absorption of the knowledge of the experts (e.g. teachers). Learning methods are based on absorbing and remembering. Assessment is simply checking what the learner has 'acquired'.

Transitional knowing stage

There is partial certainty and partial uncertainty. Baxter Magolda describes the transitional knowing stage as one in which there are doubts about the certainty of knowledge – learners accept that there is some uncertainty. Authorities may differ in view because there is uncertainty. Learners see themselves as needing to understand rather than just acquire knowledge so that they may make judgements as to how best to apply it. Teachers are seen as facilitating the understanding and the application of knowledge, and assessment concerns these qualities, and not just acquisition.

continued

Independent knowing stage

Learning is seen as uncertain – everyone has her own beliefs. Independent knowers recognize the uncertainty of knowledge, and feel that everyone has her own opinion or beliefs. This would seem to be an embryonic form of the more sophisticated stage of contextual knowing. The learning processes are changed by this new view because now learners can expect to have an opinion and can begin to think through issues and to express themselves in a valued manner. They also regard their peers as having useful contributions to make. They will expect teachers to support the development of independent views, providing a context for exploration. However, 'In the excitement over independent thinking, the idea of judging some perspectives as better or worse is overlooked' (Baxter Magolda 1992: 55).

Contextual knowing stage

This stage is one in which knowledge is understood to be constructed, but the way in which knowledge is constructed is understood in relation to the consideration of the quality of knowledge claims and the context in which they are made is taken into account. Opinions must now be supported by evidence. The view of the teacher is of a partner in the development of appropriate knowledge.

Materials B/C: Fictitious quotations from 'learners' at different stages of epistemological development

Absolute

Julia: I like clear lectures where the lecturer does not mess around giving us lots of different theories for everything – but just tells us what we need to know and we can get on and learn it.

Emma: I am not sure why we have such a long reading list for this subject. I mean, why does someone not just write a textbook on the subject and then we could learn from the textbook? Lecturers sometimes confuse me, the way they wander around the subject.

Samuel: In our tutorial, it came out that there are differences of opinion about how much different mammals 'plan' their actions. I suppose it is just that people have not done the research yet. There does not seem much point in disagreeing about it when the work has not yet been done.

Mohammed: I do not understand why we have to do this referencing game. It all seems such a chore. I mean it disturbs my writing and I can't flow. Knowledge is knowledge, isn't it? Facts are facts. Why does anyone have to own a fact and have their name put beside it?

Transitional

Janine: I have been a bit confused by the way that the two lecturers I have had in this subject have dealt with the Battle of Samargo. They seem to have different attitudes to it. One said that it came about because of political reasons and the other said that it resulted from an uprising of the poor. I don't know how to handle these different attitudes. I have an examination coming up and I feel I'd better know the right answer – or maybe it is that I have to understand it and that is what matters.

Charlie: Learning in sociology seems hard. I had got good at writing clear lecture notes either from the lecture or from the web. This teacher won't give us notes. She won't even give us straight lectures. We all thought it was a game at first but now we have had a semester of it, I guess I have to quite enjoy the thinking that I am forced to do and I can discuss the ideas better because I have had to think.

Isaac: I thought I came to college to stuff my head with what is known. Now I feel confused because there are lots of things that are not certain. I have to think about what I do with those ideas. College learning is different from what I thought.

Christina: I like subjects where I know where I am, like physics. In English there are different ways of thinking about things. Physics theory is physics theory and that is what you learn. In English it is OK to have different views. You have to understand how the views work.

Independent

Ella: I used to think that everything was so certain – like there was a right answer for everything and what was not right was wrong. Now I have become more aware of people arguing over issues, debating. I suppose it is a matter of coming to your own conclusions and sticking to those.

Kay: I do statistics. It seems at first that statistics is statistics – a kind of truth – but now I see that you can make statistics back up any argument. I suppose it is a matter of deciding what line you are taking and then making the statistics work for you.

Resource 8, *Critical Thinking*, © Jennifer Moon, Routledge 2008.continued

Dale: It is good in seminars now. I see that my mates sometimes have made a different sense of the lectures on politics than me. It's not that one of us is right and the rest not right – but that we have to get good at justifying the way we see it.

Michael: I was asked to critically analyse some theories about delinquency last semester. I wasn't sure exactly what was meant by that. I thought it was probably about discussing each of them and arguing my case for the one I thought to be right.

Contextual

Elke: I like having to work in groups now in social work. It is amazing that we have all developed such different perspectives since we have come back from placement. We are much better at listening to each other. I know that I am all the time trying to understand how each of us justifies our views and listening to others helps me to put together my own thoughts.

Krishna: The tutor I have got now would have driven me mad last year. He just sits there and says, 'OK, what do you think about this theory of coastal erosion?' He goes quiet and we discuss it. Then he will make the odd remark that usually sets us off again. I jot down some notes so that I take everything into consideration when I have to write it all up.

Francesca: I understand better why we have to put down references. The quality of the reference and the way I have used it provides the evidence for the viewpoint that I take and enables others to check the evidence I have used. I used to think referencing was just about showing that I was not plagiarizing.

Darren: When I was reading this chapter, I was thinking 'how does this fit?' and 'why does the author seem so sure about this?' and I was relating it all to my views and I think my views might have changed now. I will have another look at it and decide where I stand.

Resource 8, *Critical Thinking*, © Jennifer Moon, Routledge 2008.

RESOURCE 9

An exercise designed to raise awareness of epistemological beliefs 1

(see Chapters 8 and 11, section 3)

Introduction

There is a fundamental difficulty in helping learners progress from relatively descriptive and non-critical absolutist approaches to writing, towards contextual processing of ideas. It is that while we may wish to explain to them how it is that we might hope that they process knowledge, they may not be at the stage of understanding the nature of the knowledge required for that understanding to take place. They might 'go through the motions' of writing in a sophisticated manner without really understanding what they are doing.

The exercises below have been designed to support learners in their development from absolutist processing of ideas towards more sophisticated stages (using Baxter Magolda's terminology – Baxter Magolda, 1994). This exercise may be used as a means of explicitly introducing the phases of development of understanding of the nature of knowledge (e.g. Baxter Magolda's scheme) or they may be used to demonstrate how the processing of critical thinking can shift from simple description to more sophisticated processing without direct reference to any hierarchy of epistemological beliefs.

Method

This exercise is best run with learners seated and working in small groups. They are introduced to the underpinning ideas – either in terms of epistemological development or the way in which written representation of critical thinking needs to shift from the descriptive into more sophisticated modes. Where the stages of epistemological development are to be made explicit, short descriptions of Baxter Magolda's four stages could be provided as a back-up to the exercise (see Resource 8, materials A). The exercise could be run once before the descriptions are given, and then once again, now with the second scenario (Resource 10), when learners have the descriptions and they can then work on identifying the stages directly.

The participants are given a scenario with three named students involved. The scenario is as follows:

> Three students are in a tutorial. They are asked to write a few paragraphs in response to an issue that is given to them by their tutor.

---

     continued

The topic is capital punishment and the issue to be discussed is: 'What do you think of capital punishment? Should it be used automatically when police, or those whose jobs are to protect the public, are the victims of murder?'.

(To make the responses in the scenario reasonably compatible, the arguments of the students are all in the same direction and the texts are approximately the same length and clearly therefore are not full arguments. Attention should be focused on the quality of the reasoning.)

Copies of the responses of the three students (Selma, Joe and Susan) are supplied to the participants and they are asked, in groups, to decide which is the most sophisticated response to the given argument and which is the least sophisticated response, and then to point out why they have decided on this sequence. It is the verbalization of this reasoning about the quality of critical thinking that is central to this exercise. The participants could be asked to write notes on a flipchart sheet so that their responses can be compared with those of other groups.

A valuable way of extending the value of material like this is to ask learners themselves to develop scenarios to illustrate the progression from absolutist thinking to contextual thinking or the progression from simple descriptive pieces to the more sophisticated argument (if the terminology of epistemological development is not used).

The responses of the students are on the opposite page:

(Least sophisticated is Selma, then Joe, then Susan.)

Selma says: I am asked to consider if capital punishment should be used when people kill police and others who might protect us. I believe that it is always wrong to kill and that means that it is wrong for the murderer to kill, but it is also wrong for the state to kill the murderer. I realize that some people would want to make an exception for the police because they might be more scared of the death penalty than of a long sentence in prison and perhaps would choose not to kill the police. However, if capital punishment is morally wrong then it just is wrong to kill the murderer too and there can be no exceptions. I think that it is wrong because religion tells me it is wrong anyway.

Joe says: It is right that there should be discussions about capital punishment and that people will hold different views on it. I think that capital punishment is wrong, but I realize that my position could be challenged by the argument that those who protect us, like police and security guards, deserve some protection from those who might kill them in the course of their duties. There could be an argument, therefore, just for the use of capital punishment for the killers of this group. However, other things are relevant: killing someone, whether in crime or in carrying out the death penalty, is final, and mistakes have been made. On the whole, I believe that it is much easier not to have exceptions. I can understand why people want the death penalty, but my opinion is that it is wrong.

Susan says: It is a massive decision to take the life of another. There have been many erroneous decisions made and the consequences of making a wrong decision outweigh the value of capital punishment as deterrent. In principle I believe that capital punishment should never be used because it turns the state into a murderer, setting the wrong example to those who, themselves, would murder.

It is important to re-examine my argument when it applies to those who protect us because there could be said to be impelling reasons to use capital punishment as deterrent in these situations. The threat of capital punishment could be seen to provide greater protection to those who risk danger to protect us. I think that is an important point, but my arguments above still convince me that we should not use capital punishment.

                    continued

210

An exercise designed to raise awareness of epistemological beliefs 2

(see Chapters 8 and 11, section 3)

The instructions for this exercise are the same as those for Resource 9. The task is the same and the scenario is similar, with three students being given a topic for written discussion.

In this scenario, the point for discussion is: 'At this stage in the evolution of humans, we should be coming to a point where we do not expect to eat meat'. It is discussed by Martina, Thomas and Mandi – and (to simplify the comparisons) they are all vegetarian.

(Most sophisticated is Mandi, then Thomas, and then, least sophisticated, Martina.)

Mandi: I have always been vegetarian and I feel strongly about it, but it is my choice. From my point of view, my justifications for being vegetarian are strong: for me a mark of what I call 'civilized living' is the avoidance of killing animals. If *I* would not kill an animal to eat it, how can I let someone else do it for me? I also consider that there is good evidence that vegetarian living is healthier. I cannot say, however, that eating meat or not is linked to human evolution. I recognize that, for example, our teeth are still designed for eating some meat and it is more difficult to get proper nutrients from a vegetarian diet. I would say that it is a sign of our civilization and evolution that we have individual choice and can decide on our own patterns of nutrition and live with those who choose other ways.

Martina: I am vegetarian and I believe that eating meat is not right. I have never eaten meat and nor does anyone in my family. Animals are living on this earth with us and they have a right to their lives. Some people say that they are vegetarian when they eat fish but fish is a kind of meat, so they are kidding themselves and others. It is a sign of a lack of evolution of civilization that people eat meat still, so I would agree that at this stage we should not expect to eat meat. I do recognize that it would be difficult to change other people's views on this. I have tried to talk about it with others, so I do not know how this evolution could come about properly.

Thomas: I have always been vegetarian but I have started thinking about why I have these views on the eating of meat that are not in common with the views of most of my friends who eat meat without even questioning it. It is a matter of opinion how you see it and what you do about it and I would say that is what it should be. The argument, however, suggests that those who do eat meat might be or should be (I realize that there is a difference here) on the way to being vegetarian. I do not agree that eating meat or not is linked to being civilized or not or evolving or not. It is just that we now feel we have a right to have an opinion on it.

RESOURCE 11

An exercise designed to raise awareness of epistemological beliefs and their effects on teaching, learning and the relationships between learners and teachers

(see Chapters 8 and 11 section 3)

This is another exercise based on the Baxter Magolda scheme for epistemological development and it is designed for teachers or for advanced students. The exercise can be used either to introduce a discussion about the processes of teaching for new teachers, or to help learners to understand epistemological development. In the exercise there are statements from twelve fictitious students directly about their experiences of learning and four statements from teachers about their teaching. Three student statements and one teacher statement belong to each of the four Baxter Magolda stages (Resource 8, material A). The aim of the exercise is for participants to match the quotations (teaching and learning) to the appropriate stage of epistemological development. To prepare the exercise, the sixteen quotations are copied – preferably onto card – and cut into slips. Participants work in groups and each group will have a set of quotation slips and each individual will need a description of the stages (taken from Resource 8A). The 'answers' in this exercise could be given out orally or printed for each group.

Quotations about learning and teaching

Student – Jan: Good learning for me is when I listen really well in class and get down exactly what the teacher says – she is there to tell us what we need to know, after all. I don't like it when I have to work out what is the best way of explaining something when only one way can be the right one.

Student – Tony: I realize that learning is not just a matter of getting facts down. We need to know about research and there are obviously things that have not been discovered yet. We have to be able to apply knowledge and to cope with situations of uncertainty. That is more than just learning facts.

Student – Frederick: I like to make up my own mind about things and that is how it should be. Sometimes the ideas come from teachers, other times from other sources. When things are uncertain or not clearly agreed, I have to be clear what I think.

Student – Mette: There are lots of things that are uncertain. To learn and make knowledge is to put ideas together, to make sense of them and to be able to say they make sense, knowing that they might make different sense to another person.

Student – Andres: We have to be objective – to know the facts about a matter. We put them down and make sure that we do not colour them with our biases.

Student – Sam: We do not know everything and sometimes different people hold different views about a theory or idea. We have to learn to judge which theory is right so we have to learn to think. Being objective is a way of avoiding personal bias and finding the true answer.

Student – Elke: There is lots of uncertainty. Knowing facts only takes us so far and we have to learn to take a stand based on what we know and an understanding of objectivity.

Student – Mike: Knowledge is basically subjective since we come to it by relating new ideas to what we know already. We have to seek to be as objective as we can be in our judgements by recognizing, and where possible taking account of, subjective influences.

Student – Sue: In biology, we are given lecture notes on exactly what we have to know for the test. That is what I call good education – clear and to the point – and no more than what we need to know.

Student – Joanne: We were given several theories in chemistry to explain a particular phenomenon. Our tutor did not make it quite clear which was most right – I guess that he wants us to think.

Student – Ed: In our politics seminar we argued about the position of Israel in the Middle East conflict. It felt good to be holding my own. Nothing that any of the others said made me waver at all from what I think. I cannot start to see how the others got to how they think.

Student – Hugo: In theology we listened to interviews with prominent theologians arguing for the existence of God. I was open to persuasion, almost willing them to give me an understanding of how they hold their faiths. My mind was not changed, though now I want to know more of what they all mean by 'faith'.

Teacher – Tom: As a teacher, my duty is to give them what I think that they need to learn. We go through the syllabus systematically and I make the material as easy as possible for learning.

Teacher – Helen: I cover the syllabus, but I try to get learners to think as they will have to cope on their own, applying ideas and sorting out right and wrong for themselves.

                    continued

214

Teacher – Leo: I help the learners to engage in their own thinking. They need to read around a topic so they can develop their own views. I keep challenging them to nurture their development and expect them to come back at me.

Teacher – Andrew: We are all in this game of learning and developing knowledge. I facilitate the knowledge making process, but recognize that sometimes my understanding is changed by contact with their ideas.

'Answers'

These students and teachers are grouped in the following manner:

Absolute views of knowledge:
Jan, Sue, Andres and Tom (teacher).

Transitional views of knowledge:
Tony, Joanne, Sam and Helen (teacher).

Independent views of knowledge:
Frederick, Elke, Ed and Leo (teacher).

Contextual views of knowledge:
Mette, Hugo, Mike and Andrew (teacher).

Resource 11, *Critical Thinking*, © Jennifer Moon, Routledge 2008.

RESOURCE 12

Critical review or analysis of an article

(see Chapter 11, section 3)

This material is designed either for use by learners undertaking review, or by tutors who want to guide the reviewing work of their students. It does not cover the issue of the critique of the actual methodology of research.

Writing a critical analysis or review of another's argument is a complex activity which involves a number of proficiencies both in the ability to communicate and understand text – to read and to write – and in the ability to demonstrate understanding of the process of critical thinking. This description of critical analysis could be used alongside the Framework for Critical Thinking and its Representations (Resource 7) and examples of articles for review. It goes through the features of a review process considering the ways in which elements of a text might raise issues that warrant critical comment or concern. The assumption here is that the piece to be reviewed is an academic article. The same ideas can be applied – sometimes with a change of vocabulary – to the review of 'everyday' written material like a newspaper article that puts forward a particular case, or the review of a film or of marketing material, in which case the level of interest and enjoyment may warrant comment. We use the terms 'reviewer' for the person undertaking the review and 'author' for the author or authors of the article.

Purpose of the review and recognition of the audience

A review is written for a purpose. The purpose may be that the reviewer needs the material for the development of her own arguments in research, for writing a book or other material, to keep up to date, for interest and so on. If the article is read for a research purpose, it may matter whether it is in the early stages of the work, when the purpose may be part of 'getting to know the field' – or later. If it is later on, then the purpose may be more specific – perhaps as supporting or opposing evidence in the arguments being made. The purpose of the review may also be simply to communicate the information to others (as in reviews in journals) or to indicate the quality of an article to the editor of a journal who may or may not want to publish the article. **The purpose of the review should guide every process in the reviewing.**

216

Sometimes defining 'purpose' sufficiently clearly is a problem – particularly when the requirement is to 'get to know the field'. There is then little guidance as to what is important. It is usually students who are in this anomalous position – for example when trying to decide on a topic for research. Once one is working as a 'researcher', the review process is only likely to start when there is actually a focus – an 'idea in mind'.

Closely linked with purpose is consideration of the audience for the review. The audience may be the reviewer herself or – it may be the readership of a journal, a research funder, or colleagues at a research seminar. The perception of the needs or purposes of the audience is likely to shape the writer's purpose (above) and the manner in which the review is presented.

A deep critical thinker will think metacognitively too. She should look into her approach to the task beyond the overt purposes of the review. She might examine her feelings about this article. Is she in any way seeking to promote or downplay the value of the work – or is she neutral? Supposing the author of the article has reached and supported a theoretical conclusion towards which the reviewer is also working – or promotes an opposing view – this could influence the reviewer's feelings about her review.

We look later at the purpose of the author.

Explicit features of a text to be taken into consideration

The title of the paper may or may not illuminate the content of the paper. Titles can often misdirect or they may be unclear. **Sections, headings and subheadings** may or may not guide the reader appropriately through the article. Research articles usually start with an **abstract**, which is often written as something of an afterthought and which may or may not appropriately indicate the content. This may or may not matter for the purpose of the reviewer.

The **content of an article** may be theoretical or it may describe a research process. It will usually start with context-setting and end with a return to a reconsideration of that context that is modified in accordance with the developed argument or research outcomes. Often the latter section (which might often be 'implications') is somewhat lacking, the focus being on the research and not its broader implications. Sometimes this inadequacy in the pattern of writing reduces the direct value of written-up research.

A **reference list** is another written feature of an article under review. Obviously what is important is not just what references have been utilized by the author, but how their content has been incorporated. However, the perusal of a reference list is often helpful in the initial phase of reviewing an article because it should indicate the field of theory on which the article is based. It may also raise some quality issues. For example, it should be sufficiently long; there should not be too many secondary citations; it should contain references to work that is of key importance to the field of study. The reference list may often be one of the earliest features of an article to consider. It contains much information.

(We have said above that consideration of the methodology and conduct of any research or theoretical argument is beyond the scope of this book – but is likely to be relevant.)

Implicit features of an article that should be considered by a critical reviewer

There is often a hierarchy of status among the journals in which articles are published – so the **location of the publication** says something of its nature. An assumption that might justifiably be made by a reviewer, is that an article from a high-status journal has been subjected to severe peer review, though even that can be worthy of question.

The author will have had a **purpose in communicating the article**. It is inevitable that her purpose will have shaped and skewed her authoring and this should be considered by the reviewer. The purpose of the author may feature in **assumptions** that she has made in the writing. For example, she may have based new thinking on insufficiently questioned theory or 'findings'. Assumptions may be made in interpretation of data or generalizations from data. Sometimes **vocabulary** is inadequate or misused or hides assumptions, and this can distort the manner in which work is reported. For example, the use of the word 'learning' when it is teaching to which reference is made, can distort the whole focus of educational writing. Our vocabulary is not always 'up to' the adequate conveyance of new ideas. Assumptions are also carried in the **overall style of writing** of an article. The style may carry hidden persuasion or reveal a bias on the part of the author that is not justified by her stated purpose. The work may be based on **generalizations** that are too great.

The **theoretical basis** of the article is often a matter of choice for the author (albeit sometimes even a career choice of following one rather than another theoretical orientation – e.g. behaviourism versus cognitive psychology). There may be other theories that could equally have provided a basis for the work (including, sometimes, those from other disciplines). With other theoretical frameworks, the outcome of research could look different.

There is much **reasoning** in the writing of an article – for example with regard to the links between the theoretical underpinnings and the methods chosen; between the introductory section and the research; in the way in

218

which the conclusions are derived from data; and in the discussing of the wider implications of the article. The reviewer needs to look carefully at the reasoning processes – with particular concern for any 'leaps', or **unevidenced assertions**. It is right that ideas are sometimes shifted out of their context and applied to other issues. This furthers knowledge, but the **language should be careful and appropriately tentative**.

Broader considerations

It may or may not be relevant to consider whether the article is well written (does it communicate well?) to consider whether it is enjoyable to read, interesting, stimulating, well timed and other such issues.

RESOURCE 13

Progression in critical thinking and its representation in writing in undergraduate education – a tentative guide for the purposes of pedagogy

(see Chapters 8 and 11 section 3)

This represents a tentative set of descriptors for the progressively increasing capacity of students for critical thinking and its representation in writing. It is based on the literature of progression in learning, critical thinking, and particularly on work on epistemological development. In terms of that work, the progression covers the transition from absolutist thinking towards, but not as far as, contextual thinking (a stage that would normally be fully reached after the first degree) (Baxter Magolda, 1992). The progression is a continuum and it is not assumed that students will shift along it in an even manner. Their capacity for critical thinking and its representation in writing will interact with the complexity of the material with which they are dealing. The guide is to be regarded as tentative.

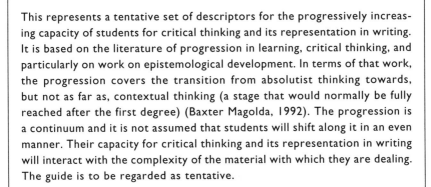

Position in terms of epistemological beliefs	Pedagogical implications
Students at the beginning of undergraduate education are likely to be at the beginning of the shift from absolutist /dualistic thinking	
They are often somewhat daunted by the 'expert culture' of higher education and this may knock back their confidence in self-expression (voice) and in their understanding of knowledge. They are beginning to understand that knowledge is not an accumulation of facts but are bemused by uncertainty and the idea of theory unless these concepts are	**The nature of teaching** at this stage is often somewhat fact-driven. It is helpful for future development of critical thinking if students are set tasks to solve alone or in groups (in some form of problem-based learning). The general principle is that students should be just beyond their 'comfort zone' in terms of thinking. **General tasks of learning and thinking.** Learners should: • be given plenty of examples of what is expected of them in critical thinking (in all of the situations below) • be helped to become aware that knowledge is not made up of 'facts', that

continued

explained regularly. They tend to start by seeing teachers as experts who will pass them the knowledge that they need.	uncertainty exists and that judgements need to be made
	• be exposed to the idea of critical thinking as fundamental to their progress in HE, the concepts of evidence, evaluation, conclusions or judgements. This should be illustrated in everyday material
	• be given tasks in which they deal with making judgements in everyday situations to illustrate critical thinking
	• be exposed to the idea that teachers/ experts are also learners, and can 'get it wrong'
	• meet experts in their discipline in the process of disagreeing, and there should be discussion of this in terms of the content and in terms of the idea of disagreement between experts
	• be involved in discussion about the idea of 'a theory', and the idea that several theories can legitimately be held about the same thing (illustration from own discipline – but done simply)
	• be exposed to uncertainty (e.g. as illustrated in everyday life and in the research fields of their discipline)
	• be engaged in tasks in which they have to seek for evidence to justify a claim in everyday life
	• be given some tasks in which they make their own judgements and have a chance to express their own voices about an issue – probably an everyday example
	• be introduced to the idea of developing conceptions of knowledge in a manner well illustrated by everyday issues in thinking
	• be exposed to general discussions about how knowledge is 'produced' – publication, media distortion, expert agreement, common usage, etc.

Writing – there should be practice in:

- being precise and clear
- being able to draw a conclusion from the provision of written evidence
- being able to summarize the main points of an argument – such as introduction of the issue, the evidence, the reasoning about evidence and the conclusion and/or judgement made
- referencing. Students need to understand referencing as an acknowledgement of other people's work

During the middle period of an undergraduate programme, learners need to be supported in shifting towards a stage of contextual/relativistic thinking

This is a time when there can be considerable differences in a classroom with some learners still at an absolutist stage and some having moved beyond. In general, the discussion of the nature of critical thinking needs to be continued in an explicit manner.

Teaching may still be fact-driven, and yet we need students to be beginning to realize that teachers have a viewpoint on issues and may not agree with each other. When alternative theories are introduced there is a tendency to present them as 'something that you need to know' (i.e. as a 'super-fact') rather than as a real uncertainty. This is a kind of absolutist teaching of contextual ideas.

General tasks in learning and thinking.
Learners should:

- be given examples within their discipline of good-quality critical thinking and attempted critical thinking where there is inadequate reasoning, or assumptions are made, etc.
- be shown how assumptions in research in their discipline have led to distorted judgements/conclusions
- be exposed to situations in their discipline where experts clearly disagree
- be shown how knowledge has been constructed within their discipline (e.g. by following the history of one line of research thinking)

	• be given case studies or sample ideas from real issues in their discipline where, with guidance, they assess evidence and make a judgement • be exposed to teaching/tutorial situations in which issues of real uncertainty in their discipline are discussed • be required to make judgements that have direct significance for themselves or others (e.g. this could be in a work placement or work experience) • experience responsibility for significant actions – in or out of class • be introduced to the manner in which knowledge is produced and agreed in their discipline • be involved in well-illustrated discussion about how knowledge has come to be produced in their discipline (including the notion of peer review) – and sources of distortion. **Writing – there should be practice in:** • improving clarity and precision • in the drawing of effective conclusions • the demonstation of critical thinking in written form, using straightforward material from their discipline (probably with given or guided seeking of evidence) • demonstration of critical thinking in writing about an everyday issue in which there is expression of the learner's own voice, and encouragement in creativity in seeking one's own evidence • using referencing as a matter of course.

The further shift: this is the final stage of undergraduate education

Few students will be consistently recognizing and working with a contextual view of	**The teaching** of final-year undergraduate students can be much more 'research-based', dealing with uncertain situations, and areas of disagreement in the discipline. They

Resource 13, *Critical Thinking*, © Jennifer Moon, Routledge 2008.

knowledge, but the challenges in their learning should be of this nature. This is a time when learners may tend to think that knowledge is about reaching and holding an opinion – without taking the context fully into account.	should be working within the main body of knowledge of their discipline, and exposed to 'the cutting edge', but not expected to work at that level
	General tasks of teaching and learning. Learners should: • display competent critical thinking in the relatively familiar areas of their discipline (i.e. not likely to be 'cutting edge') • have their opinions challenged whether in the written or spoken word. Challenge should be by peers or teachers • be able to recognize and challenge assumptions • question – their general attitude towards the discipline should be one of questioning • be expected to argue a case in their discipline • be exposed to situations in which they make judgements for which they have to take responsibility. This may be in a placement or work experience situation. **Writing tasks:** Learners should be able to judge the competence of their own writing and that of others (peers). There is usually some kind of undergraduate dissertation, which contains a literature review and a small piece of research. This is an opportunity for learners to demonstrate critical thinking in a literature review, skills of evaluation and the making of discipline-related judgements, also the writing of a conclusion to their own work.

Resource 13, *Critical Thinking*, © Jennifer Moon, Routledge 2008.   continued

224

Learners should now understand referencing as a matter not only of properly acknowledging sources, but also as a means of judging the quality of a piece of work (how many and which references are used, how have they been used, etc.).

General statement: The discussion of the nature of knowledge should be revisited. By showing learners how their views of knowledge have changed over their undergraduate education, it is possible to make ideas around the notion of the contextual knowing stage explicit, and to help learners to make sense of their 'learning journey'.

References

Abouserie, R. (1995) 'Self esteem and achievement motivation as determinants of students' approaches to studying', *Studies of Higher Education*, 20 (1), 19–26

Adams, R., Dominelli, L. and Payne, M. (2002) *Critical Practice in Social Work*, London, Palgrave

Alberti, R. and Emmons, M. (1970) *Your Perfect Right*, San Luis, Calif., Impact Publishers

Alexander, P. and Dochy, F. (1995) 'Conceptions of knowledge and beliefs: a comparison across varying cultural and educational communities', *American Educational Research Journal*, 32 (2), 413–442

Andrews, R. (1997) 'Learning to argue', in M. Riddle (ed.), *The Quality of Argument*, School of Lifelong Learning and Education, University of Middlesex, pp. 9–16

Angelo, T. (1995) 'Classroom assessment for critical thinking', *Teaching of Psychology*, 22 (1), 6–7

Astin, W., Vogelgesang, L., Ikeda, E. and Yee, J. (2000) 'How service learning affects students', paper from Higher Education Research Institute, University of California at Los Angeles, January

Augstein, S. and Thomas, L. (1973) *Developing Your Own Reading*, Bletchley, Open University Press

Back, K. and Back, K. (1982) *Assertiveness at Work*, London, McGraw-Hill

Bailin, S., Case, R., Coombs, J. and Daniels, L. (1999a) 'Common misconceptions of critical thinking', *Journal of Curriculum Studies*, 31 (3), 269–283

Bailin, S., Case, R., Coombs, J. and Daniels, L. (1999b) 'Conceptualising critical thinking', *Journal of Curriculum Studies*, 31 (3), 285–302

Barnett, R. (1997) *Higher Education: a critical business*, Milton Keynes, SRHE and Open University Press

Barnett, R. (2006) 'Willing to learn: being a student in an age of uncertainty', paper given at iPED (Inquiring Pedagogies Research Network) Conference, University of Coventry, September

Barnett, R. and Coate, K. (2005) *Engaging the Curriculum in Higher Education*, Buckingham, SRHE and Open University Press

Baron, J. and Sternberg, R. (1987) *Teaching Thinking Skills*, New York, W. H. Freeman

Barrell, J. (1995) 'Teaching for thoughtfulness', *www.ncrel.org/sdrs/areas/rpl_esys/thinking.htm*

Baxter Magolda, M. (1992) *Knowing and Reasoning in College Students; gender-related patterns in students' intellectual development*, San Francisco, Jossey-Bass

Baxter Magolda, M. (1994) 'Post college experiences and epistemology', *Review of Higher Education*, 18 (1), 25–44

Baxter Magolda, M. (1996) 'Epistemological development in graduate and professional education', *Review of Higher Education*, 19 (3), 283–304

Baxter Magolda, M. (1999) *Creating Contexts for Learning and Self-authorship*, San Francisco, Jossey-Bass

Baxter Magolda, M. (2001) *Making their Own Way*, Sterling, Va., Stylus

Baxter Magolda, M. and King, P. (2004) *Learning Partnerships*, Sterling, Va., Stylus

Beard, C. and Wilson, J. (2002) *The Power of Experiential Learning*, Kogan Page, London

Belenky, M., Clinchy, B., Goldberger, R. and Tarule, J. (1986) *Women's Ways of Knowing*, New York, Basic Books

Bell, J. (1995) *Evaluating Psychological Information*, Boston, Allyn and Bacon

Bendixen, L. and Rule, D. (2004) 'An integrative approach to personal epistemology: a guiding model', *Educational Psychologist*, 39 (1), 69–80

Bensley, A. and Haynes, C. (1995) 'The acquisition of general purpose strategic knowledge for argumentation', *The Teaching of Psychology*, 22 (1), 41–46

Bernstein, D. (1995) 'A negotiation model for teaching critical thinking', *Teaching of Psychology*, 22 (1), 22–24

Blom Kemdal, A. and Montgomery, H. (1997) 'Perspectives and emotions in personal decision-making', in R. Raynard, R. Crozier and O. Svenson, *Decision-making*, London, Routledge, pp. 72–89

Bloom, B. (1956) *A Taxonomy of Educational Objectives*, New York, Longmans Green

Bonnett, A. (2001) *How to Argue*, Harlow, Essex, Prentice Hall

Bowell, T. and Kemp, G. (2002) *Critical Thinking: a concise guide*, London, Routledge

Bradford University (n.d.) Mission information, www.brad.ac.uk/admin/conted/tls/aim1.html

Brennan, J. and Osbourne, M. (2005) 'The organizational mediation of university learning', The Social and Organizational Mediation of University Learning Working Paper 2, York, Higher Education Academy

Brockbank, A. and McGill, I. (1998) *Facilitating Reflective Learning in Higher Education*, Milton Keynes, SRHE and Open University Press

Brookfield, S. (1987) *Developing Critical Thinking*, Milton Keynes, SRHE and Open University Press

Brookfield, S. (1990) 'Using critical incidents to explore learner's assumptions', in J. Mezirow, *Fostering Critical Reflection in Adulthood*, San Francisco, Jossey-Bass, pp. 177–193

Brookfield, S. (1998) 'Critical thinking techniques', in M. Galbraith, *Adult Learning Methods*, Malabar, Fla, Kreiger Publishing, pp. 317–336

Brown, K. and Rutter, L. (2006) *Critical Thinking for Social Work*, Exeter, Learning Matters Ltd

Brown, S. and Dove, P. (1999) 'Peer and self assessment', Birmingham, Standing Conference on Educational Development (SCED)

Brownlee, J. (2001) 'Epistemological beliefs in pre-service teacher education students', *Higher Education Research and Development*, 20 (3), 281–291

Bruce, C. (1994) 'Research students' early experiences of the dissertation literature review', *Studies in Higher Education*, 19 (2), 217–229

Cannon, D. (2002) 'Learning to fail; learning to recover', in M. Peelo and T. Wareham, *Failing Students in Higher Education*, Buckingham, SRHE and Open University Press, pp. 73–84

Capossela, T. (1993a) *The Critical Writing Workshop*, Portsmouth, NH, Boynton/Cook

Capossela, T. (1993b) 'Using William Perry's scheme to encourage critical writing', in

T. Capossela (ed.), *The Critical Writing Workshop*, Portmouth, NH, Boynton Cook, pp. 36–70

Carey, S. and Smith, C. (1999) 'On understanding the nature of scientific knowledge', in R. McCormick and C. Praechter, *Learning and Knowledge*, London, Paul Chapman Publishing and Open University Press

Chanock, K. (2000) 'Comment on essays: do students understand what tutors write?', *Teaching in Higher Education*, 5 (1), 95–105

Claxton, G. (2000) *The Intuitive Practitioner*, Milton Keynes, Open University Press

Clegg, S. and Bradley, S. (2006) 'The implementation of progress files in higher education; reflection as national policy', *Higher Education*, 51, 465–486

Coles, M. and Robinson, W. (1991) 'Teaching thinking. What is it? Is it possible?' in M. Coles and W. Robinson, *Teaching Thinking*, Bristol, Bristol Classical Press, pp. 1–23

Cooper, J. (1995) 'Cooperative learning and critical thinking', *Teaching of Psychology*, 22 (1), 7–8

Cottrell, S. (1999) *The Study Skills Handbook*, Basingstoke, Macmillan

Cottrell, S. (2005) *Critical Thinking Skills*, Basingstoke, Palgrave Macmillan

Csikszentmihalyi, M. (1990) *Flow: the psychology of optimum experience*, New York, Harper and Row

Damasio, A. (2000) *The Feeling of What Happens – Body, Emotion and the Making of Consciousness*, London, Virago

Davies, P. (2003) *Increasing Confidence*, London, Dorling Kindersley

de Bono, E. (1976) *Teaching Thinking*, Harmondsworth, Penguin

de Bono, E. (1982) *de Bono's Thinking Course*, London, BBC

de Bono, E. (1983) *Practical Thinking*, Harmondsworth, Penguin

Dewey, J. (1933) *How We Think*, Boston, Mass, D. C. Heath and Co.

Dickson, A. (1992) *A Woman in Your Own Right*, London, Quartet Books

Donaldson, M. (1992) *Human Minds: an exploration*, Harmondsworth, Penguin

Dublin Descriptors (2004) 'Dublin qualification descriptors', *www.unibuc.ro/uploads35714/Dublin_descriptors_2004* (accessed June 2006)

Duignan, J. (2003) 'Placement and adding value to the academic performance of undergraduates: reconfiguring the architecture – an empirical investigation', *Journal of Vocational Education and Training*, 55 (3), 335–345

Durkin, K. (2004) 'Adapting to Western norms of academic argumentation and debate: the critical learning journey of East Asian students', Thesis submitted for PhD, Bournemouth University

Dweck, C. (1999) *Self Theories: their role in motivation, personality and development*, Philadelphia, Psychology Press

Eisenschitz, A. (2000) 'Innocent concepts? A paradigmatic approach to argument', in S. Mitchell and R. Andrews, *Learning to Argue in Higher Education*, Portsmouth, NH, Boynton / Cook, pp. 15–25

Eisner, E. (1991) 'Forms of understanding and the future of education', *Educational Researcher*, 22, 5–11

Emmet, E. (1964) *Learning to Philosophise*, Harmondsworth, Penguin

Ennis, R. (1987) 'A taxonomy of critical thinking dispositions and abilities', in J. Baron and R. Sternberg, *Teaching Thinking Skills*, New York, W. H. Freeman, 9–26

Ennis, R. (1990) 'The extent to which critical thinking is subject-specific: further clarification', *Educational Researcher*, 19 (4), 13–16

Ennis, R. (1996) *Critical Thinking*, Upper Saddle River, NJ, Prentice-Hall

Fisher, A. (2001) *Critical Thinking, an introduction*, Cambridge, Cambridge University Press

Fisher, K. (2003) 'Demystifying critical reflection: defining criteria for assessment', *Higher Education Research and Development*, 22 (3), 313–324

Flew, A. (1975) *Thinking about Thinking*, Glasgow, Fontana Collins

Ford, P., Johnston, B., Brumfit, C., Mitchell, R. and Myles, F. (2005) 'Practice learning and the development of students as critical practitioners – some findings from research', *Social Work Education*, 24 (4), 391–407

Furedi, F. (2005) 'I refuse to hand it to students on a plate', *Times Higher Educational Supplement*, 25 March

Garnham, A. and Oakhill, J. (1994) *Thinking and Reasoning*, Oxford, Blackwell

George, J. and Cowan, J. (1999) *A Handbook of Techniques for Formative Evaluation*, London, Routledge Falmer

Gibbs, L. and Gambrill, E. (1999) *Critical Thinking for Social Workers*, London, Sage

Gillen, T. (1992) *Assertiveness for Managers*, Aldershot, Hants, Gower

Gilligan, C. (1998) *In a Different Voice*, Cambridge, Mass., Harvard University Press

Giltrow, J. (2000) 'Argument: a term in talk about student writing', in S. Mitchell and R. Andrews, *Learning to Argue in Higher Education*, Portsmouth, NH, Boynton/Cook

Gleaves, A. and Walker, C. (2006) 'How does digital caring differ from physical caring?', Paper presented at Scholarship of Teaching and Learning Conference, London, May

Gold, J., Holman, D. and Thorpe, R. (2002) 'The role of argument analysis and story telling in facilitating critical thinking', *Management Learning*, 3 (3), 371–388

Goleman, D. (1995) *Emotional Intelligence*, New York, Bantam

Goleman, D. (1998) *Working with Emotional Intelligence*, London, Bloomsbury

Halonen, J. (1995) 'Demystifying critical thinking', *Teaching of Psychology*, 22 (1), 75–81

Hannay, R. (2006) 'Working at problems: placing work at the centre of media practice education', paper presented at Coventry IPED conference, 11–12 September, University of Coventry

Harri-Augstein, E. and Thomas, L. (1991) *Learning Conversations - the Self Organized Learning Way to Personal and Organizational Growth*, London, Routledge and Kegan Paul

Hart, M. (1990) 'Liberation through consciousness raising', in J. Mezirow and associates, *Fostering Critical Reflection in Adulthood*, San Francisco, Jossey-Bass

Hastie, R. and Davies, R. (2001) *Rational Choice in an Uncertain World*, London, Sage

Hatton, N. and Smith, D. (1995) 'Reflection in teacher education – towards definition and implementation', *Teaching and Teacher Education*, 11 (1), 33–49

Hettich, P. (1997) 'Epistemological approaches to cognitive development in college students', in P. Sutherland, *Adult Learning: a reader*, London, Kogan Page

Hines, R. (1988) 'Financial accounting: in communicating reality, we construct reality', *Accounting Organizations and Society*, 13 (3), 251–261

Hinett, K. (2002) 'Assessing failure or failure to assess?', in M. Peelo and T. Wareham, *Failing Students in Higher Education*, Buckingham, SRHE and Open University Press, pp. 172–183

Hinton, A. (2006) 'Effective communication and assertiveness: a guide for students', Oxford Brookes University, *www.brookes.ac.uk/student/services/health/assertiveness/html*

Hofer, B. (2004) 'Introduction: paradigmatic approaches to personal epistemology', *Educational Psychologist*, 39 (1), 1–3

Hofer, B. and Pintrich, P. (1997) 'The development of epistemological theories: beliefs about knowledge and knowing and their relation to learning', *Review of Educational Research*, 67 (1), 88–140

International Baccalaureate (2005) Website for International Baccalaureate in relation to theory of knowledge, *www.ibo.org/diploma/curriculum/core/knowledge* (accessed June 2006)

Jackson, B. (1997) 'Argument and learner autonomy', in M. Riddle, *The Quality of Argument*, School of Lifelong Learning and Education, University of Middlesex, pp. 17–24

Jacobs, A. (2000) 'From a student', in S. Mitchell and R. Andrews, *Learning to Argue*, Portsmouth, NH, Boynton/Cook Heinemann

Janis, I. (1982) *Groupthink*, Boston, Houghton Mifflin

Kaasboll, J. (1998) 'Teaching critical thinking and problem defining skills', *Education and Information Technologies*, 3, 101–117

Keeley, S. and Shemberg, K. (1995) 'Coping with student resistance to critical thinking', *College Teaching*, 43 (4), 140–147

Kegan, R. (1994) *The Mental Demands of Modern Life*, Cambridge, Mass., Harvard University Press

Kember, D. (2001) 'Beliefs about knowledge and the process of teaching and learning as a factor in adjusting to study in higher education', *Studies in Higher Education*, 26, 205–221

King, P. and Kitchener, K. (1994) *Developing Reflective Judgment*, San Francisco, Jossey-Bass

Kiniry, M. and Rose, M. (1993) *Critical Strategies for Academic Thinking and Writing*, Boston, Bedford books of St Martin's Press

Kinney, J. (1980) 'Why bother? The importance of critical thinking', in R. E. Young, *Fostering Critical Thinking, New Directions for Teaching and Learning*, San Francisco, Jossey-Bass, pp. 1–10

Kitchener, K., Lynch, C., Fischer, K. and Wood, P. (1993) 'Developmental range of reflective judgement; the effect of contextual support and practice on developmental stage', *Developmental Psychology*, 29 (5), 893–908

Kloss, R. (1994) 'Helping students through the Perry scheme of intellectual development', *College Teaching*, 42 (4), 151–159

Kneale, P. (2003) *Study Skills for Geography Students*, London, Hodder

Knight, P. and Yorke, M. (2002) 'Employability through the curriculum', *Tertiary Education and Management*, 8, 261–276

Kuhn, D. (1999) 'A developmental model of critical thinking', *Educational Researcher*, 28 (2), 16–26

Kuhn, D. and Udell, W. (2001) 'The path to wisdom', *Educational Psychologist*, 36 (4), 261–264

Laming, D. (2004) *Human Judgment*, London, Thomson

Lea, M. and Stierer, B. (eds) (2000) *Student Writing in Higher Education*, Buckingham, SRHE and Open University Press

Lillis, T. (2001) *Student Writing*, London, Routledge

Lindenfield, G. (1986) *Assert Yourself*, Wellingborough, Northants, Thorsons

Lipman, M. (1991) *Thinking in Education*, New York, Cambridge University Press

Lonka, K. and Lindblom-Ylanne, S. (1996) 'Epistemologies, conceptions of learning and study practices in medicine and psychology', *Higher Education*, 31, 5–24

Lucas, U. and Tan, P. (2006) 'Developing a reflective capacity: the role of personal epistemologies within undergraduate education', paper presented at 14th international Student Learning Symposium, University of Bath, 4–6 September

McDade, S. (1995) 'Case study pedagogy to advance critical thinking', *Teaching of Psychology*, 22 (1), 9–11

McDrury, J. and Alterio, M. (2003) *Learning through Storytelling*, London, Routledge Falmer

McKay, J. and Kember, D. (1997) 'Spoonfeeding leads to regurgitation: a better diet can result in more digestible learning outcomes', *Higher Education Research and Development*, 16 (1), 55–67

Marshall, L. and Rowland, F. (1998) *A Guide to Learning Independently*, Buckingham, Open University Press

Marton, F. and Booth, S. (1997) *Learning and Awareness*, Hillsdale, NJ, Lawrence Erlbaum Associates

Marton, F., Hounsell, D. and Entwistle, N. (1997) *The Experience of Learning*, Edinburgh, Scottish Universities Press

Maudsley, G. and Striven, J. (2000) 'Promoting professional knowledge, experiential learning and critical thinking for medical students', *Medical Education*, 34, 535–544

Meyer J. and Land, R. (2003) 'Threshold concepts and troublesome knowledge', enhancing teaching-learning environments in undergraduate courses project, Occasional Report 4, University of Edinburgh

Meyers, C. (1986) *Teaching Students to Think Critically*, San Francisco, Jossey-Bass

Mingers, J. (2000) 'What is it to be critical? Teaching a critical approach to management', *Management Learning*, 31 (2), 219–238

Mitchell, S. (1997) 'Quality in argument: why we should spell out the ground rules', in M. Riddle, *The Quality of Argument*, School of Lifelong Learning and Education, University of Middlesex, pp. 25–30

Mitchell, S. (2002) Thinking Writing website, *www.thinkingwriting.qmul.ac.uk* (accessed December 2006)

Mitchell, S. and Andrews, R. (eds) (2000) *Learning to Argue in Higher Education*, Portsmouth, NH, Boynton/Cook Heinemann

Mitchell, S. and Riddle, M. (2000) *Improving the Quality of Argument in Higher Education*, Final Report, Department of Lifelong Learning and Education, Middlesex University

Moon, J. (1975) 'Some thoughts on study skills', *Reading*, 10 (3), 24–34

Moon, J. (1993) 'What do you expect at my age?', a feasibility study of assertiveness training for older adults, dissertation presented in part fulfilment for MSc in Health Promotion, University of Wales College of Medicine, Cardiff

Moon, J. (1999) *Reflection in Learning and Professional Development*, London, Routledge Falmer

Moon, J. (2001) *Short Courses and Workshops: improving the impact of learning and professional development*, London, Routledge Falmer

Moon, J. (2002) *The Module and Programme Development Handbook* London, Routledge Falmer

Moon, J. (2004) *A Handbook of Reflective and Experiential Learning*, London, Routledge Falmer

Moon, J. (2005a) 'Progression in higher education: a study of learning as represented in level descriptors', in P. Hartley, A. Woods and M. Pill (eds), *Enhancing Teaching in Higher Education*, London, Routledge Falmer

Moon, J. (2005b) 'Coming from behind: an investigation of learning issues in the process of widening participation in higher education'. Final Report (March 2005) ESCalate website, *www.ESCalate.ac.uk/index.cfm?action=grants.completed* (accessed December 2006)

Moon, J. (2005c) 'We seek it here . . . a new perspective on the elusive activity of critical thinking: a theoretical and practical approach', Higher Education Academy Education Subject Centre – ESCalate, University of Bristol and *www.ESCalate.ac.uk* and search for title or author (accessed June 2006)

Moon, J. (2006) *Learning Journals: a handbook for reflective practice and professional development*, 2nd edn, London, Routledge Falmer

Morgan, A. (1995) *Improving Your Students' Learning*, London, Kogan Page

Morgan, N. and Saxon, S. (1991) *Teaching, Questioning and Learning*, London, Routlege

Mortiboys, A. (2005) *Teaching with Emotional Intelligence*, London, Routledge

Mumm, A. and Kersting, R. (1997) 'Teaching critical thinking in social work', *Journal of Social Work Education*, 33 (1), 75–84

Murdoch, I. (1954) *Under the Net*, Harmondsworth, Penguin

Nelson-Jones, R. (1994) *Thinking Skills*, London, Cassell

Nickerson, R. (1987) 'Why teaching thinking?', in J. Baron and R. Sternberg, *Teaching Thinking Skills*, New York, F. W. Freeman, pp. 27–41

Odum, E. (1968) *Ecology*, New York, Holt, Rhinehart and Winston

Palmer, B. and Marra, R. (2004) 'College student epistemological perspectives across knowledge domains: a proposed grounded theory', *Higher Education*, 47, 311–335

Paul, R. (1987) 'Dialogical thinking – critical thought essential to the acquisition of rational knowledge and passions', in J. Baron and R. Sternberg, *Teaching Thinking Skills*, New York, F. W. Freeman, pp. 127–148

Paul, R. and Elder, L. (n.d.) Website *www.criticalthinking.org*

Paul, R. and Elder, L. (2004) *The Miniature Guide to Critical Thinking*, Foundation for Critical Thinking, obtainable from *www.criticalthinking.org*

Paul, R., Elder, L. and Bartell, T. (n.d.) 'Study of 38 public universities and 28 private universities to determine faculty emphasis on critical thinking in instruction', *www.criticalthinking.org/aboutCT/Research.shtml* (accessed June 2006)

Paulsen, M. and Wells, C. (1998) 'Domain differences in the epistemological beliefs of college students', *Research in Higher Education*, 39 (4), 365–384

Peelo, M. (2002) 'Setting the scene', in M. Peelo and T. Wareham, *Failing Students in Higher Education*, Buckingham, SRHE and Open University Press

Peelo, M. and Wareham, T. (eds) (2002) *Failing Students in Higher Education*, Buckingham, SRHE and Open University Press

Perry, R. (1997) 'Perceived control in college students: implications for instruction', in R. Perry and J. Smart (eds), *Effective Teaching in Higher Education*, New York, Agathon Press, pp. 11–60

Perry, W. (1970) *Forms of Intellectual and Academic Developments in the College Years* New York, Holt, Rhinehart and Winston

Perry, W. (1985) 'Different worlds in the same classroom', *http://isites.harvard.edu/fs/html/icb.topic58474/perry.html* (accessed March 2007)

Phelan, P. and Reynolds, P. (1996) *Argument and Evidence*, London, Routledge

Phillips, V. and Bond, C. (2004) 'Undergraduates' experiences of critical thinking', *Higher Education Research and Development*, 23 (4), 277–294

Plath, D., English, B., Connors, L. and Beveridge, A. (1999) 'Evaluating the outcomes of intensive critical thinking instruction for social work students', *Social Work Education*, 18 (2), 207–217

Poulson, L. and Wallace, M. (2004) *Learning to Read Critically in Teaching and Learning*, London, Sage

QAA (Quality Assurance Agency) (2001) Qualification descriptors, *www.QAA.ac.uk* (accessed December 2006)

Ranyard, R., Crozier, R. and Svenson, O. (1997) *Decision Making*, London, Routledge Falmer

Read, B., Francis, B. and Robson, J. (2001) 'Playing safe: undergraduate essay writing and the presentation of the student "voice"', *British Journal of the Sociology of Education*, 22 (3), 387–399

Resnick, L. (1987) *Education and Learning to Think*, Washington DC, National Academy Press

Riddle, M. (1997) *The Quality of Argument*, Department of Lifelong Learning and Education, Middlesex University, Trent Park, London

Ryan, M. (1984) 'Monitoring text comprehension: individual differences in epistemological standards', *Journal of Educational Psychology*, 76 (2), 248–258

Schommer, M. (1990) 'Effects of beliefs about the nature of knowledge on comprehension', *Journal of Educational Psychology*, 82 (3), 498–504

Schommer, M. (1993) 'Epistemological development and academic performance among secondary students', *Journal of Educational Psychology*, 85 (3), 406–411

Schommer, M. (1994) 'Synthesizing belief research: tentative understandings and provocative conclusions', *Educational Psychology Review*, 6 (4), 293–319

Schommer, M. and Walker, K. (1995) 'Are epistemological beliefs similar across domains?', *Journal of Educational Psychology*, 87 (3), 424–432

Schon, D. (1982) *The Reflective Practitioner*, San Francisco, Jossey-Bass

Schon, D. (1987) *Educating the Reflective Practitioner*, San Francisco, Jossey-Bass

Scriven, M. and Paul, R. (n.d.) Defining critical thinking, *www.criticalthinking.org/aboutCT/definingCT* (accessed June 2006)

SEEC (2001) SEEC level descriptors 2001, *www.seec-office.org.uk/creditleveldescriptors 2001.pdf* (accessed June 2006)

SEEC (2006) Website *www.seec-office.org.uk/creditleveldescriptors2001.pdf* (accessed December 2006)

Service learning (n.d.) Service learning website for information, *www.servicelearning.org* (accessed December 2006)

Shah, I. (1979) (ed.) *World Tales*, Kestrel Books, Allen Lane, Harmondsworth

Shaw, M. (1994) 'Affective components of scientific creativity', in M. Shaw and M. Runco, *Creativity and Affect*, Norwood, NJ, Ablex Publishing Corporation, pp. 3–42

Smith, M. (1975) *When I Say 'No', I Feel Guilty*, New York, Bantam Books

Sternberg, R. (1987) 'Teaching intelligence: the application of cognitive psychology to the improvement of intellectual skills', in J. Baron and R. Sternberg, *Teaching Thinking Skills*, New York, F. W. Freeman, pp. 182–201

Strong-Wilson, T. (2006) 'Bringing memory forward: a method for engaging teachers in reflective practice on narrative and memory', *Reflective Practice*, 7 (1), 101–113

Sweet, D. and Swanson, D. (2000) 'Blinded by the enlightenment: epistemological concerns and pedagogical restraints in the pursuit of critical thinking', in S. Mitchell and R. Andrews, *Learning to Argue in Higher Education*, Portsmouth, NH, Boynton / Cook, pp. 40–52

Team technology (2006) Assertiveness course, *www.teamtechnology.co.uk/assertiveness/ how-to-be-more-assertive.html* (accessed December 2006)

Thinkingwriting (n.d.) *www.thinkingwriting.qmul.ac.uk* (accessed December 2006)

Tobin, K. (1987) 'The role of wait time in higher cognitive functioning', *Review of Higher Education Research*, 57 (1), 69–75

Topping, D., Crowell, D. and Kobayashi, V. (1989) *Thinking across Cultures, The Third International Conference on Thinking* Hillsdale, NJ, Lawrence Erlbaum Associates

Toulmin, S. (1988) *The Uses of Argument* (9th edn), Cambridge, Cambridge University Press

Underwood, M. and Wald, R. (1995) 'Conference style learning, a method for fostering critical thinking with a heart', *Teaching of Psychology*, 22 (1), 17–21

Van Den Brink-Budgen, R. (2000) *Critical Thinking for Students*, Oxford, How to Books

Vygotsky, L. (1978) *Mind in Society: the development of higher psychological processes* Cambridge, Mass., Harvard University Press

Wallace, M. and Poulson, L. (2004) 'Critical reading for self critical writing' , in L. Poulson and M. Wallace, *Learning to Read Critically in Teaching and Learning*, London, Sage

Wallace, M. and Wray, A. (2006) *Critical Reading and Writing for Postgraduates*, London, Sage

Watton, P., Collings, J. and Moon, J. (2002) *Independent Work Experience: an evolving picture*, SEDA paper 114, Birmingham, Staff and Educational Development Association

Yinger, R. (1980) 'Can we really teach them to think?', in R. Young, *Fostering Critical Thinking*, New Directions for Learning and Teaching, San Francisco, Jossey-Bass, pp. 11–31

Yorke, M. and Knight, P. (2004) 'Self theories: some implications for teaching and learning in higher education', *Studies in Higher Education*, 29 (1), 25–37

Yorke, M. and Knight, P. (2006) 'Curricula for economic and social gain', *Higher Education*, 51, 565–588

Young, R. (ed.) (1980a) *Fostering Critical Thinking, New Directions for Teaching and Learning*, San Francisco, Jossey-Bass

Young, R. (1980b) 'The next agenda: practical reasoning and action', in R. Young, *Fostering Critical Thinking, New Directions for Teaching and Learning*, San Francisco, Jossey-Bass, pp. 91–97

Young, R. (1980c) 'Testing for critical thinking', in R. Young, *Fostering Critical Thinking, New Directions for Teaching and Learning*, San Francisco, Jossey-Bass, pp. 77–90

Index